# MEXICAN GOVERNMENT IN TRANSITION

BY ROBERT E. SCOTT

# *Mexican*
# *Government*
# *in Transition*

Revised Edition

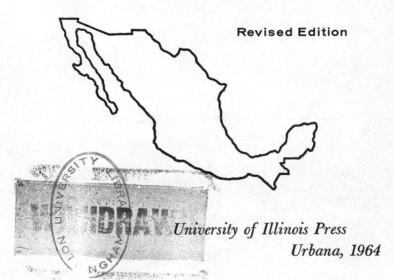

*University of Illinois Press*
*Urbana, 1964*

# Contents

# *Introduction*

In the study of government and the process of politics, it is important to distinguish a generalizing and scientific approach from the particularizing limitations of simple empirical data-gathering. Seeking thus to demonstrate broader patterns or processes in the relationship called politics is not to deny the importance of fact as a basis of knowledge but it does suggest that masses of facts do not of themselves provide the materials for a science of politics. Collecting facts by what might be called implicit selectivity is to establish an almost intuitive standard of description, one that may provide tools for understanding events in a particular political situation but fails to supply a more general hypothesis for description that can state relatively constant relationships between the events in one aspect of politics being studied and those in others. This is especially so in the study of distinct political systems from country to country.

The present volume attempts to study Mexico's evolving system of politics through such a generalizing approach, applying methods which can be and are utilized to describe the political process in other, quite different countries. It considers the multifold social, psychological, and physical conditions which go to make up the Mexican political culture, but relates them to action within a political system by discussing them as factors in the group approach to the study of the political process.

This generalized approach has universality in that the decision-making process and the interaction of the interest groups which participate in it are common to all political systems, no matter what the constitutional structure or the values under which the government machinery is operated. In this sense, it provides what may be a real basis for comparing Mexico's governmental system with those of other countries throughout the world.

But even without regard to universality and the possibility of comparing political systems, within the rather specific goal of this study—describing the operation of Mexico's political system—this methodological approach has real merit. By providing an internally consistent and logical frame of reference, it supplies meaning and coherence to the usual unsystematic enumeration of social and economic conditions and related historical events, the tenuous descriptions of constitutional tenets and political organisms, and the listing of the particular political leaders involved in these things, all of which are so much a part of the study of foreign governments. By no means does this kind of approach ignore such data; instead, it discusses facts in terms of the real business of government, Mexico's or any other, that is, the deciding of public policy.

Understanding the work of government involves more than consideration of isolated institutional phenomena and the possible effect upon it of individuals who manipulate the machinery of government. Government activity is, after all, nothing more than the actions of individuals in a position (officially or otherwise) to decide and act in public matters, and institutions have meaning only because they represent habits followed by so many individuals in a society that the habits form a discernible pattern. It is not the individual, nor even the shared and consistent value, which turns a number of separate individuals into a group, but their action as a group that is politically important. Similarly, it is the gradual adjustment of the means by which competing groups participate in the deciding of public policy affecting their needs and desires that provides a system of politics.

From a methodological viewpoint, classifying a body of activities, in this case political activities, as a system makes for a more precise analysis of the relationships involved. By definition, the observer must view everything that occurs in that system as systematically and continuously related. There can be no unexplained phenomena, although careful study may prove that a given puzzling event or activity is not really a part of the system under study but of another in the same universe, operating simultaneously though not necessarily interdependently. Again, system presupposes cause in political activity as a matter of predictable relationship between two variables; this presupposition saves the investigator from falling into the trap of viewing one factor as somehow exerting force or pressure upon the other while the latter remains passive. Social (including political) relationships simply do not occur this way.

These introductory paragraphs may have convinced the reader that this is a volume riding a hobbyhorse of methodology. It is not. On the contrary, even the most casual glance at its content should convince him that substantive fact fills by far the largest part of the book's pages. In a study of this type an understanding, a full understanding, of a country's political culture is absolutely essential. So is a clear view of formal constitutional structure and the government agencies established by law. The values which motivate individuals, the institutionalized habits which bind these individuals into groups, and the formal organs of government through which part if not all of their political activities take place are the raw material out of which we shall build our description of Mexico's real process of politics. The principal difference between this and other studies of Mexican government, at least with regard to substantive materials, is that the data is presented within a particular frame of reference, based upon what is hoped to be an internally consistent and logical method.

CHAPTER 1

# Government in Transition

## Purpose of This Study

This study of Mexico's government considers the development of systematic government over a period of almost fifty years in a country involved in a basic social and political revolution. Taking into account the disruption wrought upon an existing political system by the invasion of new factors into the culture, the economy, and the social patterns which shaped that system, this volume attempts to demonstrate how these dynamic new factors synthesize with the most viable and enduring aspects of the older system in the gradual evolution of a new working system of politics.

Such interest in how government and the process of politics operate is nothing new. Ever since the dawn of history, human beings have been concerned with the problem of understanding these things, with making government work, and manipulating it to their own ends. Probably the first crude attempts to discover a rational basis for human relations and to channel the nonsocial impulses of his fellow man into a workable system of government were made at a subconscious and nonverbal level by some early human soon after man reached that stage of development at which absolute naked force was replaced by some less violent arrangement among the people who lived in a single community.

From that day to this, innumerable theories about the nature of government have sanctioned all kinds of devices to hold the members of society within bounds. Tradition, religious injunction, caste systems, written and unwritten constitutions, all have played their parts to this end. And, where these social and political controls fail, resort to force is used again, in the form of criminal law and sanctions exercised by the state against recalcitrant individuals.

Also as old as history is the disruption of working political systems by shifts in the factors which control the structure and operation of a society. So is the failure of the dominant group manipulating the political process for its own ends to recognize the need to adjust to meet the challenge of new conditions and the demands of new and effective interest groups which grow out of those conditions. As a consequence, resort to revolution is another almost inevitable part of the age-old evolutionary political pattern, a direct result of attempts to hinder change in the political process so as to protect the vested interests of a ruling faction.

What is new in today's world is the manner in which what is usually called Western technology has affected these political relationships throughout the world. It and the values it represents have resulted in a tremendous speed-up both of the rate at which change invades once stable communities and of the rate of growth of the difficulties such communities must face in trying to adjust their political systems to that change.

Technology, with its instantaneous communication, its speedy transportation, and vastly expanded industrial productivity, has made once tradition-bound and underdeveloped peoples aware of the wide world. It has also given them some sense of the possibility of change in their status, whether that change be a greater share of the world's goods or a stronger voice in the concerns of government. During the twentieth century, in fact, change has begotten change. Hand in hand with material advances goes the spread of ideas, pointing up very real differences in the position of the masses and the ruling elite, differences which sometimes seem to have existed forever in most of the countries of the world.

As the relationship of dominance between ruling and ruled is challenged, revolutions occur, real revolutions based upon widespread social, economic, and political reform, and often accompanied by strife, bloodshed, and breakdown of government. For despite its great gifts, technology does not necessarily provide the broadly shared and institutionalized habit patterns or the political mechanisms which might allow a peaceful transition from the older social and political systems to the new. The older system, based perhaps upon tradition or other nonpragmatic understandings of human relationships and controlled by a select few, cannot evolve easily into a Western-oriented system based on rapid change, material values, a growing specialization of function, and an ever-widening politically active citizenry.

In their hope of achieving all of the advantages of Western life as quickly as possible, many of these awakening countries have sought to model themselves upon those Western nations which have succeeded in developing stable and integrated political systems. But the outward trappings of Western government—constitutionalism, parliamentary systems, separation and division of powers, not to mention democracy—cannot operate successfully within an environment that has not yet accepted fully the value systems and the institutions upon which Western government is founded. Too often in these non-Western states, therefore, social and economic dislocation, which grows out of the changing conditions engendered by exposure to Western influence and which arises just as the government is adopting alien political concepts, has resulted in political disequilibrium, as the old devices for political adjustment and control fail in the new situations.[1]

Obviously, not all of the peoples of the world have been affected to the same extent by exposure to the practices and values of the West. In many countries the façade of Western constitutions and political agencies simply hides the traditional control by a governing elite, or has been the means by which one ruling elite replaces the other. In others, as has been suggested, the new governmental machinery is inadequate to balance the increasingly numerous and conflicting demands made upon the political system, because it is not based upon widely shared values and institutionalized habit patterns.

But a few countries—all too few—have been able to face the problems of rapid change, of Westernization, if you will, and to evolve a workable political system out of the old and new factors

---

[1] Two anthropological studies of culture change, the first general and theoretical and the second specific and applying to individual cultures, are Julian H. Steward, *Theory of Culture Change* (Urbana, 1955), and Margaret Mead, ed., *Cultural Patterns and Technical Change* (New York, 1955). Both are well worth reading for an understanding of the problems incidental to Westernization.

in their changing environment. Sometimes the initial price of the adjustment is high, collected at the cost of internal stability, material development, and even of human lives. But in the long run the result is worth the price, for a country's problems can be solved, responsible government can be established, and a political system to operate the organs of government effectively can be formed. Or at least these things can be accomplished to the degree that the cultural, social, and economic conditions of the country permit. Mexico is such a country.

## Mexican Government in Transition

The Mexican Revolution and the governmental system it produced have been evolving ever since 1910. Even before that, certain changes had begun to make their effects felt, effects which led finally to the resort to violence. It is precisely because Mexico has been so long on the road and traveled so far toward transition from non-Western to Western-type politics that study of its experience and consideration of the system of government produced by that experience have value in the world-wide context. In a very real sense, Mexico provides the political scientist with a laboratory example of a government in transition.

Any attempt to list and discuss here all of the conditions leading to the Mexican Revolution would be difficult and perhaps unnecessary. Probably the most important in terms of this study was the gradual appearance on the Mexican scene of the social and political effects of Western industrial technology, which got an earlier start in Mexico than in most underdeveloped countries because of the development program of General Díaz and his *científicos*. And without a doubt the propinquity of the highly industrialized United States on Mexico's northern border speeded up this process. Thus, the procession of events which later spread throughout the entire world began their classic pattern one generation earlier here.

As changing conditions produced new interests and new groups who demanded that these interests be accommodated, improved communications brought into sharp focus the truly deplorable plight of the landless masses. By 1910, leaders from an expanding but unsatisfied *mestizo* middle class could channel the desperation of the landless *peones* into effective action, and the pressures upon the governmental system reached an intensity which made the Revolution a reality.

Because it could not satisfy all of the interests which had to be considered, the old political system of Mexico was ruptured. But this did not mean that a new, all-inclusive system of politics sprang into being overnight. Quite the contrary, for by definition no real revolutionary situation produces such a system. If adjustment and inclusion in a nationwide system had been possible, no revolution would have taken place at all. Moreover, the very occurrence of the Mexican Revolution so speeded up the degree of change in the factors of human existence which most directly affect politics that it took some time before ordered and patterned relationships could again evolve. Since 1910, Mexico has passed through several stages of political evolution, only gradually working its way toward the closely integrated and systematic form of national politics and government which we term Western.

This evolutionary process can be described in several ways, depending on what one wishes to stress. It involves change in the human factors which influence politics and changes in the locus of political power, as well as changes in the structure of that power. In reality, all of these factors must be considered, for they all go to make up the pattern of the political culture which provides the environment in which the most basic of all political action, decision-making, takes place.

In one sense, we see in Mexico a system of older, less differentiated, and primarily locally controlled governments, adequate to meet the minimal demands of an underdeveloped and badly integrated country, evolving toward a complex and nationwide system of politics within which most of the growing number of separate and specialized interests can make their claims on government effective. In another sense, a revolutionary coalition controlled by men representing interests in conflict with those of the previous governing group and basing its authority upon force of arms gradually is being transformed into a political system based on much wider popular acceptance of what are hazily called Revolutionary goals, which in turn have been so watered down by the demands of practical government that they are no longer very extreme.

More important, perhaps, the national and more representative system of politics that has evolved is structured and rather clearly, if not formally, patterned, and in consistent relationship with most of the more important values and institutions in Mexico's political life. The haphazard and all too often irrational acts of personalistic leaders are being replaced by a more formalized policy-making process, rooted in the real political culture of all (or at least most) of the Mexicans and based upon the activities of an effective and rather elaborate political structure.

In addition to formal government agencies with their professional public bureaucracy, this newly developed political machinery includes a revolutionary party, known today as the Partido Revolucionario Institucional (PRI), which is composed of a surprisingly large number of organized interest associations with their own leaders and professional private bureaucracy. These associations in turn grow out of differentiated and relatively aware latent interest groups produced by the effects of Westernization. All of these factors in the political life of the nation operate within a partly observed constitutional framework, but the real governmental process takes place through the interactions of persons and interests working through the revolutionary party. Here it is that a reasonably effective set of relationships allows most major interests, both in and outside of the so-called official party, access to and consideration in the policy-making process.

Some such transition from simple to more complex political forms, from isolated and nonrelated political activities to systematic national politics, occurs in most countries where technological and economic development affect the limiting conditions of physical and social environment. As communications and economic relations develop, the inhabitants are brought into more frequent contact with one another and gradually build greater interdependence upon each other. This in turn results in greater dependence upon the central government that regulates their relations and tries to solve those new problems which are produced by technology in such bewildering array and which require greater technical and physical resources than the small communities possess.

As it occurred in Mexico, this transition takes on special interest in terms of this study, for it is a transition toward a Western society and political system. This becomes obvious if we list and discuss somewhat more formally the most generally accepted factors which differentiate Western from non-Western political systems, and indicate where Mexico stands in regard to them after nearly fifty years of revolutionary experience.

One of these factors is so all-pervading and so basic that it can only be indicated rather than discussed here. The very existence of the study, indeed of the Mexican Revolution itself, results from it. I refer, of course, to the attitude of a people toward change itself.

To the Western, and particularly the North American mind, acceptance of change is so normal, so usual, that it hardly seems a specific cultural trait. But it is. In many non-Western systems, tradition and habit are the operative cultural traits, and acceptance of change the departure from the norm. By definition, however, until the possibility and the acceptability of change are recognized by a people, they and their society cannot begin to become transformed into a Western society with a Western political system. Conversely, once change has begun to make inroads into a society, the process is apt to continue, although it is impossible to predict that the end result always will be a workable system of Western-type government. Note the difficulties which have overwhelmed the emerging Asian states in their search for effective democracy.

In cultures which have been tradition-oriented, it is not so much the incidence of change as the very existence of change itself that disrupts political stability. Probably the degree of change since World War II is greater in the highly industrialized countries than it is in most of those states just emerging from monocultural or extractive dependent economies and semifeudal social systems. But the effect of change is much greater in the latter, for a whole new concept of society and of government must be formed, and an entirely new set of political relationships has to be hammered out on the forge of practical politics.

In some cases, as in the case of Mexico, a large section of the country's inhabitants have to be integrated into the national society, and still larger portions of the citizenry must be directed into effective political action, where they can influence the decisions of government so as to maximize the advantages of the newly accepted possibility of change. For most of its inhabitants, though not all of them, Mexico has accomplished the acceptance of change; the whole process of turning *indios* into *mestizos* revolves about the new attitudes which have been adopted.

This leads us directly into a discussion of the rather more specific factors which differentiate Western from non-Western systems of politics. A recent discussion of the political process of non-Western states now undergoing influence from the outside characterized them as follows:[2]

1. In non-Western countries there is a high rate of recruitment of new elements into political activity;

2. In such countries there is a lack of consensus about legitimate forms and purposes of political activity;

3. There is a tendency toward charismatic leadership;

4. There is a lower degree of integration among the active participants in the political process than in Western systems;

5. Actors in the political process of non-Western societies have less clearly defined and less specific roles than do those in Western societies;

6. The political process in non-Western states is likely to be composed of interests which are less formally and explicitly organized than are those in Western countries;

7. In non-Western countries, not all of the potential political elements manifest themselves in so continuous a manner as those in the West are apt to do.

Even the reader with a most superficial knowledge of Mexico's politics since 1910 should be struck by the high degree of applicability of most, even all, of these criteria to Mexico during the early days of the Revolution. Every serious study of Mexican government reflects one or more of them.

But equally striking to the careful observer of Mexico's political system as it has evolved during the past decade is the fact that many of these characteristics either no longer apply, or do not apply nearly so much as they once did. Mexican politics has become more patterned, more inclusive, more continuous, perhaps more sophisticated. It has, in short, become systematized into a working political culture in the Western sense.

Most of this book is devoted to explaining the conditions of transition from the earlier non-Western situation and to describing the political system resulting from that transition. Here I shall do little more than set up a number of guideposts to point up just how far development of Mexico's peculiar version of a Western system of politics has affected these seven characteristics of non-Western politics. They will be spelled out in detail in later chapters.

---

[2] George McT. Kahin, Guy J. Pauker, and Lucian W. Pye, "Comparative Politics in Non-Western Countries," *American Political Science Review*, XLIX (December, 1955), 1022-41.

The first characteristic of non-Western countries is the high rate of recruitment into national political awareness and activity occasioned by the first impact of outside ideas. No one could for a moment deny that such recruitment has occurred in Mexico, for integrating the Indian and the village-dwelling peasant into the broader Mexican nation and its political life has been one of the strongest goals and major achievements of the Mexican Revolution. But this recruitment process has been going on in Mexico for almost fifty years and, considering the very high proportion of Mexicans who were not aware of, much less active in influencing, national public policy before 1910, the process is very nearly complete. Certainly the rate of initial recruitment is much lower now than it was before, say, 1940.

Today, the principal problem is not so much making previously isolated peoples aware of the nation as it is acculturating them to play a more active and positive role in the political life of that nation. This, too, is being accomplished. The leaders of the Mexican Revolution, perhaps for their own political advantage, but for whatever reason, have encouraged the organization of numerous functional groups to participate in Mexico's political system and in so doing have supplied mechanisms for speeding up the process of political acculturation.

A second characteristic of non-Western political processes is the lack of consensus about the legitimate forms and purposes of political activity. Here, again, Mexico has progressed amazingly in achieving a broader area of shared social and political values and goals than one might have imagined possible only a few years ago. Given the general Latin tendency toward doctrinaire political stands and factionalism, such a change is impressive—all the more so because this expanding consensus of opinion far exceeds the growth that might have been expected simply as a result of some fifty years of enforced revolutionary "legitimacy," or even the nationalizing effects of improved communication and transportation. The newly found consensus results from adoption of a much more pragmatic approach to the forms and functions of government which, in turn, probably reflects the breakdown of doctrinaire attitudes during the military phase of the Revolution. If the move toward pragmatic politics is not yet complete, it has invaded both the so-called revolutionary party and most of the opposition parties and factions.

The third characteristic of non-Western government, charismatic leadership, is so endemic in Latin American states that one might be tempted to pass over it lightly after conceding its existence in Mexico. Without a doubt it would have been correct to do so during the early days of the Revolution, when the strong Latin tendency toward personal identification with an effective leader, together with low levels of education and poor communication, limited chances for understanding of and loyalty to abstract government. These factors naturally led Mexicans toward such personalistic leadership.

Today this situation no longer obtains. Although some outward vestiges of personalism and charismatic leadership do manifest themselves from time to time, the office of the president has become institutionalized and his actions restricted by a formalized pattern of duties and responsibilities to a much greater extent than appears on the surface. The personal role of the president, in which he could make capricious political decisions based on face-to-face contacts and individual likes or dislikes, has diminished markedly. This is due to the development of a structured political system and an official revolutionary party which serves that system, more than to expanding loyalty to the formal constitution. Nonetheless, present-day political conditions in Mexico have brought a greater adherence to the outward forms of constitutional government and an end to charismatic leadership in the country.

With regard to the next characteristic of non-Western political systems, it is true that Mexico has not yet achieved a complete integration of the political actions of the participants in its system of politics. Even ignoring the ever-decreasing number of unassimilated Indians, who by definition are not part of the Mexican "nation," a large number of the Mexicans who have just been brought into that nation—the peasant *mestizos*—are not wholly integrated into the political system. But by the very token that these people have been drawn into the broader Mexican nation, the areas of important decision-making at the village or local level have become more and more restricted and those at the national level broader. The nature of the Western-type society and economy that have begun to absorb them calls for action beyond the local scope. Roads, schools, electrification, irrigation dams, and the like must be provided by those with the technical skill and capital, which in Mexico means the national government. Inevitably, this weakens the role of the older, traditionally established village governments but makes all of the Mexicans more dependent upon each other.

Mechanisms auxiliary to the legal governmental agencies are also at work in the integration process. The very nature of a national economy based on commercial crops sold for money, which in turn is used to purchase manufactured goods, has produced a class of middlemen—tradesmen who provide a link between the isolated villager and his nation. Where they are available, so do roads and radios and newspapers, all of which are multiplying daily. Finally, the revolutionary party, through its local leaders and particularly through its functionally organized subsidiary associations, works constantly to expand the "Mexican" as opposed to the "village" values.

The fifth broad difference between the two systems suggests that actors in the political process in non-Western societies are apt to play less clearly defined and less specific roles than those in Western societies. As compared with the United States, this is still rather true in Mexico. Nonetheless, as Mexican society becomes more complex, the need for and the degree of functional specialization of activity also expands. As a corollary of increasing specialization, differences in the interests of individuals and groups of individuals fall into sharper focus, creating competition among them. As the political system becomes more structured and as the number of things which government can do to and for specialized functional interest groups grows, the participants in the political process become more circumscribed in the nature of their political roles. If at one time a political leader could represent a large number of undifferentiated persons, today he finds it increasingly difficult to continue to satisfy them as their more specialized interests diverge. Improved education is making more trained and able leaders available in Mexico. These are beginning to represent the specialized interests in the political process, putting an end to some of the old-style polyfunctional leadership.

This phenomenon is closely related to Mexico's position in regard to the next characteristic of non-Western countries. Mexico has long since incorporated into its political system a large number of formally and explicitly organized interests. It was suggested earlier that the more recent leaders of the Mexican Revolution encourage the organization of such functional interest organizations, which are then assimilated into the official party. Quite naturally, as each such association forms, both its rank-and-file members and its leaders begin to play a more clearly defined and specialized role in the process of politics, one in which substitutability of roles is much more difficult.

The pattern is not identical with that in the United States by any means. In the first place, in Mexico most, though not all, of the real interest groups and formal functional interest associations are related to, rather than differentiated from, the political parties, particularly the official party. Secondly, there is a good deal less interaction between the rank and file on the one hand and the leadership and bureaucracy on the other in Mexico's formal organizations, with a consequently weaker sense of responsibility in the hierarchy. In this sense there may be some substitutability of role, as a leader sells out his followers for immediate personal gain. Improving educational standards, together with increasing political sophistication among Mexico's masses, are, however, reducing the degree of irresponsible activity by political leaders in this respect. Finally, because of certain quirks in his personality, the individual Mexican is not likely to have so great a number of "overlapping memberships" in various interest groups or functional interest associations as does his North American counterpart. More of this later.

Despite these dissimilarities to the United States as a political prototype, Mexico has been able to evolve its own Western-style political system, one which works. Most, if not all, of the potential political elements can and do manifest themselves in a continuous manner, for the emerging political system provides suitable machinery to allow the proliferating interests of a plural society to articulate and transmit their demands within the political process, though this may not always be outwardly apparent in the formal agencies of government. Note, too, that opposition political movements may and do exist and that opposition newspapers not only are tolerated but exist in an environment of press freedom unsurpassed in Latin America.

Given the revolutionary roots of the present ruling administrations, and given the general tendency of Latins toward unyielding doctrinaire attitudes, the extent of accommodation of interests provided by Mexico's political mechanisms is little short of amazing. Integration of new interests into the official party through their functional interest associations is an accomplishment in itself. But one might have expected that the accommodation process would stop there, that the "legitimacy" of the Revolution and its goals would preclude any consideration of interests and organizations not formally affiliated with the revolutionary party. This is not so. Although the Church, or certain kinds of industries and businesses, or management as a class, does not participate formally in the activities of the official party, where real political decisions are made, the present system takes their existence into account. In matters of major concern to such interests, some form of adjustment takes place, reflecting the relative power of the interests found in the official party and those outside of it. This is not to say that in matters of elections, local and national, the revolutionary party does not act like a well-oiled political machine. It does, imposing its own candidates over those of the opposition when and if necessary. But for all of this, the degree of consideration for individual interests, as opposed to outsiders' political ambitions, is remarkably high.

Whether the interests outside of the official party can make their voices heard as effectively as those within, and whether those within represent perfectly the needs and desires of the rank and file, is another question, one which must be answered in the body of this study. But at least, by shoring up the constitutional agencies, the revolutionary party provides machinery approximating that necessary for the effective operation of a Western-style system of politics. Within this political mechanism the normally uncompromising attitude of Latin American interest groups has been subjected to the discipline of a structured agency operating a political process in which most, if not all, of the major social and economic interests of most regions of the entire country are represented on a relatively continuous basis.

In sum, then, according to most of the criteria by which Western as opposed to non-Western political systems are characterized, Mexico has advanced toward the West. There is a relatively high degree of participation in, or at least awareness of, politics, and rather highly developed and specialized interest groups and associations exist and act in politics. This in turn means that some of the traditional power agencies such as the Church, landowners, and military officer cliques are counterbalanced and kept in relative check. Similarly, there is continuity of political action by parties, particularly by the revolutionary party, which seek to form coalitions of existing interest groups; in practice, therefore, these parties have replaced their inflexible personalistic or ideological bases with a more pragmatic one, though they may not admit or even know it. All of these conditions are vital to the development of a Western-style political system.

If at present the mechanisms which aggregate conflicting interests and translate them into general public policy operate more within the revolutionary party and the quasi-legal mechanism of the presidency than in the formal constitutional agencies, they do provide a means by which the interests of most citizens and interest groups both in and out of the party can be considered. This aggregating function exists not as an isolated phenomenon but as part of a systematic adjustment of the factors which operate in the decision-making or political process.

The fact that these mechanisms and the values which motivate them are peculiarly Mexican in their form does not mean that the political system itself cannot be classed as Western. On the contrary, by the very fact that Mexico has achieved a synthesis of older habits and values with those resulting from change, the country has fulfilled the most basic of all requirements for a Western political system—a single system based on the needs, necessities, values, ~~RUBBISH~~ and desires of a nation—in short, a workable and working system that includes the entire country. If to do so, the system concentrates effective political power in a single central authority, negating constitutional federalism and even the checks and balances of presidential government, this is more in accord with Mexican reality than a law that does not accurately reflect the country's conditions and value system.

## Groups and the Political Process

The term "political process" which has been used so frequently in the foregoing ought to be defined more carefully. It is nothing more than an abstract way of describing the interplay among the effective factors which participate directly or indirectly in political decision-making at any given level of government. Such a term has the advantage of being neutral in the question of whether decisions should be reached only by those agencies formally designated as "legislative" by a formal constitution, or whether all of the effective deciders, in or out of the legislature (in or out of the formal government, for that matter) should be recognized as participating in the process of deciding policy. In short, "the political process" is a convenient term for describing what really happens in reaching public decisions, as opposed to what should happen from a formal or legal viewpoint.

Any discussion of the political process must presuppose that the deciders have authority to carry out their decisions, whether because they hold office in a legal government with sufficient institutionalized strength to enforce its laws, or because they represent a combination of interests whose united strength and agreed-upon course of action outweighs any possible combination of power factors opposing the decision. This is a particularly useful concept in a country such as Mexico, where constitutional government is observed in form but the effective decision-making takes place elsewhere, in this case in the interaction of interests in and around the revolutionary party.

But this in turn leads to a further difficulty. In describing this "interaction of interests," some meaningful definition of "interests" is required. In this study we use what is known as the "group approach" for the systematic study of interest groups and their role in the political process. This method attempts to measure influence in terms of a specific question, as well as the factors interacting to affect the decision of the question at hand. That is to say, rather than measuring the number of votes for political candidates or the number of members a specific interest group or faction may claim or really have, this group approach seeks to isolate the specific groups of citizens who have sufficient interest to act (or in a negative sense, to react) in the process of reaching and enforcing a given policy, and to measure the effectiveness of their action or reaction upon the whole process of making the decision.

This study, for example, attempts to describe the political environment and the conditions under which the president of Mexico is nominated by the official party and, after the formality of an election campaign, operates in the executive office. The nomination procedure and the operation of the presidency as a mechanism for balancing all of the conflicting interests in Mexico's political process were selected because nowhere else in the political system does a policy decision stir up quite as much interest-group activity.

It is the activities of these groups we wish to study, for the study of politics is really the study of groups at work, tracing the relationships among them as they seek their objectives, distinguishing the elements in their activities associated with success or failure, and tracing the factors in the political environment which cause them to form and determine the manner in which they operate. As Bentley, Truman, and others have pointed out,[3] such interest groups may be latent or manifest. There may be little or no interaction among the participants in a group, only a sense of similar reaction to a given stimulus. Or the group may be organized formally into an association, with specified goals, internal discipline, recognized leaders, and a bureaucracy. A group may be inarticulate and, in fact, a negative rather than a positive factor in a given situation, or it may be vocal and highly influential. But in every case, the group is an action-related concept, even though that action may be expected only after the decision is made and put into effect.

Obviously, the more specific and clearly recognized the goals which unite a group and the more effectively organized and internally disciplined it is, the more successful the group will be, other things such as numbers, status, strategic location, or relative economic position being equal. Thus, in Mexico, as elsewhere, a formally organized "association," a labor union, perhaps, with clearly defined and perhaps limited goals, with a high degree of interaction among its members, an agreed-upon set of rules (a charter or a constitution), good internal discipline, and a permanent leadership with a bureaucracy to aid it, is infinitely more effective in those matters with which it concerns itself than a latent but unorganized interest group of equal numbers, such as parents of school children. But the latter, in turn, is more influential in policy decisions to which its members react because of some sort of shared attitude or opinion than would be an equal number of noninterested or nonaware (though not necessarily nonaffected) citizens, such as Mexico's Indians would be.

A formal association will have both a more continuous and a more widespread influence on governmental policies than will temporary interest groups which spring up in response to a particular stimulus. Because, in fact, almost no activity of government is com-

[3] Arthur F. Bentley, *The Process of Government; A Study of Social Pressures* (Chicago, 1908); David B. Truman, *The Governmental Process* (New York, 1951). The best available short summary of the group concept is Phillip Monypenny, "Political Science and the Study of Groups: Notes to Guide a Research Project," *The Western Political Quarterly*, VII (June, 1954), 183-201, from which part of the above was adapted.

pletely isolated from any other, permanently organized functional interest groups may bring pressure in matters which at first glance seem far beyond their competence. A Mexican farm group may, for example, support road building because the program opens market roads for its members. But it may oppose expanded educational expenditures because its leaders see the program as eating into available money for direct farm aid without commensurate increases in rural schools. Again, a given group may support an entirely unrelated policy as part of a political deal, in return for similar cooperation from the interest group whose objective it assists. Unorganized and latent interest groups are in no position to act in this way.

Using this group approach to consider the operation of the political process encourages conceiving of political policy-making as an active process, rather than as a description of the formal agencies and the constitutional mechanisms of government which ostensibly make decisions. Insofar as it applies to the political process, the structure of government can profitably be studied by reading the formal constitution of a country or commentaries upon it.[4] But this will not tell the reader how politics really operates in any country, least of all Mexico. Consideration of interest groups and associations offers meaningful insights into the process of politics, not simply because such groups exist, but because they act. Using them as units in the policy-making relationship makes for a description of the structure of political power rather than of the structure of government.

Considering the political process in an active sense is important because decision-making on any given policy is a continuous process. Even in the United States, where policy decisions and formal law relate very closely, decision-making continues after the law is passed. If necessary, administrative rulings can ease or stiffen the application of a decision and, ultimately, the law can be amended. In Mexico, where real decision-making operates, to a much greater extent, outside the formal agencies of

---

[4] Mexico's constitution can be found in Russell H. Fitzgibbon, *The Constitutions of the Americas* (Chicago, 1948). Commentaries include William P. Tucker, *The Mexican Government Today* (Minneapolis, 1957); Gabino Fraga, *Derecho Administrativo* (6th ed.; Mexico, D.F., 1956); Felipe Tena Ramírez, *Derecho Constitucional Mexicano* (Mexico, 1955). A review of any or all of these will quickly demonstrate how little they say about how the political process really operates.

government, alteration of a given policy is even more responsive to group pressures. A classic example of the manner in which formal action follows political action is the practice of granting the Mexican president extraordinary powers to legislate by decree, which in turn constantly have to be cut back by new constitutional provisions. Despite this, because the president is the single most powerful factor in the political process, legal authority continues to flow to him because the interests active in the political decision-making process look so consistently to the chief executive for policy decisions that sooner or later the law again reflects this authority.

Quite naturally, differences in the political culture and the environment in which interest groups operate as they seek to influence public policy make the operating of the political process somewhat different in Mexico from that in other countries, the United States, for example. So, too, there are differences in the nature of groups themselves, in the framework of relations within which they interact, and in the role they play, individually and collectively, in making public decisions. Important as these differences are, however, they must not be overemphasized, for the policy-making process itself is basically the same in every political system.

## The Political Process in the United States

North American interest group relationships can be characterized by a predominance of functionally specific, bureaucratized, associational-type groups, together with large numbers of civic and ethnic interest groups. A relatively high degree of membership participation in internal decision-making takes place within each group and, as a corollary, its leaders and bureaucracy also feel a relatively high sense of responsibility to the rank and file.

The average person in the United States tends to belong to numerous interest groups, several of which may compete for his loyalty and influence his thinking in a given decision-making situation. Because of this overlapping membership, there is a greater tendency to keep the relationship and function of interest groups separate from that of political parties. A party too closely identified with specific interest groups cannot hope to attract enough votes to win a national or, in most cases, a state or local election. In bidding for the support of as many as possible of these semi-independent interest groups, the party must abandon extreme stands and doctrinaire views, adopting a moderate, compromising policy so that it can be all things to all men.

Because in the United States there are two major parties, each bidding for the support of the same interest groups, they become increasingly similar in their activities and in the goals so piously stated in their platforms. In the North American political system, therefore, the primary function of each of the major parties is not so much to represent a limited number of specific interest groups in conflict with those represented by the other party as it is to reduce the conflicts of interest and adjust the differences among as many as possible of the interest groups competing in the political arena. This aggregating of conflicting interests initiated by the political parties carries over into the formal agencies of government, where the process of adjustment continues.

Because the leaders of the major political parties hold public office, or, perhaps more correctly, because those who hold public office are the principal leaders of the major parties, there is a high degree of incidence between those who wield the political power to make public policy and those granted that authority under law. At the same time, there is a strongly ingrained popular support for constitutional government. Therefore, the legally established legislative agency—congress at the national level, state legislatures and so on—resolves public policy questions, with varying degrees of participation by the executive, the judiciary, or even agencies outside the formal government, depending upon the matter at hand.

In short, in the United States the work of articulating group interests is performed primarily by organized and semi-independent associations; that of evaluating the relative strength of each interest in conflict on a given issue and attempting to reconcile and adjust the conflict is done by politicians as members of the two major parties; and the final aggregation of interests and deciding of public policy is carried out by perhaps the same politicians, but this time as members of the government.

### The Political Process in Mexico

Mexico's decision-making process has many of the characteristics of a Western political system, even though it is not identical with that of the United States. Certainly it cannot be described simply as an "informal and intermittent process of communication between and among class and status groups such as large landholders and businessmen, and cliques of bureaucrats and/or army officers,"[5] as it may in most non-Western countries.

Although the principal mechanism for balancing the interests participating in Mexico's political process operates under the aegis of the revolutionary party rather than through the constitutionally established government agencies, it is no less permanent and little less formalized than its North American equivalent. Because real political power and formal legal authority do not coincide so completely as they do in the United States, access to policy-making is not quite so easy and decisions do not always reflect so satisfactory an evaluation of the relative power positions of the interests involved. But access is possible, and adjustment does take place, so that Mexico has worked out a stable political system.

As in the United States, the basic units operating in the policy-making process are not class or status groups, but a relatively large number of specialized and bureaucratized associational-type, functional interest groups. Not unexpectedly, given the rate of social and economic change, the number of latent interest groups evolving into formal associations and the splitting of the latter into even more specialized groups is greater here than in the more static North American environment.

Within every interest group or functional organization, there is a whole continuum of slightly different interests bound together by more or less shared values and common goals. The persons holding interests on the periphery of the omnibus group may split off as their interests become more specialized and in greater conflict with those of the rest of the group. Or, as the group becomes a formally organized association, the degree of group discipline exercised may become so great as to force a particular faction to change its goals or to get out, unless the faction itself is strong enough to force the association to compromise with it. In Mexico this process is particularly evident because the country is just at the stage in Westernization where the rate of increase in specialization is most marked.

Some class and status groups, such as the Church, the prerevolu-

---

[5] Gabriel A. Almond, "A Comparative Study of Interest Groups and the Political Process," Report of the Planning Session Held at the Center for Advanced Study in the Behavioral Sciences, Committee on Comparative Politics, Social Science Research Council, Stanford, California, April 5-10, 1957, *American Political Science Review*, LII (March, 1958), 270-82.

tionary aristocracy, and an increasingly large professional and managerial class, still have a role in the political process, but with the exception of the present government bureaucracy and the army, most of the old-style, less specialized, and nonfunctional groups operate outside of the official party. Those groups and associations more representative of modern, industrialized, and urban Western society (trade unions, farm groups, student organizations, etc.) more often than not are assimilated into the revolutionary party.

There is one important exception to this last statement. Outside of the official party machinery are the most important business associations, functionally organized Chambers of Commerce, of Light and of Heavy Industry, Associations of Employers, and the like. These *cámaras* are not formally affiliated with the revolutionary party for several reasons. They have not affiliated, partly because they do not fit into the historical context of the Mexican Revolution as a mass movement for reform, and partly because they are a relatively new phenomenon which came into being with industrialization, after the broad outlines of the revolutionary party had already crystallized; but they stay outside the party mainly because their members do not always find it necessary or expedient to submit to the limitations of party discipline.

Though they are not part of the party organization, the *cámaras* have friends at court in the form of political and functional organization leaders who are silent (and sometimes not so silent) partners in business enterprise. We shall see that one major factor that strengthened the revolutionary party's 1958 presidential candidate in his struggle for the nomination was his ability as Labor Minister to avoid almost all strikes by promoting compromise between business and labor; he paid a price for this record, however, in a period of labor unrest during his campaign and first days in office.

Internal relationships in Mexico's interest groups long tended to differ rather sharply from those in the United States. To some extent they still do, for change comes slowly in social situations. Membership participation in internal decision-making for the individual group was much less marked, and the leadership-bureaucracy much less apt to feel a sense of responsibility to the rank and file. In fact, unlike their North American counterparts, leaders in mass membership associations more often than not were middle-class intellectuals rather than recruits from the rank and file which the organization existed to represent. The resulting lack of identi-

TRITE

fication of the leadership with the membership because of a paucity of shared experiences and values was heightened by the average Mexican's strong personalistic desire to improve his own position without regard to any other individual. *unlike in USA*

Although both interest group and governmental bureaucracies are more highly specialized in Mexico than in most other Latin American states, all of this made for the kind of polyfunctionalism in the leadership of groups mentioned earlier, particularly when the leaders penetrated the elective offices and bureaucracy of the government. In actuality, the nature of the sector organization in the revolutionary party still encourages this dual representational-administrative role. Where such polyfunctionalism does occur, the leadership quite often demonstrates a lack of loyalty to the organization which originally gave it political power, identifying personal with associational goals. In the face of spiraling living costs, just such weak protection of organized workers' interests by labor politicians, who were more interested in seeking union peace to assure themselves public office than in representing their followers, resulted in the relatively high degree of support won by radical elements who tried to capture control of several key unions during 1958, both during and after the presidential election campaign. The amount of political independence demonstrated by the rank and file was great enough to win success for one or two of these movements, so that the threat forced the entrenched labor bureaucracy to seek a general increase in wages in order to protect its own position. On the other hand, once the radical opposition leaders managed to capture a union, they in their turn did not *REDS UNDER THE BED* hesitate to manipulate its activities to further their own ends. The clearest example of this is the series of politically motivated strikes inspired during February and March, 1959, by Demetrio Vallejo, a Communist-tinged labor leader who had wrested control of the railroad workers from more moderate hands a few months previously. The government broke the strike by use of troops, and large numbers of strikers lost their previously protected jobs as a result. Neither under the moderates nor under the radicals was the well-being of the rank and file a primary consideration of the union leadership.

But if interest group leadership is not perfect, and it is not, rank-and-file interests are so much better represented now than they once were, and the alternatives offered by competing groups outside of the official family are so unattractive, that most rank-and-file members go along with it. And a number of control factors are operative. The tendency toward refinement of objectives, with consequent splintering into more specialized interest groups, has already been suggested. Within each of these new groups, as education and political sophistication spread, the general membership begins to demand more and more from its leadership. This is made the easier because for every successful leader in Mexican politics there are five lean and hungry potential leaders ready, willing, and anxious to capture his position. The most dangerous threat to a leader generally is his first assistant. Thus, each interest group has a kind of built-in responsibility mechanism, one which operated in the case of the 1958-59 labor unrest just mentioned.

Another difference from the North American pattern, attributable to dissimilar social values, is the relative lack of overlapping memberships held by individual Mexicans in competing groups or associations. Mexico has developed a Western-type, plural society, and a Mexican may well participate in more than one group. But it is quite unlikely that on a given issue he will find himself in a situation where he must choose among organizations playing different and even contradictory roles. This is partly because the number of interests which are likely to motivate him still is smaller than it would be if he lived in the United States, and partly because most formally organized social and functional groups are subsumed in the three sectors of the revolutionary party, which adjusts differences before they become fully public. But most of all, it is because the Mexican usually tends to identify his own interests—social, economic, and political—with some personalistic leader, whose indication of proper political response to a given situation will motivate the individual.

By now it must be obvious that Mexico's political system does not keep the function and relationship of organized interest groups separate from those of the political parties, in spite of the specialized and formally independent functional associations which make up the membership of at least two of the three sectors of the revolutionary party. Instead, the revolutionary party encourages the organization of new associations as latent interest groups become ready to formalize their relationships, or it absorbs citizens into the existing organizations as they enter the "Mexican nation." Similarly, the official party often supports factions of existing associations in their attempts to break off to form new organizations when their specialization of interest so requires.

This tendency to associate interest groups and associations with political parties is not peculiar to the official party. Indeed, it is a part of the personalistic political relationship that so long has been a part of Mexico's political culture. If, as will be suggested later, the tendency is beginning to break down with the advent of Western social and political conditions, *personalismo* still plays an important role in Mexican politics. Most of the opposition parties are based upon a cluster of small, weak interest groups of one kind or another. Even the PAN, which demands an end to associational party structure, consists of a number of rather specialized interest groups which will be identified later.

A note of caution is in order here. The reader must have noticed that speaking of personalistic ties as a motive for political support directly contradicts the "interest" concept inherent in the group approach, making groups more nearly analogous to the sociologists' primary group, whose unity is based upon face-to-face contact in social or family relations, rather than upon shared objectives or re-action to a given political stimulus. In Mexico, groups run across the whole spectrum, from one type to the other, but even in the true functional interest group some vestiges of the personalistic rela-tionships still exist. They may be found in an organized interest group as the relationship between leader and follower, or between the leader of a functional group and a national political figure. This is part of the heritage of *personalismo* mentioned above. Its exist-ence need not preclude use of the interest group approach in Mexico, for the interest that motivates a given person need not be material, or rational for that matter. Even an emotional identification can unite individuals into an effective interest group, so long as the identification results in action by individuals because they see the leader as a personification of their own motivating interest.

Generally speaking, however, the interest groups and associations which are found within the revolutionary party are less affected by personalistic influences than by functional and material aspirations. Too many of them have survived changes in their leadership, both at the local and national level, too many have adjusted to changing attitudes on the part of their membership, to be classed as the per-sonal property of specific leaders. Moreover, by now they are so formally structured, and their role in the political process so well defined, that the old manipulation by blindly trusted leaders in most cases has long been impossible.

Much the same is true of many, but not all, of the groups which cluster about the small opposition parties. Here personal identification with a leader is stronger. This helps explain why a few functional interest associations such as labor unions may associate themselves with a person who at best is a supplicant outside of the decision-making machinery of the revolutionary party and at worst an enemy of the Revolution whose supporters are apt to be punished by the withholding of aid and comfort by government agencies. But even here, personalistic tendencies on the one hand and official retaliation on the other are falling before the growing Westernization of the country. The dissident group (or its leadership) really may seek to use its support of the opposition leader as a lever by which to pry concessions out of the government. Economic activities have become so interrelated and political relationships so stabilized that the trick actually works. Instead of immediate and terrible sanctions, the group may win its desires in rough proportion to the intensity of group pressure it can wield.

This occurs because, despite the lack of bidding between two or more relatively equally matched parties for support from competitive interest groups, the revolutionary party, like its North American major party counterparts, is an increasingly moderate, middle-of-the-road party. In providing the machinery for solving the problem of specific demands made by all of the varied interest groups and associations found in an increasingly diverse and complex plural society, the official party forces most of them into the government coalition. The price of being "inside" is, of course, moderation of demands and discipline of activities. Their only alternative is to bring pressure from the outside, which can be done, though less effectively. But it is of note that interests outside of the official party not only can exist but do exist with some slight hope of success.

To a great extent, this same pattern of group relationships and moderation of demands is found in the stronger opposition parties, if one can call parties which have little or no real strength by this term. That is to say, the most dangerous recent opposition parties have consisted of temporary coalitions of unsatisfied or dissatisfied groups, led by ambitious leaders, which cluster around what appears to be a strong opposition presidential candidate. Because of the presence within it of groups with basically competing interests, the major campaign strategy of an opposition party has been to claim to be able to out-Herod Herod in achieving carefully vague and broad "Revolutionary" goals. The pattern even fits the smaller, more specific, politically weaker and (perhaps for this reason) more permanent opposition parties. While most of them started as rather doctrinaire parties, they have modified their stated policies greatly, for this is the only way in which they can hope to compete with the revolutionary party in attracting support. So far they have not succeeded, but the very fact that they act in this manner indicates a growing political pragmatism in Mexico.

In my opinion, the existence of opposition parties, and particularly their evolution from highly specialized class and single interest organizations toward broader, more nearly pragmatic parties like the official party, makes Mexico's political process a great deal more like that of the United States than appears on the surface. For all of its overwhelming power, the revolutionary party is bidding for widespread support just as do the Democrats and Republicans, but against latent coalitions of forming and existing interest associations which could and probably would turn themselves into effective political agencies if the incumbents should fail to bid successfully.

As long as the present official party continues to work out a formula for satisfying a majority of the strongest influence associations, dissatisfying as few as possible, not only the aggregating function but the decision-making process itself will reside in it and not in the formal government. But as Mexican society becomes more complex, more specialized, balancing the competing interests becomes more and more difficult and the need for internal discipline more acute. Here, we shall see, is a responsibility of the institutionalized president and consequently a major source of presidential power.

Sooner or later the official coalition may not be able to juggle all of the power factors successfully and if some other party can gather up and organize the unsatisfied interest groups which drop out of the "revolutionary coalition," it will more nearly equate in political power with the incumbents. When and if this happens, if the institutionalized links of national economy and social interaction are strong enough to keep the political system operating peacefully, presidential elections will become real bidding contests and the analogy to the North American style of Western politics will become even stronger.

Because of their generalized, pragmatic nature, two quite similar parties bidding for support from the various interest associations probably will emerge. Articulating of group interests will be performed by the interest associations, the major work of aggregating interests will be done by the party system, but now decision-making will pass to the legal agencies of government because neither party will hold a preponderance of power factors within its own organization. Inevitably when this occurs, the identification of specific interest associations with one or the other of the two parties will weaken, as their leaders begin to shop around for the best available offer in return for political support.

Or, if the revolutionary myth proves too strong for the evolution of broadly based opposition parties, the present one-party system may continue, with interaction among the conflicting interests in the policy-making process taking place within the official party. The inability of General Henríquez Guzmán to capture any politically significant part of the revolutionary aura for his Federation of Peoples' Parties during the 1952 presidential campaign, despite obvious efforts to do so, suggests that the two-party pattern will take some time to evolve. Lack of a broadly supported opposition candidate during the 1958 presidential campaign substantiates this opinion.

As of now, the developing economy has been able to keep up with some, if not all, of the demands of the proliferating interests it evokes, and the official party's political organization still is strong enough to control internal disputes. The present structure of political power in Mexico strongly discourages dissatisfied elements from leaving the official fold to form opposition parties. The initial impetus of an important figure in the revolutionary party leaving to form an opposition movement may carry along some support of this type, but when the new grouping cannot wield enough political power to carry the presidential election, a constant stream of penitents return to the official fold. Some come individually, some as entire interest associations, and in a few cases an entire party tries to reinstate itself through some sort of "united front" with the revolutionary coalition.

Only as Western social and economic conditions begin to operate more effectively in the political culture will the political demands of interest groups become so complex and competitive that the revolutionary party machinery may not be able to satisfy enough of them. If this occurs, it probably will involve multiplication of the specialized interests participating in politics, together with a basic change in nature of membership in such interest groups, creating multiple political motivating forces not now present. Certainly the introduction of education, the expansion of social sophistication, and the spread of political awareness have accelerated the weakening of personalistic relationships and the growth of overlapping memberships in interest groups and associations which can and do find themselves in competition on given public policy issues.

One indication that this process leading toward the last step in the transition to a full Western-type political system may already be occurring lies in the composition of, and the role played in the political process by, the so-called Popular sector of the official party. This sector is not composed of functionally specialized groups, as are the Farm and Labor sectors, but of a central core of government bureaucrats and a large number of heterogeneous associational-type groups such as civic betterment groups, professional groups (medical men, lawyers, engineers, architects), even student and women's groups. Its central sector organization, the National Federation of Popular Organizations (the CNOP), is controlled and manipulated by professional politicians.

In recent years, after a slow start compared with the more internally homogeneous functional sectors, the Popular sector has been becoming stronger and stronger in the revolutionary coalition. It tried unsuccessfully a few years ago to replace the sector system in the party with a system based more on individuals or at least on less monolithic interest associations. The move failed, but another may succeed in the near future. Certainly the Popular sector's strength is growing, for during 1956 and 1957, in anticipation of the 1958 election, the official party stepped up its drive to add individual memberships, as opposed to functional association affiliations, and placed these new members in the Popular sector. After the inauguration of President López Mateos this drive for individual members continued. In fact, it was greatly intensified by the new president of the Central Executive Committee, General Alfonso Corona del Rosal, who stressed broadening the base of popular membership as part of a more general democratization of party practices and procedures.

Nonetheless, in the foreseeable future the functional interest associations will continue to be a very important factor in the structure of political power in Mexico. One might almost say that, with the political process centered in the machinery of the revolutionary party and with that party organized primarily in functional sectors as it is, for the present at least Mexico has an informal but very real semicorporative form of government. This despite the formal constitutional system, with its federal and presidential systems copied from the United States model. The real decision-making process short-cuts the constitutional distinctions of state-national and executive-legislative-judicial authority. Access to government and to decision-making is not through state or national government agencies so much as it is through the interest association, the sector with which it is affiliated and, finally, through the party leadership to the ultimate core of power that centers in the president. As was suggested earlier, this holds even for interests not formally within the revolutionary coalition, interests such as the Church and the *cámaras* of commerce, industry, and the like.

Despite the departures from formal constitutional norms, the system that is evolving in Mexico is basically a "good" one, in that it provides for most of the political contingencies which arise as the country moves toward Westernization. Mechanisms are provided for the voicing of demands by both latent and manifest interest groups and for communicating these demands through the revolutionary party, which aggregates them into workable policy questions, to those who have real authority to decide public policy matters. So, instead of an unstable pluralism, as in France or Chile, Mexico has an organized and stable plural society.

But Mexico does not yet have a "perfect" political system. No country does. The lack of coincidence between formal constitutional and actual political practice makes for a lack of preciseness in the operation of decision-making and, particularly for the politically uninitiated, for a certain degree of confusion as to just how to accomplish a given political end. As one Mexican businessman once put it, "The official party is like a cathedral; you can get whatever you want by going there, praying hard enough and lighting enough candles. But you must know in which chapel to pray."

No political system ever is perfect, for perfection is a static concept, while politics is just the opposite, being rooted in action as it attempts to adjust the differences which arise constantly among peoples and groups of peoples in a society. Mexico's political system is an adequate one, surprisingly adequate in the face of all of the rapid adjustments required as a result of industrialization and the spread of commercial agriculture, and all of the other by-products of Westernization. The system is both internally consistent and logical in terms of traditional Mexican values, as affected by the newer invading influences from outside and by some of the myths of the Mexican Revolution. And, very important, the Mexican political system is flexible enough to accommodate rapid changes in the social-economic situation and the new interests pouring forth. It is so "open-ended," in fact, that this study makes no attempt to list all of the interest groups and associations affecting politics, but only to indicate some of those which have already demonstrated a degree of stability by their activities in, around, or against the revolutionary party. To do otherwise would suggest a false sense of permanence in a dynamic political system that is stable but still very much in transition.

CHAPTER 2

# The Physical and Social Setting

## The Emerging Nation

Since the Revolution, the forces of change—of progress, if you like—have been at work forging the separate parts of Mexico into a more unified nation, and there is a growing body of citizens who look upon themselves not only as inhabitants of village, state, or region, not primarily as revolutionaries or antirevolutionaries, but as Mexicans. This process of national unification is by no means complete, nor is it ever likely to be, considering that the mind-set of the Mexicans is a product of centuries during which dividing influences have left their impact upon the people. But for practical political purposes, some of the recent changes in the limiting conditions of geography and economics, with resultant changes in human institutions, have produced national integration to an extent never before possible.

This is an important forward step. Consider for a moment Mexico as compared with the United States. Mexico's northern neighbor has four times its territory and over five times its population. And yet, in spite of great size and large numbers of citizens, in spite of manifold personality differences throughout the country—social, economic, ideological, geographic—as a nation the United States is a homogeneous polity. By far the greatest part of its people participate in a single value and conceptual system. More important from the viewpoint of this study, they share a single political system, one in which limited, responsible, and popular government rates high on the scale of importance. It is a system in which so broad a zone of political agreement exists that there is room for individual differences within the system itself. Not so in Mexico.

Until recently there was no one Mexico, only a number of isolated and separate peoples. The inhabitants of the country were divided by external controls—difficult terrain, poor transport, lack of physical integration. They were divided, too, by internal controls—cultural differences, psychological barriers to cooperation, a history of mutual suspicion and civil war. Where the political system of the United States tended to be homogeneous, that of Mexico was heterogeneous. Even now, with the growth of a more nearly national society, many of the habit patterns resulting from this separatism remain institutionalized in the Mexican system of politics.

The limiting conditions of geography have had great influence over social and political life in Mexico, so that the changes the Revolution has brought in this field are of particular importance. The individual as such can have little influence over the barriers established by geography. If he lives in a country like Mexico, where movement from place to place long has been difficult, chances are that he will not know his neighbors or have been able to work out a common set of values or political habits. Only since the technological advances of the industrial revolution has it been possible to overcome the barriers to communication and provide geographic integration. Geographic integration has been the key to social integration, which in turn results in national political integration.

## The Geographic Setting[1]

The political map of Mexico shows a tapering isthmus narrowing from north to south. It is divided into twenty-nine states, two federal territories, and a federal district surrounding the national capital, Mexico City. But even in political terms a political map of Mexico has much less meaning than a relief map of the country, for the latter stresses the all-important dimension of physical contour.

Altitude, for example, determines climate and crops in Mexico and consequent concentrations of people. Mountains and valleys, which do not show on a political map, separate these concentra-

---

[1] I make no attempt to present more than an outline of Mexico's geography here. See the bibliography for more comprehensive sources.

tions of inhabitants from each other in regional and village groups; this grouping has had a profound effect upon Mexican society and politics. State boundaries, on the other hand, are artificial divisions which in Mexico have been of little real importance in the daily life of the citizens.

In few countries have the diversities of landscape and climate more dramatically divided a people. Some two-thirds of Mexico is broken by spectacular mountain peaks and rugged land surfaces where the inhabitants measure distances and differences of climate more meaningfully in terms of up and down than of east and west. The last third of Mexico's territory is more or less level, but the level spots are widely separated from one another. The great limestone plain of the Yucatán Peninsula is far from either the east or the west coastal lowlands, which in turn are separated from the intermontane basins of the central highlands and the valley bottoms in the great mountain ranges by the mountains themselves. The northern half of the country receives too little rain; the rest enjoys adequate annual rainfall, but most of it at the wrong time of the year for efficient agriculture. Similarly, a few parts of the country are cool the year around because of their altitude; other areas which are nearby but lie at the foot of the mountains remain warm or hot all of the time. Many areas of the country are subject to periodic floods, for example, along the Río Grande (or Río Bravo as the Mexicans call it), and even Mexico City has serious drainage problems. Along the coastal lowlands of both the Pacific Ocean and the Gulf disastrous floods have also occurred. Unfortunately, in some areas floods alternate with drought conditions.

The core of the Mexican nation is a vaguely triangular highland that includes about a third of Mexico's total area. It narrows in width and rises in altitude gradually from the northern border of the country to a point just south of Mexico City, and lies cradled between the eastern and western mountain ranges—the Sierra Madre Oriental and the Sierra Madre Occidental—which separate the highland from the coastal plains on the Gulf of Mexico and the Pacific Ocean. This central highland is further separated from southern Mexico by lower and broader mountains between it and the Isthmus of Tehuantepec.

Internally the central plateau is not an integrated geographic or political unit, because its rough surface configuration breaks it into semi-isolated regions. To the north the terrain is lower and less rugged, the climate drier, and the population sparser. Farther south, on the *mesa central* proper, the valley basins in which most of the Mexicans live lie among the mountains at seven to eight thousand feet above sea level, with peaks towering another five to ten thousand feet above the clusters of villages. Toward this central and more populous section of the highland core the mountains become more continuous, isolating the basins and their inhabitants from each other.

Despite its lack of internal integration, the *mesa central* was the heartland of the Aztec empire at the time of the Conquest and it remains the nucleus of the Mexican nation today. Internal disaffection may have developed among the peoples of the great mountain valleys from time to time, but outside pressures and the advantages of cooperation among themselves always have led to re-establishment of the area as a political entity. Today most of the industrial and economic life of Mexico engendered by Western technology centers in the central plateau. The resultant interaction, together with increased social relations because of improved communication and transportation, tends to unite the inhabitants of this central highland area, so that more than ever they are the core of the Mexican nation.

The concentration of population, together with the stressing of industrialization in this central zone, have made for serious problems among the rural population. If some of the excess farm workers had not been drained off by movement to the cities and by emigration as *braceros* to the United States, the pressures upon the central government from this region would be much greater. As it is, the politically aware portion of the rural inhabitants of this central plateau area are an important group to watch. As interest groups, they still are more latent than active, but improved communications mean more interaction among them, and traditionally it is from this crowded part of the country north and west of Mexico City that political action in the form of revolts has most often sprung.

Distance and cultural differences have inculcated a sense of regionalism in the sections of Mexico surrounding the central plateau so that they are less firmly tied to the central core. Regionalism long was a cause of national political weakness, for it promoted the local independence mentioned earlier. With the advent of improved communications and a truly national economy, however, there is no

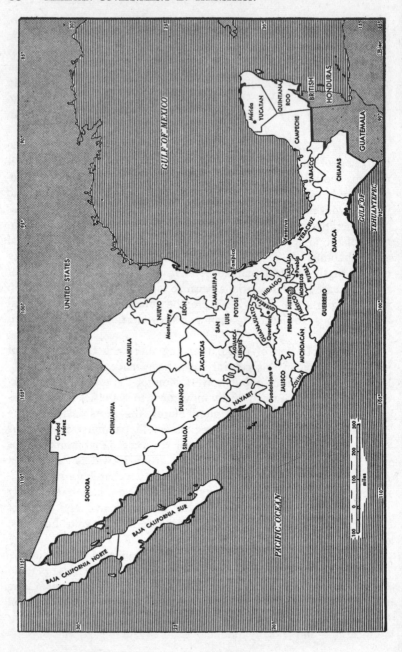

question that today the peripheral regions are part of the modern Mexican nation. These outlying areas are: (1) the highlands in the northwest; (2) the highlands of Chiapas; (3) the highlands of Oaxaca; (4) the low-altitude coastal strips which lie along the edges of central Mexico on the Pacific and the Gulf; and (5) the broad, low plain on the Gulf side of the Yucatán Peninsula.

In the northwest the relatively rough topography and high altitudes of southern California extend into Mexico on both sides of the Gulf of California. The area, which includes the peninsula of Baja California and parts of the states of Sonora and Sinaloa, is separated from central Mexico by the mountainous Sonora Desert. It was long a source of political localism and economic isolation, but recently attempts have been made to bring it into the orbit of the national capital. As improvements in internal communication within the area have increased, as transportation to Mexico City has improved, and as private and public investment from the capital has expanded, a closer identification with the center has developed.

In 1951 the president of Mexico recommended to congress that the northern section of the territory of Baja California be made Mexico's twenty-ninth state; by the end of 1953 a state constitution had been approved, a state government was operating, and representatives from Baja California (Norte) had been elected to Congress. One of the deputies was a woman, the first in the national legislature. Nonetheless, Baja California still remains somewhat isolated from the rest of the country, as the struggle over customs privileges for the area around Tijuana demonstrates. In 1955, for the first time, the central authorities tried to end the duty-free import privileges enjoyed by the region on the grounds that the Mexican interior could compete favorably with the United States in supplying its needs. After a trial period this proved incorrect and many of the free import privileges were reinstated. Because of its proximity to the United States, the tourist trade and commercial agriculture (cotton and truck gardens) based on irrigation have made Baja California one of the richest regions of Mexico.

The highlands of Oaxaca, which lie south of the valley of the Balsas River in the broad mountain belt between the *mesa central* and the Isthmus of Tehuantepec, are somewhat similar to the central plateau in surface configuration and linked to it by relatively easy travel routes. As late as 1952, however, the citizens of Oaxaca held a series of mass meetings to assert their strong feelings of local independence against the centralization of political authority in Mexico City. The meetings came to nothing with regard to local autonomy, but they demonstrated the tenacity of regional attitudes in Mexico. Despite being the birthplace of Benito Juárez and therefore, one might think, having a predilection toward reform, Oaxaca has never warmed to the Revolution of 1910, probably because the Revolution bore with it greater central authority. As a consequence, the revolutionary government has done relatively little for the area until recently. Only in 1957 was Oaxaca linked to the national electrical grid, and the area still is one of the most underdeveloped and unintegrated rural regions in the country. Greater attention may be paid to this region in the future, however, for it was included in the first extended campaign trip of the revolutionary party's 1958 presidential candidate, Lic. Adolfo López Mateos.

Separating Oaxaca from the Chiapas highlands is the low and semitropical Isthmus of Tehuantepec, historically a major barrier between the central plateau and the south of Mexico. It is still difficult to cross by surface transportation, and its sparse population is among the least integrated into national life in all of Mexico. Beyond it, the far southern portion of Chiapas is situated in a range of mountains known as the Sierra Madre de Chiapas, which faces the Pacific Ocean but really is the beginning of the mountainous area of Central America. In fact, during the viceregal era Chiapas was administered as a part of Central America and only the circumstances of the revolt from Spain placed the territory within the Mexican fold.

The relatively few people who live in this area are found mostly in the valley of Chiapas; if they were not somewhat dependent economically upon the center for markets for their cattle, corn, and coffee, they would be almost completely isolated from the rest of Mexico. Not until 1955, with the opening of the railroad across the Isthmus of Tehuantepec from Veracruz on the Gulf side to Tapachula on the Pacific side, were many of the people of Chiapas linked by economical land transportation to the rest of Mexico, for the highway and feeder-road system is still far from complete in this part of Mexico.

The narrow Pacific coastal lowlands are economically dependent upon the highlands overlooking them. Much the same might be said for the Gulf coast lowlands, although as far south as Tampico the latter are much wider and economically much more important than their Pacific counterparts because of petroleum production. Economic strength is particularly lacking in the sparsely populated and isolated Gulf coastal area that begins to broaden near the Isthmus of Tehuantepec and expands into the entire Yucatán Peninsula. In hopes of strengthening the economies of the states along the entire lower Gulf coastal area, early in his administration President Ruiz Cortines inaugurated a "march to the sea," with a program to improve harbors, transportation, and marketing facilities for the shrimp fishing and other maritime industries. He also transferred some 14,000 square kilometers of forest and farm land from the national territory of Quintana Roo to the states of Campeche and Yucatán as a gesture of aid to the southeast. This did not entirely satisfy the authorities of the state of Yucatán, who asked in December of 1955 that the whole of Quintana Roo be incorporated into their state. They did not get their wish, but more attention has been paid to the area since then.

Probably this was because the state of Yucatán is the clearest example of isolation, separatism, and economic woe in the Mexican union. Not until 1950, with the completion of the Southeastern Railroad, which took fifteen years to build, was there a land tie between the peninsula and the north, and as late as 1958 Yucatán had no roads across the isthmus to the economic heart of the country, the *mesa central* and Mexico City. The *yucatecos* once declared their independence of Mexico and requested admission to the United States, and to this day they of all the Mexicans have managed to preserve the separate identity of their "Socialist Party of the Southeast" as the Popular sector of the official party in their state.

In addition to the economic difficulties of the other coastal states, the collapse of the wartime henequen boom and the failure of the government-sponsored henequen growing and marketing collective in 1954 left Yucatán badly off indeed. Much of the central government's program of relief for the Gulf coastal area appears to stem from a growing awareness of Yucatán's problems, with possibly a touch of recognition that Yucatán is far enough away from Mexico City to demonstrate its impatience in ways which might give other peripheral areas unfortunate ideas. Major political difficulty is not very likely to arise, though, for Yucatán's political separatism and its traditions of independence have tended to weaken and disappear as the state has become dependent upon Mexico City for economic aid and as a market for its products.

The Mexico City government has made real efforts to integrate the southeastern part of the country into the national economic life. At the end of his term, in 1958, President Ruiz Cortines pointed to the completion of the southeast road linking Quintana Roo with the remainder of the Yucatán Peninsula as one of the proudest achievements of his administration. Previously, during 1957, he had requested former President Cárdenas to visit the entire region (the states of Yucatán, Campeche, and Tabasco, and the territory of Quintana Roo) in order to study and suggest solutions to its problems. Finally, in addition to Oaxaca, Adolfo López Mateos came to the southeast on the first major campaign trip of the 1958 presidential campaign, demonstrating the continuity of interest in this region felt by the official party.

Mexico today corresponds to a logical geographic pattern, covering about the same area as that dominated by the Aztecs before the Spanish conquest, and in spite of sizable contractions of the northern and southern border areas during and since the wars for independence, the present Mexican territory includes just about the effective extent of Spanish viceregal rule. The loss of Central America during the independence era is not surprising, considering the less than firm ties between this outpost of empire and the core of strength in the Mexican central highlands. Only the accidents of history and a still extant internal disunity in Central America enabled Mexico to retain possession of Chiapas and Yucatán in the south. Similarly, in the north it was highly unlikely that the expanding power of the United States would fail to detach Texas, Alta California, and the lands between, for the almost unpopulated northern desert separated these territories from Mexico proper.

The lands left to Mexico, for all of their difficulties of geographic diversity, permit just enough internal integration to form a nation, particularly with the growth of technological progress. So, in spite of all the problems of separation and isolation which have plagued Mexico's internal politics and which still leave their mark, the country is now united by the ties of increasingly efficient land transportation and the instantaneous communication of radio and telegraph, as well as by an expanding national economy. All of this makes for a growing sense of national being among an increasing number of the Mexican people which, in turn, makes evolution of a national system of politics possible.

## The Population of Mexico

Mexico is a crowded country, if not in terms of total area per capita, certainly in terms of arable land and other natural resources available for immediate use. Some 33,000,000 people live in its 760,375 square miles, and as a consequence of recent improvements in social and medical standards the population increases about three and a half per cent every year.[2] Because of this high birth rate, which adds about a million people to the total population each year, and the large number of deaths during the violent phase of the Revolution, Mexico is a country of relatively young people, with well over half its inhabitants under twenty years of age.

The Mexicans are unevenly distributed throughout their country. Most of them prefer the cool highlands, where slope and altitude make much of the land unusable even for the incredibly patient and hard-working Indian farmer, rather than lower climes where more rain and flatter land might provide a more satisfactory living. About seventy per cent of the people live in the half of the country that lies at over 1,000 meters (roughly 3,300 feet) above sea level, with the greatest proportion on the central plateau, where fourteen per cent of the national territory supports over forty-eight per cent of the inhabitants. In order to be absolutely accurate, one really ought to say seven per cent of the national territory, for half of the *mesa central* is unusable mountains.

Here on the central plateau it is that many of Mexico's larger cities are found. In addition to the capital, Mexico City, six of the nine cities classed by the 1950 census as being over 100,000 in population are found here. In descending order, they are Guadalajara (377,928), Monterrey (333,422), Puebla (211,203), Torreón (128,976), San Luis Potosí (125,557), and León (122,646). Obviously all of them have grown since 1950. In 1958, for example, Guadalajara had 435,000, Monterrey 390,000, and Puebla 240,000 inhabitants.

Density of population drops off sharply as one moves down and away from the central highland region toward the coastal lowlands or the northern desert. The only cities of over 100,000 population in

---

[2] As of June, 1959, the official estimate of Mexico's population was 33,300,000. Between 1943 and 1958 the death rate declined some 50 per cent, from 21.9 to between 12 and 13 per thousand. This and all other data not otherwise identified come from the *Dirección General de Estadística* in Mexico City.

these outlying areas are Mérida (142,838), Juárez (122,566), and Veracruz (101,515). Numerous attempts by the national government to open these less crowded areas to colonization through large-scale irrigation projects and development schemes for resettlement of farmers from the *mesa central* have not changed the population pattern notably. Incidentally, expansion of population and the fact that the largest numbers of persons are located in less propitious farming areas are sources of constant worry to government planners because of the present inability of Mexico to expand agricultural production sufficiently to feed the new mouths appearing every day.

Even the opening up of large new tracts of land by completion of irrigation projects has not been able to keep up with the expanding population. This problem is exacerbated by two nonphysical factors over which the government has not been able to extend any really effective controls. They are an insistence of Mexican farmers on growing and consuming corn in areas poorly suited to its cultivation, and a tendency of newly settled farmers to leave the lands they have been granted because of homesickness and because the new lands are so isolated that commercial farmers cannot get their crops to markets.

### The Village

Even in the more thinly populated districts where the land cannot support a higher concentration of people, the Mexican usually does not live alone, for Mexico is a country of villages.[3] Less than one per cent of Mexico's people live on what are classed as isolated farms or other such holdings. Since before the Spanish conquest the peasant has lived in a town and worked the outlying fields, so that village life has a meaning for the rural Mexican that far transcends his understanding of distant and to him abstract political entities such as state or nation. Out of this age-old system of towns has grown the modern unit of Mexican local government, the *municipio*.

The boundaries of the *municipio* generally include not only the *cabecera*, or seat of local government, but also the surrounding farm lands and any smaller communities which may exist. Thus, it is roughly analogous to the county in the United States. According to the 1950 census, Mexico's 2,349 *municipios* were composed of

---

[3] A general view of Mexican village life is available in Sol Tax (ed.), *Heritage of Conquest* (Glencoe, Ill., 1952). A more specific study of a single village is Oscar Lewis, *Life in a Mexican Village: Tepoztlán Restudied* (Urbana, 1951).

99,028 such communities, or an average of over forty per *municipio*. Obviously they were not large; their population may be broken down as follows: [4]

| Number of inhabitants in community | Communities | | Population | |
|---|---|---|---|---|
| | Number | Per cent | Total number of inhabitants | Per cent |
| 1 to 100 | 68,837 | 66.5 | 1,825,593 | 7.0 |
| 101 to 500 | 24,825 | 25.1 | 5,844,253 | 22.7 |
| 501 to 2,500 | 7,356 | 7.4 | 7,220,230 | 28.0 |
| 2,501 and up | 1,010 | 1.0 | 10,900,934 | 42.3 |
| *Total* | 99,028 | 100.0 | 25,791,010 | 100.0 |

Typically, then, well over half of the Mexican population live in communities of less than 2,500 persons and some sixty-five per cent in towns and villages of less than 5,000 inhabitants. Until very recently, these villages were isolated from one another and from the main currents of national life. These barriers to intercommunication led to a sense of inwardness, *localismo* as the Mexicans call it, so that the individual villager tended to view the outsider with suspicion. To some extent the rural citizen still identifies himself with his own community and may have markedly different daily habits and work patterns from those of the inhabitants of neighboring towns or villages. In many cases he has little or no conception of the nation or national life and values.

The Constitution of 1917 sought to establish the *municipios* in which these smaller communities lie as independent and active centers of local government, but most of them have neither sufficient population nor wealth to provide necessary governmental or social services. Gilberto Loyo, later Minister of Economy under President Ruiz Cortines, pointed out some years ago that about half of the existing *municipios* were too small to support necessary services, suggesting that a minimum of 50,000 inhabitants was required for efficient local government.[5] Since then, costs of everything, including government, have been multiplied by inflation, but the 1950 census shows that the average *municipio* had a population of only

---

[4] *México en Cifras*, 1952 (Mexico, 1953), introduction.

[5] Quoted in Nathan L. Whetten, *Rural Mexico* (Chicago, 1948), pp. 524 ff.

about 11,000 and not even the most optimistic population estimates could forecast that the average *municipio's* size would grow to 25,000 people in 1960. Add to this the fact that most of the villages which make up the *municipios* are poor, land-hungry in a country where about 56 per cent of the labor force still depends on agriculture for its livelihood and where the Revolution was fought primarily for land.

All this might not be very significant if the *municipios* were free to attempt to solve their own problems, but they are not. With most of the major local taxes, including the one on land, in the hands of the state governments, the local administrations do not have adequate fiscal resources. Nor do most of them have control over their own budgets, which in most states must be approved in the state capital. And, generally speaking, the municipal president and other local officers are at the mercy of the governor, who can remove them almost at will.

Nonetheless it would be incorrect to leave the impression that the state governments are very meaningful entities in Mexico's politics. Both constitutionally and politically they are of small importance. Most major decisions are made at the national level and carried out by federal agencies. Where and if the states administer substantive programs, they act usually as agents of the central authorities. Politically the governors, who control the other branches of the state government, are little more than viceroys of the national president; in fact, they frequently are described as such by opposition newspapers. In another study I have demonstrated that federalism as defined in the Mexican constitution simply does not exist in practice.[6] For reasons detailed there, I believe that it is correct to say that although the states may dominate many of the actions of the *municipios*, they run a poor third in the race for political importance in Mexico. They are neither near the source of power at the top of the political system nor near the people at the bottom.

It might be worth while to mention in passing the public fiscal situation in Mexico, to show the relative position of local, state, and national government regarding income and to suggest both the political reasons for and the consequences of the situation. During 1956, the last year for which complete figures are available,

---

[6] "Some Aspects of Mexican Federalism, 1917-1948," unpublished Ph.D. thesis, University of Wisconsin, Madison, 1949.

combined government income at all levels totaled 12,789,419,754 pesos. Of this, the national government took 10,193,521,754 pesos (79.7 per cent), the 29 states took 1,414,793,000 pesos (11.1 per cent), the Federal District took 797,747,000 pesos (6.2 per cent), and the 2,349 *municipios,* including all of the other large cities in the country, took 383,358,000 pesos (3 per cent). Compare the figure for the Federal District, almost twice that of all other municipal governments combined, with the 12 million pesos taken in by Monterrey, a city of nearly 400,000 people.

The very high degree of hierarchical control over finances, which permits the central government to take the lion's share and dole out grants to the state and local administrations and allows the states to exercise strong controls over local budgets, is a natural outgrowth of traditional Spanish centralism and the disordered political situation during the Revolution. Mastery over fiscal resources is just one of the many weapons Mexican government leaders have forged to assure domination of their political subordinates. As Westernization proceeds and the political system becomes more rationalized, pressures to reduce this superimposed control from above have begun to mount. During 1959, for example, both the National Congress of Municipal Governments, representing the local administrations, and the national Senate, speaking for the central government, began separate studies of the need for improved fiscal resources for the *municipios.*

## The City

With regard to both formal government and informal politics, the larger towns and cities play a more important role than do either the states or the outlying villages in a hierarchical pyramid of relationships that has its apex in the national capital. Thus, three-fifths of the Mexicans live in the 98,000 smaller villages, but for political leadership they look to and in turn are influenced by the inhabitants of a thousand larger communities. These include 151 towns of over 10,000 population, which look upon the surrounding smaller towns and villages as political tributaries. The larger towns then consider each of the nine cities of over 100,000 people as a kind of regional capital which can exercise leadership over them.

Finally, and almost literally, all roads lead to Mexico City, for in addition to being the press and radio center, the capital is the transportation hub of the country. Like Paris, it is the social, cultural, and economic heart of the nation, as well as its political capital. Picture in the United States a city with the principal attributes of New York, Chicago, Los Angeles, and Washington. To the Mexicans their capital is that city. Although its physical setting is somewhat unsuited for a large urban center, Mexico City and its environs have a far larger population than all nine other major cities combined. The capital itself, with over three and a half million residents, almost equals this total. The Federal District has some four and a half million inhabitants and is growing at an almost unbelievable rate, about seven per cent annually, or twice as rapidly as the rest of the country.

Mexico City drains leadership from the periphery much as Rome used to do, and as the Eternal City used to do also, the Mexican capital sends back trusted agents to govern the rest of the country. The promising student, the ambitious lawyer, the seeker for culture, the strongest politician, each gravitates from the village toward the larger towns and cities and ultimately to the national capital. Once there, if he becomes a successful member of the dominant revolutionary clique, he may rise in his political fortunes and in time even return to his former home as representative of the central authority. Governors, senators, deputies, even state university rectors are recruited from among the successful political and administrative officers who long have lived in the national capital. Their election or selection to office is assured by the all-powerful organization of the official party.

### Urbanization

But if Mexico City has added over two million citizens to its population since 1940, the other cities of the country also have continued to grow. The number of those with over 100,000 people rose to nine in 1950 and cities with more than 50,000 inhabitants totaled twenty-four. If measured in terms of urban areas, using *municipios* as the basic unit, the growth is even more impressive. Between 1940 and 1950 *municipios* with more than 100,000 inhabitants rose from four to sixteen, and those with more than 50,000 people nearly doubled in number, totaling fifty-four. Proportionately, larger towns and cities loom much more important in the total population than they once did. This tendency toward urban expansion is one of the most interesting phenomena in Mexico's postrevolutionary development pattern, from a political as well as a sociological viewpoint. Given present estimates, this tendency should be even more pronounced by the time the 1960 census data is published.

It is in the larger towns and cities that the most obvious manifestations of Western-type society and politics are found. Here it is that those parts of the population most aware of the advantages of political action are concentrated. Here it is that specialization of function has proceeded farthest. So here it is too that the associational interest organization has its strongest impact, and the interaction of unorganized citizens most often turns latent interest groups into effective influences over political policy deciders. Unfortunately, urbanization and the full effects of Westernization have yet to reach a high proportion of the nineteen million rural Mexicans, much less the unintegrated Indian villages.

Islands of backwardness lie in the midst of more highly developed regions, just as they did under the viceroys and during the nineteenth century. As recently as 1955, in the state of Querétaro, superstitious Indians lynched a rural medical team they thought had bewitched them. And in 1956, in Chiapas, a New York artist was beaten to death because of what was termed an old Mayan legend according to which a "white devil" would come and cast a spell over the countryside, killing the cattle.

Nonetheless, the towns and cities serve to diffuse the new values, and with them the national culture and institutions, among the people of the hinterland. Considering the obstacles Mexico once faced, Westernization has at least begun to end the material difficulties which at one time isolated a high proportion of its citizens from the nation at large. The struggle to gain the more material goals of the Mexican Revolution has been long and hard and the end is not yet in sight, for the problems to overcome are as complex as they are numerous. Only recently have schools and the other advantages of modern technology begun to reach out from the principal cities to the back country in any appreciable amount. Some villages remain without potable water or electricity, and entire areas still lack easy access to the rest of the country. Gradually, however, the inhabitants of these isolated areas are being reached.

It is through the more urban areas that the process of integration is carried out. As economic centers they provide markets for rural cash-crop agricultural production, supplying in exchange the mass-produced goods the farmers need. As administrative centers they translate into action the government's policies on education, irrigation, road construction, and all the other matters which so concern the isolated areas. As political centers the urban areas house the headquarters of the revolutionary party (and of others, where they exist), as well as providing an arena for the activities of the agrarian functional interest associations which do spread out into the back country. As social centers they provide facilities for religious services, motion picture and radio entertainment, and the production of regional newspapers. In a very real sense, they are the funnels through which all of the by-products of Westernization are channeled to the rural population.

All of this has meaning in the political sphere, for the broad ramifications of integration into the nation entail not simply the involvement of the rural masses in a system of cash-crop production and consumption of mass-produced goods, but the by-products of such involvement. As the wide world reaches in toward the rural Mexican and he in turn reaches out to the wide world, he becomes more and more aware of government and of political action. The role played by the state in controlling and directing change, and its augmented function as a provider of services beyond the capabilities of the rural peasant, are part of a pattern of more nearly national political life that accompanies technical progress and the growth of interdependent economic enterprise.

As the inhabitant of the once isolated community becomes enmeshed in relationships with the urban area, the new values characterized by economic motivation and the more specialized activities of urban life begin to affect him. The old, single-class, village community is replaced by one in which class and/or economic distinctions exist. The new way of life sets a higher value on economic and social success, both of which may be identified with political activity and certainly can be increased by organization of and action through special interest groups. Urbanization, therefore, is a vital ally of Westernization in making Mexicans aware of government and in broadening the base upon which Mexico's government rests.

Under these circumstances, the trend toward urbanization is politically significant in Mexico. Even excluding the move toward larger cities, the increasing proportion of Mexicans who live in what are classed in census data as urban communities (2,501 or more inhabitants) as opposed to rural areas suggests that Mexico is becoming more nearly typically Western. In 1930, 71.6 per cent of the Mexicans were classed as rural; in 1940 this proportion fell to 65.4 per cent; in 1950 to 57. 4 per cent. By 1960, if present estimates prove correct, the rural population should be only 54 per cent. Obviously, the highest urban concentration is found in the Federal District, with 94.5 per cent so classified; the lowest is in Oaxaca, with only 20.6 per cent urban inhabitants.

The use of the figure 2,500 as the breaking point between urban and rural has been challenged as unrealistic by several sociologists who point out that it was adopted by the Mexicans from United States census practice without due regard to conditions in the smaller and less highly developed country. Whetten, for example, suggests that few if any Mexican towns of less than 10,000 population ought to be classified as urban,[7] and anyone who has visited or lived in many towns or villages smaller than this can testify that isolation and poverty still prevent the inhabitants of most of them from sharing the physical advantages or mental outlook enjoyed by their North American counterparts in towns of equal size. The 2,500 figure is, however, officially recognized in Mexico and for that reason is used here. If the percentage of rural inhabitants has not decreased as speedily as the official data suggests, the pattern of expanding urbanization, with all of its by-products, still is quite marked in Mexico.

### Town vs. Country

Tragically, in the larger cities, where one might have hoped for better conditions, some of the worst aspects of modern Mexican social and economic life are found. Not in the jungle of Tehuantepec or in a semi-isolated rural district of Chiapas, but behind the façade of skyscrapers and brightly colored murals of Mexico City does one note the highest rate of infant mortality. Many of the rural people who come to the city are unprepared for life there, either socially or economically. They are faced with new problems originating in culture conflicts, disorganization of older living habits and customs, difficulties of personal adjustment, dislocation of both the family and the broader social structure. They have neither the skills to earn a living in the new environment nor the education to learn

---

[7] See Nathan L. Whetten, *op. cit.*, pp. 34-36,

the skills. They end up in unbelievable slums. As a result of inadequate housing, overcrowding, lack of sanitary facilities, and bad water, coupled with lack of preparation among the new inhabitants, these slum districts have the worst health record in the country. Some of Oscar Lewis' research indicates that where families from the same village live together in the same *vecindad* or multiple dwelling unit, family ties and village culture carry over to a surprising extent, but this of itself makes adjustment to the urban, more Westernized environment just that much slower and more difficult.[8]

Even though it may not appear on the statistician's graph or add to the national cash income, the subsistence farm of the backwoods Indian can at least keep him and his family alive and away from concentrations of people who spread disease. In the city, the individual is trapped in an economic situation where inflation has multiplied prices five times since 1939, without any corresponding increase in lower class income, except among the organized workers. During 1954, the income of more than a quarter of the families in the Federal District, which includes Mexico City, was below 300 pesos a month, and five per cent of the households lived on less than 100 pesos, at that time about U.S. $12.50. Although the cost of living in Mexico is appreciably lower than in the United States, the booming economy is accompanied by inflation, making life not at all easy for many of the people who live in Mexico City and other larger urban communities. For 1958-60, just after the courts had nullified the legality of fixed ceiling prices on articles of prime necessity, a new minimum wage was fixed—twelve pesos a day in cities and ten in rural areas, an increase of one peso a day over the old minimum. At the time, one peso was worth eight U.S. cents. The government continued its attempts to keep down the price of basic foodstuffs through low-cost sales of primary articles at cost price in its CEIMSA stores, but inadequate numbers of outlets, long lines, and recurring shortages of stock largely negated the attempts. Moreover, from personal observation I know that many country people worked for three to four pesos a day, and city laborers for six pesos, and considered themselves lucky to find work, even at those rates. All of this was a prime cause of the labor difficulties mentioned in Chapter 1.

---

[8] Oscar Lewis, "Urbanization without Breakdown," *Scientific Monthly*, LXXV (July, 1952), 31-41.

But for all of these difficulties, the urban population, or at least that portion of it which is sufficiently acclimated to Western values to know how to organize into effective interest groups, on the whole has benefited more from industrialization and change than has the farmer in the backlands. The 1950 census showed somewhat less than five million adult workers in agriculture, a million in industrial work, a quarter million in communications and services, with 100,000 more in mining. For all of their larger numbers, farmers came off a poor fourth in the value of their annual production. The figures in U.S. dollars were: farmers, $200; industrial workers, $1,000; communications and services, $1,700; and miners, $2,500. Individual income obviously reflected the value of goods produced or services rendered, even taking into account the unmeasured value of food and other goods produced for home consumption on the farms. One estimate suggests that in 1950 farmers received only U.S. $120 average cash income.

During the past decade or so, however, the tempo of material development has increased throughout the entire country. Between 1939 and 1951, for example, manufacturing production doubled; between 1951 and 1955 it doubled again. It is clear to anyone who has observed Mexico for any length of time that some of these gains are beginning to reach out to the rural districts, encouraging integration of the rural masses into the national life, but at much too slow a rate to bring very many of them into effective political participation in the near future.

Since 1950, the total number of persons in the working population has increased, but the relative number and the relative position of each group in the economy remains about the same. Before a more equitable share of the benefits of industrialization and technical progress can filter down to the rural population, the political imbalance between village and city must be adjusted.

During the discussion of the national budget for 1954, a rural deputy demonstrated graphically how great is the difference between what rural Mexico needs and what it gets. He complained that more than twice as much per child was allotted for education in the Federal District than was granted in country areas, where illiteracy is highest. Since state supplements to national expenditures for education within their boundaries are often theoretical at best, this is an important point. Particularly in the poorest rural states such as Oaxaca, where the need is greatest and the resources are weakest, the lion's share must come from the national government, which controls most of the fiscal sources of Mexican government.

During 1955, public expenditures for education ran to two million pesos daily, with a larger proportionate share allotted to nonurban areas than previously, but the favorable balance still lay with the cities. In all, a third of all children of school age, at least three million of them, never entered a classroom, and well over a third of all Mexicans over six years of age (8,946,638, to be exact) could not read or write. Until more Mexicans, and especially more rural Mexicans, are brought into contact with the wide world through schools, the influence of Western values will not permeate their society very deeply and therefore will not influence their political values systems either.

To put it another way, some ten million of the nineteen million persons in rural Mexico have scarcely been touched by modern techniques. They do not wear shoes or eat wheat bread; instead they wear sandals or go barefoot and they eat *tortillas* of corn. Because the material changes engendered by Westernization and spread by the Mexican Revolution have not been exported in sufficient quantities from the cities to the country areas, the more gifted rural inhabitant, whose eyes are opened to the wide world by education and experience, is lured away from the land by the attractions of the city. The less gifted and less fortunate peasant then proceeds to replace him on the land with one of Malthus' children.

Not unexpectedly, with the most intelligent persons, those best adapted to Western political life, drained from their role as potential rural leaders, the inhabitants of the smaller villages continue to play at best a secondary role in the formal politics of Mexico. By far the greatest part of them have only the haziest conception of state and national affairs and less idea about the nature of the political process. Even those who theoretically are members of a functionally organized farm group have only a tangential relationship with either the national political system or formal constitutional government, through the leaders of their associations, who work with and sometimes are put into office by the state or national political machine.

Mere learning to read and write, or to wear shoes, or to eat wheat bread will not materially alter the political habits of these people, but it can open the door to change. It already has begun to do so for almost half the rural population. As Westernization comes to rural Mexico, the possibility of truly national government for all the country's citizens follows. But the process is slow and until the people can be fitted into some more comprehensive pattern of social and political action, many of the citizens will remain as they are now, outside of direct influence upon the political process, except as their traditional differences are exploited by the *políticos* who dominate the organizations to which they belong or the districts in which they live.[9]

---

[9] Perhaps the best available source of general observations combined with exhaustive data concerning economic, social, and cultural conditions in present-day Mexico is Oscar Lewis' article, "Mexico desde 1940," in *Investigación Economica*, XVIII, no. 70 (segundo trimestre de 1958), 185-256.

CHAPTER *3*

# The Mexican People

## The Revolution and National Institutions

The problems of political integration posed by geographic barriers have been compounded by the absence of a high degree of shared values, indeed for a long time, of a truly national society among the Mexicans. Among antirevolutionaries it is popular to point to the Revolution as the principal cause of this lack of unity among the Mexican people. The theory is that the breakdown of the well-organized and operating set of social and political institutions which existed before 1910 was a terrible blow to continuity of values and political thought, and that the new governments have failed to supply any positive substitute institutions acceptable to the whole of the Mexican people. In actuality this allegation oversimplifies the matter.

The Revolution was really a final effect of the social disintegration that started with the Conquest. In setting up the kind of closed social and political system they did, the *conquistadores,* and later, during the independence era, the landed aristocracy, set the stage ─────── unhappy violence that marked the early days of the revolu──── movement. By excluding most of the Mexican people from ─────evelopment, economic advance, and political participation, ────de any really widely based governmental system impossible. ────ngs considered, the social and political system in which the land-holding, ruling class participated was quite stable. It had developed over a period of centuries, with little interruption, much less disruption, when the Spanish viceroy was replaced by strong-man presidents. The practices upon which it was built were systematically interrelated, the ethic as a whole tended to be internally consistent, so long as one stayed within the ruling clique. Each of the various persons who enacted his role in the system quite naturally sought complementary rather than contradictory patterns of action, thus strengthening the system further.

The mechanics by which the segments of this nationally active society made their relationships effective were an important part of the system of politics. More specialized interests, such as the Church or the military, had worked out a fairly well-defined rapprochement with each other and with the more general portions of the society, so that a comparatively well-integrated over-all relationship existed. Of course, power struggles occurred, but they erupted within and among the factions of the ruling clique, rather than between them and the masses. If social reforms such as those offered by Juárez were instituted from time to time, the interests of this closed society were sufficiently interrelated and the political potentialities of the masses so limited as to counteract reform in short order.

No social-political system ever is in such perfect adjustment that it is static, not even so very limited a one as that of prerevolutionary Mexico, but the influence of strong personalistic leaders such as Díaz over the power factors to be controlled generally was enough to contain the fluctuations of political activity so as not to disturb the ruling elite unduly. The remainder of the Mexicans either did not know enough to seek to participate or were excluded as unprepared and unworthy of participation, for the theories of positivism and Social Darwinism found a fertile field in the minds of Díaz and his *científicos*. Consequently, the aristocracy considered national government their private preserve and, as far as they observed it, the national constitution as a set of rules for a kind of private game played among themselves.

In truth, a high proportion of the Indian inhabitants had no conception of a Mexican nation, much less the status, the education, or the economic independence to enable them to play any real role in the formal processes of political decision-making. They had relatively little sense of the class distinctions existing between them and their masters, for the traditional tendency of the Indian to isolate himself made for little day-to-day competition. The lack of any group consciousness or banding together against oppressors made the relationship more nearly a caste than a class system. Even among those with a broader outlook, who otherwise might have shared a sense of the nation, the barriers to easy communication weakened any real chance for the compulsory conformity with minimal basic nationwide institutions such as government, law, education, or a national economy which might have worked to develop a common heritage. Inevitably, a great number of different cultural, social, and economic types and classes resulted, so many that Mexico could not be said to have a single nationwide social or political system.

Only as the social and technological changes growing out of Westernization began to make themselves felt in Mexico did the weaknesses inherent in the old aristocratic system become apparent, as the expanding middle class, made up mainly of mixed-culture *mestizos,* sought participation in national life. The institutions which broke down during the Revolution failed precisely because they did not represent the whole population, or even this growing politically aware portion. The very occurrence of the Revolution demonstrates the inadequate adaptability of the institutions in question, for they could not provide channels through which the problems and desires of the *mestizos* and the less clearly observed difficulties which harassed the Indian masses could reach the government. A system based on such institutions could hardly hope to supply continuity of political thought on a national scale for an indefinite period of time.

Little wonder then, that the Revolution threw this select political system out of adjustment as it effected changes in most of the factors influencing the social process. It weakened the status of the former governing elite just as the revolutionary leaders flung open the floodgates of politics to admit hitherto unrepresented and still unprepared peoples to the national life. So many of the factors in economic and political life changed so speedily that they could not ommodated systematically in the political system, and its ning was disrupted as institutionalized patterns of action own. In Mexico during the 1920's and 1930's, therefore, the social disequilibrium and of political instability was very

Nonetheless, the Revolution did not, could not, abolish Mexican society or the strongest institutions in that society. Little by little, the social and political systems have been adjusting to change, acquiring legitimacy in the process. Only time, working with the increased opportunities for interaction among the Mexican people made possible by technology, can offset the conditions which for so long tended to exaggerate distinctions among these people and acted to minimize the core of shared traits which make for an integrated nation. By now, however, even the leaders of opposition parties speak—for campaign purposes at any rate—of how they could accomplish the goals of the Revolution more effectively than the official party. This does not mean that the newer institutional practices which have developed within the revolutionary system of politics are wholly representative of the entire Mexican people, but they are more representative than their predecessors and, I submit, they provide mechanisms which may permit continuing expansion of their representative function.

## Continued Diversity

Despite these changes, which are bringing more and more people into effective national life, not all Mexicans are satisfied with the degree of national unification that has been achieved to date under the Westernization movement for which the Revolution of 1910 stands. They seek that feeling of security which comes of sharing in a really homogeneous society, so they search for some almost metaphysical concept that can bind the Mexicans together. This is reflected in the unending striving among Mexican intellectuals to discover "the most precious values of the Mexican soul," as it was once put to me.

The theme of *Mexicanismo* recurs constantly in their thoughts and in their writings. This, that, or the other thing is Mexican, truly Mexican, purely Mexican—the highest praise they can bestow on a book, a picture, a man, or even a theory of politics.

This fixation on Mexicanism is at once proud and pathetic; it indicates a love of nation and at the same time a seeking for the unity of purpose that makes a nation. But until very recently that unity of purpose has never existed in Mexico, because of those physical and mental barriers which divided the Mexicans into local factions and antipathetical groups, each of which wished to recast Mexico into its own mold. Even today, with the changes brought about in the country since the advent of Western technology, no all-inclusive society that completely satisfies the disparate interests represented in these groups has yet evolved.

Many non-Mexicans have their own mental picture of the typical Mexican. Whatever it is, it is wrong; as yet there is no typical Mexican. Certainly, no one who knows frenetic Mexico City or solid, industrious Monterrey can accept as typical the picture postcard image of an incredibly lazy man clad in white pajamas, leaning against an adobe wall with his sombrero over his eyes. Nor could the intelligent observer credit the picture of a puffy-faced, over-dressed man with dark glasses—the guide, shopkeeper, or minor political leader—as representative of modern Mexico.

A few moments reflection should convince anyone that both pictures are purely fictional. Mexico has not yet conquered its diversity sufficiently to have produced a typical, stamp-pressed, semiautomaton citizen such as those who seem to inhabit North American suburbia. True enough, Westernization has begun the process of evolving a national economy and a national political system, but the differences among the Mexicans who are being drawn into the national life still are so clearly defined as to preclude any easy generalization about them en masse. They differ in their ways of life, in their standards of living, even in their patterns of thought; they have a fairly sharply defined class system, although it is not so rigid as that of other Latin American countries with large Indian populations.

From the standpoint of politics, clearly the most obvious and important division lies between those segments of the population who take an active part in nationally oriented political life and those who do not. Here again, there can be no clear-cut distinction, for there is an overlap between those who do not yet participate and others who are slightly more politically aware. They exist in a shadow-zone where apolitical Mexicans are evolving into citizens who do feel the influence of government in their lives, who have some interest in the political process, and who are able to organize into groups in order to participate in political policy-making.

Despite the common denominator of understanding of national life and shared political mechanisms, among those portions of Mexican society which already are politically active there is a whole hierarchy of differing values and interests. Various segments of the population demonstrate greater or lesser understanding and intensity of interest in different aspects of the political process. Depending upon the conditions in which they act, whether urban or rural, industrial or white collar, fully or only partly integrated into national life, these parts of the Mexican people (and the interest groups which represent them) are more or less active, effective, and influential in policy-making.

Luckily, in considering the Mexican national political system we can concentrate upon the composite activities of interest groups at the state-national political level and, to some extent at least, upon the role of those most active politically. This is not to ignore the Indian or the latent but unorganized group, but to keep them in their proper perspective. The emphasis must be on the more generalized and effective portions of the national political culture, in this case the *mestizo* and the functional interaction of the groups in which he operates.

Let us turn, then, to consideration of the major subcultural groups in Mexico, to show their role in the society, their relative size and their tendency toward (or against) effective national political action, as well as the degree of latency in them as potential factors in the political process. We do this because, although the subcultural segments of the political culture must be treated separately from the composite national political system, the two are so interrelated that they cannot be understood and evaluated properly in isolation from each other.

In order to point this up, we group the Mexicans into six broad subcultural types, each of which has its peculiar place in the modern social-political system. These types are: (1) the Indian; (2) the peasant, including *ejiditarios* and small farmers; (3) the small town dweller; (4) the urban proletariat; (5) the metropolitan middle class; and (6) the metropolitan upper class.[1] These six subcultural types reduce in terms of political awareness and influence, as well as role in the social system, to four broad classes: (1) unintegrated Indians; (2) a peasant *ejiditario* and small farmer-urban proletariat lower class; (3) the small town and urban middle class;

---

[1] For purposes of this typology, I have adapted the system of classification suggested by Charles Wagley and Marvin Harris in their "A Typology of Latin American Subcultures," *American Anthropologist,* 57, no. 3, (June, 1955), 428-51. I have deleted two types from their classification (tribal Indian and Family Owned Plantation) as nonpertinent in Mexico and combined several under the general term "peasant."

and (4) the urban upper class. I use the term "class" advisedly here; in spite of some slight easing of social barriers which accompanies revolutionary reform, and notwithstanding Mexico's rapidly expanding economy, there is still relatively little mobility among the social-economic levels which participate in Mexican politics, with the exception of unintegrated Indians moving into the *mestizo* nationally oriented society as new members of the lower economic class.

## The Indian

The way of life of the Mexican Indian is quite distinct from that of the rest of Mexico, though a few archaic sixteenth- and seventeenth-century Spanish habits and techniques seem to have been picked up along the way, probably from the *conquistadores* who settled in the midst of the stable Indian societies in order to exploit them. Usually the Indian practices a debased form of Catholicism mixed with practices from pagan religion and a cult of the saints. He tends to speak a native tongue or is bilingual. Generally the Indian is agrarian, but he has little or no sense of either the legal or the economic aspects of cash-crop production. He is not concerned with legal title to his land; as an individual he may follow the *milpa*, slash-and-burn, constantly moving type of farming, but more often as a villager he participates in farming his own *ejido* or privately owned lands and at times community-owned lands, aided by crude irrigation systems if and when water is available. In any case, most farm production is for home use or exchange in a local market, rather than for an outside cash market.

Most important, from the standpoint of national politics, the Indian tends to think of his village as separate from other villages, of himself as a member of his own distinct group, rather than as a state or national citizen. Mexican anthropologists estimate that in this sense of separatism about fifteen per cent of Mexico's population is Indian,[2] and the census of 1950 set the number of persons who spoke only Indian languages at 795,069, with two million more as bilingual because they spoke some Spanish. These figures are undoubtedly lower than they should be, for the Indian is unlikely to volunteer accurate information on such matters for fear of taxes

---

[2] Juan Comas, "Making Mexico One," *Américas*, 6, no. 3 (March, 1954), pp. 19 ff. See also Charles Wagley and Marvin Harris, *Minorities in the New World* (New York, 1958), especially pp. 48-86, "The Indian in Mexico."

and military drafts. And I am sure that the census-takers did not count each and every Indian, at least in the backlands where at times national troops were needed to protect the census-takers.

But even if these figures were substantially correct, the census definition of "Indian" is cultural rather than political, and many Mexicans classed as non-Indians because of a greater acceptance of the Spanish language, the use of shoes, and the practice of a few European customs may as yet be almost as unfamiliar with the social and political practices of national life and constitutional government as their more isolated brothers.

As noted earlier, most rural Mexicans, including Indians, are village people, with a great deal more cultural stability than nomadic people have. It is difficult to break into the habit patterns of such people, particularly as the villages have always competed with their neighbors for land and water resources, and with larger political units because of land grabs, military drafts, attempts to levy taxes, diversion of water, and the like. As a result, the villagers tend to treasure their *localismo*, often seeking to isolate themselves both physically and mentally.

In fact, most Indian villages have worked out informal but highly effective systems of discouraging change from their ancient mode of life. The villager who begins to wear shoes rather than sandals, who ignores his village obligations, or who otherwise indicates abandonment of the old ways for modern life may be ostracized in the community. Again, the village Indians often refuse to sell land outside of their own group or to deal in any way with the outsider who does enter their boundaries.

During the 1930's, one of the revolutionary theories looked to *indianismo* as one of the most deeply rooted sources of mass participation in Mexican community life and, therefore, as the best hope for stable and responsible government. Nothing ever came of the theory. Probably nothing could, for the Indian village concept does not suit the needs of the Western industrial society developing in Mexico.

In the first place, it tends to divide the country into innumerable tiny local units just when social and economic problems have become national in scope and require national solutions. Secondly, in spite of what appears at first glance, village life provides no real basis for formal government or democracy in the Western political sense of the term. There is a good deal of community action, with every man expected to participate whether he wants to or not. And every community has a single-class society in which each individual moves up through a hierarchy of village positions as he grows older. But community activity and office-holding is based more on tradition and social pressures than on a concept of formal government. It is neither representative, in the sense of village officers being selected on the basis of merit, nor responsible, in the sense that the elders seek the positions or attempt to continue in office once selected. The office-holder does not stand for office because he feels an urge to serve his fellows, or even because he wishes the fruits of office; instead, he is fulfilling a community obligation that all must face.[3]

Since there exist effective social mechanisms to maintain the one-class system, for example, by forcing anyone who becomes too well-to-do to spend his excess money on a huge village *fiesta*, there can be no incentive in the Indian village either to want office for material gain or to seek to retain office by providing better service than some competitor. This kind of localized, non-Western system can have little relation to the needs of Mexico's national political system, even if the Indian had any real desire to share in it, and generally he does not.

In the case of the Indian, his separatism stems not only from his geographic isolation and cultural aloofness, but from his very approach to life. The goal of the *indio* is to effect a peaceful adaptation of his own desires to the universe in which he finds himself. The *mestizo*, that is, the Mexican who is of mixed culture but who is nationally integrated, on the other hand, has adopted the Spaniard's goal of effecting control over the universe by man. As John Gillan puts it, the Indian wishes to come to terms with the universe, the *mestizo* to dominate it.[4] So long as his philosophy remains unchanged, no amount of urging will lead the nonintegrated *indio* to seek out the new concepts which would turn him into an effective and participating citizen.

Under these terms the chances of the Indian entering into formal and positive political action are slight. If it is outside his nature to

[3] Sol Tax discusses the village system more completely in his study of "The Problem of Democracy in Middle America," *American Sociological Review,* 10 (April, 1945), 192-99.

[4] "Ethos and Cultural Aspects of Personality," in *Heritage of Conquest,* pp. 193 ff.

conquer his environment, he will scarcely demand that the government do it for him. Where formal political organization exists in an Indian village, it is apt to be part of a dual system in which the tradition-oriented government is separate from the legal government that carries on political relations with the state and national governments.

Consequently, the Indian as such is scarcely even a latent force in Mexican national politics. As an individual, by his very nature he rejects the concept of action that is so important a part of interest group participation in a national political system. Collectively, the Indian rejects the nation itself. Moreover, for all his large total numbers in Mexico, there is no such thing as the "Mexican Indian" which could act as a unit, but a myriad of Indian villages, each slightly suspicious of the next, speaking some thirty-three separate indigenous languages further divided into small dialect units.

Under these circumstances, it is tempting to write off the Indian as unimportant in studying Mexico's system of politics. Indeed, having considered him here we need not return to detailed discussion of him, for the Indian takes and demands little place on the stage of Mexican politics. But he cannot be ignored completely, for the very existence of the Indian affects national life. Indirectly, his low level of production and lack of contribution to the national economy, his aloofness and illiteracy, his lack of participation in national life, can and do have an adverse effect upon the evolution of an integrated and effective system of Western-style politics. More directly, the Indian and his social characteristics have a very important effect upon Mexican politics. By definition, the second cultural subtype we shall consider—the peasant—is not very far removed from the Indian, out of whose culture he evolves, entering national life either individually as he is exposed to new influences, or collectively as a village or even an entire region is integrated into the nation. Because of this, the term peasant, as used here, indicates a Mexican in an intermediate status, sometimes close to the Indian and sometimes more advanced and nationally oriented, as in the case of the *ejiditarios* and small farmers who participate in a cash economy.

### The Peasant

The peasant's way of life includes many of the traits which mark the Indian, but with a stronger admixture of nationalizing, Western-type values and motivations. Unlike the Indian, the peasant considers himself a national of Mexico rather than of a specific village, though his real identification may be more concrete with a region than with the nation-state. He is tied to the world by the use of other than local marketing facilities to sell his surplus agricultural goods and as a source of mass-manufactured products for his own consumption. He may work an individually owned plot of land or part of a communal village holding, but he is not always fully tied to the national agrarian economy nor does he always produce primarily for a cash market.

This may be because he does not own enough good land to grow a surplus beyond the consumption needs of his family to sell in the national market. In some cases he may not own land at all, but be forced to work for some other person, as often results in families which have many sons but own little land. Many of these landless country-people are forced to make a basic change in their life patterns, either by moving to the city or by trying to obtain permission to leave Mexico itself to enter the United States temporarily as a farm worker (*bracero*). Such moves may mean more speedy acculturation of the peasants with Western-style mores than remaining in their home villages would have.

The peasant usually speaks Spanish and has somewhat more orthodox ideas of the Catholic religion than does the Indian. This, together with his choice of Western rather than tribal-type clothes and his use of shoes rather than *huaraches*, perhaps even the acquisition of literacy, mark him from his Indian brother. It is difficult to tell just how far the process of assimilation of European traits must progress before an *indio* becomes a peasant-*mestizo*, but somewhere in the transfer real differences in outlook become apparent. The peasant takes on new values from the more strongly Western-oriented *mestizo* group with whom he shares his village or town life, for the mediating of national institutions is carried on by the persons who run the stores, control the markets, and otherwise come into frequent direct contact with the *indio*-made-*mestizo*.

Within the past two decades, the number of peasants has increased markedly and the total of non-Spanish–speaking Mexicans has halved, as expanding technology brings the Indian into communication with the outside world. When an Indian community is in the process of being bound into the Western ethic, the old, ordered, single-class society of the village is replaced by partly cash-crop agricultural production and a nationally oriented system of values and activities in which technical specialization and class distinctions become more obvious and important. Both vertical and horizontal cleavages appear, as the older community relations are disorganized, secularized, and individualized.

The tendency toward disorganization may be less marked where an entire area is integrated into the national system as a unit, as was possible in Yucatán because its tightly knit society had remained intact since the days of the Maya. But even here, the growing dependence of the region upon collective and mechanized henequen-growing has led to specialization of function and class distinctions among peoples who previously had few if any such differences. This divisive tendency, engendered by commercialization of agriculture, is heightened by a corresponding dependence upon the national government for credit facilities and marketing arrangements. This dependence, in turn, can enhance the economic and political role of the person who knows how to manipulate the political process in favor of himself or, in Yucatán, his henequen-growing cooperative.

In general, as specialization of function increases and as the peasant becomes more dependent upon the mechanics of government for credit, marketing facilities, and technical assistance, the way is cleared for initiating him into the national political system that can provide these necessities of Western economic life. The process continues as the peasant becomes more and more bound into the new value system, for he begins to want the social advantages and physical improvements identified with technology—schools, roads, electricity, health facilities, all things he can get by manipulating the political process. In time, as his general wants become fairly well satisfied, he begins to organize more specialized functional interest associations to accomplish the particular goals which he as an individual or specific member of the political society may desire, as opposed to the specialized goals of his neighbors.

Nevertheless, when such syncretism occurs and the Indian becomes a *mestizo*—for obviously the criterion is one of way of life rather than of blood—he adopts only certain traits of national culture, and they have a specialized meaning on the basis of the Indian ethic, in spite of the greater participation in national life. Interest grouping in response to political stimuli will occur, but to a lesser extent than among persons more completely absorbed into a Western social-political value system. The tendency to form interest groups is less spontaneous, and the interaction from village to village or region to region is reduced by the suspicions inherent in *localismo*. Similarly, the Indian tendency to adjust to his universe carries over into the peasant in the form of a more passive attitude toward the leadership and bureaucracy in functional interest associations, so that he demands less internal responsibility from the leaders to the rank and file within such an organization.

This is reflected in the nature of the relationship between members and leaders in the Farm sector of the revolutionary party. Many of the leaders of the sector have come from outside of the agricultural masses, and almost none of them are the less Westernized agrarians classed here as peasants. Because of the low degree of intensity of reaction in a given political situation, and the lack of interaction among members of the farm group on a nationwide basis, not to mention the lack of truly effective leadership, as compared with the other sectors in the official party, the Farm sector has failed to obtain many of the advantages of Western industrialization that its numbers and relative economic position in Mexico warrant.

Nor will this problem be solved very soon, for neither the peasant in general, nor even the more specialized *ejiditario* and small farmer types who will be discussed below, has become fully enough a part of Western life to recognize how government can assist him in increasing the value of agricultural production by opening markets, building feeder roads, and training youth in scientific agriculture, so he has been slow to organize his potential strength fully to obtain these things from government. The assimilation of the peasant into national life, which would make him aware of the possibilities of government aid, probably will continue to be a slow process, because by the very nature of his isolated existence he lacks opportunities to share work, educational, sports, and even religious experiences with other Mexicans. He may not become fully acclimated in the new, national cultural-political environment during the lifetime of the present generation.

Quite obviously, the generic term peasant includes a number of very different types of farmer, both in terms of the nature of their land holdings (or lack of them) and in terms of their role in political life. By far the most numerous are the small farmers, whose land may be held in the form of either *ejidos* or freehold private property, or a combination of the two. According to the agricultural census of 1956, Mexico's 18,564 *ejidos* were divided among 2,332,914 families, making the *ejiditarios* the largest single interest group in the country.[5] Through the National Farmers' Federation (the CNC), all *ejiditarios* are nominal members of the Farmers' sector of the official party, even though they may also own a few hectares of private property. (One hectare equals 2.471 acres.)

Farmers who own only freehold land are less numerous and do not belong to the CNC. Instead, they may belong to one of two numerically small but politically effective functional interest associations, the National Federation of Small Farm Properties (*Confederación Nacional de la Pequeña Propiedad Agrícola*) and the National Harvesters' Association (*Asociación Nacional de Cosecheros*), integrated into the Popular sector of the official party on an individual member basis. Finally, some two million farm workers who own no land at all are employed by their luckier neighbors.

Among the several types of landholders there are vast differences in wealth, culture, and political awareness. The vast majority of *ejiditarios* are poor, isolated, and easily manipulated by their farm leaders in the CNC. So are many of the small farmers who own their own land. In many cases, a farm family will work only one or two hectares of "temporal" land, which receives inadequate or badly spaced rainfall. Despite efforts to integrate many of these small landholders into the national economy by supplying credit facilities and technical advisers, the program is neither so systematic nor so successful as to offer hope for immediate inclusion of most of these people in effective national life.

There is, however, a smaller but influential group of individual landholders who are both more well-to-do and more politically effective than the average. Legally, private holdings may range up to about one hundred hectares, but sometimes they are much larger because of political arrangements or parceling out among several members of a family. The persons who own and operate these holdings are well aware of national politics and economy,

---

[5] The *ejido* system, originally conceived as a communal land system, has evolved as one in which each family generally works its own share of the land, with a few notable exceptions such as the cotton-growing area of La Laguna. Some idea of the *ejido* theory and its successes and failures can be found in Eyler J. Simpson, *The Ejido: Mexico's Way Out* (Chapel Hill, N.C., 1937), and Henrik F. Infield and Koka Freier, *People in Ejidos* (New York, 1954).

else they would not be in a position to control so disproportionate a share of Mexico's relatively small total of arable land. They are the most active members of the National Federation of Small Farm Properties and the National Harvesters' Association. Consequently, these organizations represent interests different from and often in competition with those of the Farmers' sector and its leadership.

The fact that early in 1958 the CNC attacked the concept of small farm property as "anti-revolutionary" indicates the growing competition of interests in rural Mexico. During the same period, the labor movement was attempting to organize the two million rural wage workers into a farm employees union to be affiliated with the Labor sector of the revolutionary party. This is another demonstration of growing complexity on the Mexican rural scene.

The relationship of the larger cash-crop producers with the Popular sector points up one of the problems of Mexican agriculture. Although the CNC is the largest mass organization in Mexico, and the Farmers' sector the most numerous in the revolutionary party, the *ejiditario*-small farmer group is by no means the dominant power in Mexico's political process. The *ejido* farmer and the small landowner have relatively little independent political experience, so they are easily manipulated by professional farm leaders who do not spring from or feel immediately responsible to their rural constituents. Many of the more nationally oriented agriculturists, whose training and better understanding of the operation of commercial agriculture allow them to amass a larger or more valuable plot, find that their personal interests are better served by political action outside of the Farm sector. Thus, potential leadership may disappear even if the more gifted individual remains on the land, leaving the small farmer in the hands of a professional and bureaucratic leadership that springs from middle-class rather than farm sources. The same probably will be true of the wage-earning farm employees if the Labor sector succeeds in organizing them. At the same time, the farm population is less mobile and more dependent upon government for technical and financial aid than is organized labor in an industrial setting, so it is in a less effective position to bargain politically, even if it had the education which might provide initiative for such action.

Not even including the three or four million-odd unintegrated Indians, this "Rural Proletariat," as it has been called, represents some nineteen of Mexico's thirty-three million inhabitants. But in political power, its lack of any sense of class or functional unity and the low intensity of its reactions to political situations barely allow the rural portion of the population to hold its own with the much smaller Popular sector of the revolutionary party, and relatively it is at a disadvantage even with the very small Labor sector. Obviously, it is not yet an enlightened proletariat in the Marxian sense, for its members are not yet aware enough either of the operation of national politics or their own potential role in it to act collectively so as to be a decisive force in determining Mexico's political present. In the relatively distant future, with a great deal more education and integration into national life, however, the rural population could become a very important factor in Mexican politics.

The trouble is that rural Mexico is being propelled into the midst of a complex, twentieth-century, Western social and political community without time for adequate preparation. This shows up in the apportionment of services among the various factors in Mexico's national life and economy. A great deal of money is being spent for rural services—roads, schools, medical facilities, and the like—but compared with relative needs, a much higher proportion is being spent in cities and on industrial and business development. We find in rural Mexico an almost classical example of the ineffectual position in the political process of large numbers of unaware, unorganized, and unintegrated people in competition with much smaller but politically acute and organized groups.

## The Small Town Dweller

The function of the town-dwelling Mexican as a link between the rural citizen and the national society has already been mentioned, but it is necessary to identify the group more fully. In every larger market town, and even in some of the smaller villages, side by side with the peasant who has abandoned farming to become an artisan but kept his family ties and cultural values with the peasant group, there exists another, nonfarming, more specialized, perhaps even white-collar class. The members of this group are widely separated from the peasant, be he farmer or artisan, by a broader, more national outlook and a greater acceptance of Western values and motivations.

The influence of centuries upon a particular set of values and methods of measuring success cannot be wiped out in a few decades.

Culture is notoriously inelastic, particularly in the case of those groups first moving into a new class. Consequently, too many of the representatives of the peasant class who do benefit from the government's programs seek to place themselves or their children in the traditional positions of respectability. They wish to be lawyers, doctors, *agrónomos*, bureaucrats, in the towns or cities and away from the land, rather than trained farmers or skilled mechanics. In other words, they want to take a place in the existing structured class—at the top—rather than to evolve a new set of class relations. One result is that they wish to work with the government, which seems a sure way to success, rather than opposing it, which has always been a sure way to difficulty, if not to failure.

This small shop owner or businessman, minor bureaucrat, schoolteacher, doctor, agronomist, priest group even may include some members of the old, prerevolutionary landed aristocracy, who have been permitted to keep some three hundred acres of their old estates, though by choice the latter would usually seek to remain in Mexico City on the fringe of the upper class. There is an overlap in outlook and political ability between these town dwellers and the larger landowners of today mentioned just above. They also overlap with the metropolitan middle class, which will be considered shortly, for both share an adherence to nationally oriented, relatively moderate viewpoints on politics, as well as the traditional Latin middle-class–upper-class lack of respect for manual or menial labor.

These small town dwellers look down on the agrarians who work the soil as "common," and attempt to copy urban patterns as much as possible. They wear Western-style clothes and are fashion-conscious; they have radios and they hire servants if they can afford them, sometimes if they cannot. Those who practice religion are much more orthodox than their rural neighbors and, at times, more so than their more cosmopolitan urban neighbors as well. The life of this town-dwelling group is in and of the nation. They often are frustrated by a desire to live in a larger city, particularly Mexico City, where they can enjoy urban amenities. Many compromise by sending their children to the city to obtain the university-level professional training that will permit the second generation to make the move.

A major and politically significant difference between the *hacendados* of the prerevolutionary era, who used to speak for agricultural and other nonurban interests, and the present-day small town dweller lies in the nature of their relation to the mass of rural citizens and to the region in which they live. The old-time landholding gentry owned land in the peripheral portions of the country but emotionally were inhabitants of the larger cities, especially the capital, despite occasional visits to their rural estates; they had no real understanding of or two-way relationship with their tenants or the *peones* who worked for them, and little or no interaction among themselves on a regional basis. The new, transitional small town dwellers of the middle class, on the other hand, not only have a great deal more direct contact with the masses of people, despite their disdain of the rural way of life, but also interact among themselves and—very important— act as spokesmen for the interests of their region in the national capital.

These town dwellers control much of the local economic life, and often the local political organization as well, for they think in terms of state and national politics and economics. Often there is strong competition for the support of the rural Mexicans between the town political leaders, who are apt to belong to the Popular sector of the official party, and the heads of the functional farm organizations in the region who affiliate through the CNC with the Farm sector. Because of automatic inclusion of all *ejido*-members in the CNC and their more direct access to the governmental farm agencies which can aid the farmer, the Farm sector's leadership has until now been somewhat more successful in organizing the farm vote. Recently, however, the town leader has been increasing his strength, partly because he often is closer to the peasants and farmers in his region than are professional farm leaders working out of Mexico City, and partly because, with growing specialization of function among farmers, the old Farm sector cannot satisfy the competing demands of all of its members. The development of the National Harvesters' Association, which is allied to the Popular sector, is a case in point.

### The Urban Proletariat

The urban proletariat, found usually in cities of over 100,000 population where sufficient industry and service functions exist to produce them, is somewhat more difficult to classify and describe than its rural equivalent; it is less clearly defined and much more complex in its make-up because of increasing specialization. By definition, the urban proletariat consists of functionally specialized workers engaged in relatively large industrial, service, or extractive activities (steel mills, auto and electronics assembly plants, railroads, mining, petroleum production and refining) who have a reasonably high degree of identification with Western values and concepts. But within this classification, the urban proletariat consists of as broad a range of adaption (or lack of adaption) to these values as is found in rural areas, though the range in the city probably is farther up the spectrum toward Westernization.

Along its upper fringes the urban proletariat consists of union members in the skilled and semiskilled trades who have a relatively high level of technical education and quite a clear conception of the political process. Within their unions, these workers hold the leadership responsible for effective representation of rank-and-file interest and, in turn, are fairly highly disciplined. Farther down the spectrum, the workers are less skilled, less educated, and consequently less effective in demanding and obtaining their interest goals.

But the organized urban workers, whether highly skilled or less so, are more nearly an aware and politically active proletariat than the rural agrarians. The city workers have some sense of identity, some understanding of the possibilities inherent in collective action. Despite the factionalism inherent in multifold trades and industrial union organizations, until quite recently Mexican labor has been surprisingly unified on general policy questions affecting its status. Although there are a number of national labor federations embracing all kinds of heterogeneous unions, the Mexican Federation of Laborers (the CTM) is by far the largest and most important, dominating the Labor sector of the revolutionary party. It has provided leadership in attempts to unify labor activity through, for example, the United Workers' Bloc (the BUO), which in 1958 coordinated organized labor's role in the nomination and election of Adolfo López Mateos as president of Mexico.

Generally speaking, therefore, of the two great functionally specialized mass factions participating in Mexico's political process, labor as opposed to agriculture tends to get a much higher share of political and economic benefits than its numbers warrant. Industry, commerce, and transport workers combined totaled about two and a half million persons in 1955, while agriculture and associated activities had some five and a half million workers, but the two very nearly equated in government councils, and the industrial laborer, at least, enjoyed a markedly higher standard of living, protected by tariffs and uneconomic fixed rates of pay, for which the rest of the country's consumers had to pay in higher prices or lower quality goods.

This anomaly results from a number of factors. Industry long has been identified in Mexico with progress and economic independence and has been granted protectionist legislation to encourage rapid growth, while organized labor in turn has enjoyed its own favored status. Many of the labor groups which make up the Labor sector in the official party were among the earliest functional interest associations in the revolutionary movement. Grouped together in urban areas where they can interact to provide a united front to make their pressure effective, these labor groups long have exerted a greater influence than their numbers might indicate.

This does not mean to suggest that organized labor is in as strong a position as its North American labor counterparts by any means. Conditions, both social and economic, are quite different in the two countries. Mexico is neither as highly industrialized nor is the Mexican laborer as productive as the worker in the United States, and the strong cultural bias against manual labor also tends to keep salaries down. Again, just as the larger landholder uses his slightly superior understanding of national life and politics to win advantages from government over the peasant, and the organized laborer his greater sophistication to do the same, so other more politically competent Mexicans win out in the struggle with the rank-and-file union laborer.

Many of these politically more effective persons belong to the Popular sector, a few are leaders in the Farm sector, more are businessmen not formally affiliated with the revolutionary party, but unfortunately some are leaders of the Labor sector itself, individuals who betray the interests of their followers for personal advantage. Most Mexican laborers are not so astute politically that they can protect themselves from this combination of adverse factors which work to keep them weaker than North American organized labor. In spite of and sometimes because of their leadership, one union is played against another, or collective bargaining is used as a means of enriching those who should represent labor. This situation is exacerbated because of the very influential role played by the government in determining the legality of and outcome of strikes. So long as the high degree of polyfunctionalism that places not entirely loyal labor leaders in strategic positions in the government bureaucracy continues to exist, labor will continue to find itself weaker politically and economically than it would like to be.

A word of caution is in order here. Not every urban worker is a member of the more or less politically active urban proletariat I have described. A large number of the urban labor force are marginal workers, in but not of the city. Almost none of these marginal workers are a part of the elaborate union system allied with the official party. They have neither the social integration nor the political awareness that might permit them to become active participants in formal political life.

According to anthropologists who have studied urbanization in Mexico, many inhabitants of the major cities live physically within urban boundaries without ever becoming integrated ideologically into Western urban life.[6] They may live, a whole family packed together in a single room, surrounded by the material paraphernalia of industrialization—radios, television sets, electric fry pans—but to a large extent still think as they did in their village. In a sense they are political outcasts, cut off from political acculturation by the farm organization that might have worked on them in the rural areas from which they came but yet not part of the acculturating influence of the labor unions, except on a piecemeal and isolated basis.

These unattached city dwellers who are not yet essentially Westerners are a possible source of future political instability in Mexico. Unless the political machinery of the revolutionary party finds some means of bringing them into the active national political life, some antigovernment movement may capture and use them, much as the mobs in Asiatic cities have been utilized by the Communists. I suspect, however, that the official party will assimilate them,

---

[6] See for example Robert Redfield, *The Folk Culture of Yucatán* (Chicago, 1941), pp. 339 ff. for instances of this in Mérida and other Yucatecan cities. Oscar Lewis has suggested somewhat the same phenomena for Mexico City in his *Five Families: Mexican Case Studies in the Culture of Poverty* (New York, 1959).

probably through the ambitious Popular sector, which may adopt this group into its organizational structure in order to increase its own strength, much as the North American big city machines did the large immigrant population around the turn of the century. If this should happen, a major realignment of the political structure might well result, for it would probably give the nonfunctional sector of the party a preponderance of power that would allow it to carry out its obvious desire to end the functional sector organization system of representation in the party.

## The Metropolitan Middle Class

Mexico's growing middle class is both a product of and a progenitor of Westernization in the country. It was from the earliest members of this class that the revolutionary movement recruited its first leaders, and to a great extent much of the lower-echelon leadership of all three official party sectors, as well as many opposition political leaders, still comes from the middle class. Their high degree of political ability and the intensity with which members of the urban middle class carry on political action gives them an unbalanced position in the power structure. This is a quite natural consequence of their being both well trained and strategically located for political activity, as compared with most other Mexicans. The location of the middle class in areas of urban concentration, together with the fact that their education and professional training are far above the national average, permit the middle-class Mexicans to hold a disproportionately large share of the most important positions in government and business and, almost inevitably, in politics.

The members of the urban middle class identify almost completely with Western values and reflect the high degree of functional specialization found in the urban, most Westernized areas of Mexico. They, more than any other segment of Mexico's population, can be identified with the mass-produced "organization man" found in the United States, in the sense that the Mexican middle-class ethic consists of a broadly shared and rather highly compulsive core of social and political values and goals. This does not mean that the average middle-class Mexican always has closely resembled his North American counterpart. With the exception of a rather highly developed common interest in the material benefits of industrialization (which many Mexicans would deny), until quite recently the two countries' middle-class ethics represented quite different goals for their members.[7]

Traditionally, Western middle-class values, including those of the United States, have been best represented by a stable, hard-working, money-saving, rentier type, who found respectability and fulfillment in belonging to the middle class. This group, which in the West grew rather large in size, provided the broad foundation for middle-of-the-road, moderate parties, often supplying the political machinery for aggregating the competing interests of members of the lower classes, say farmers and laborers, and then turning about and adjusting their differences with the upper economic classes. In time the differences among the lower, middle, and upper classes became hazier until, as in the United States today, nearly everyone belongs emotionally if not economically to the middle class.

In Mexico, however, for a long time the small businessman, the professional, the technician, the higher level office worker, the junior-grade army officer, the government bureaucrat, did not see belonging to the middle class as an acceptable end in itself. Instead, many hoped to use the middle class as a stopping-off point on their way to the upper class, into which each dreamed of moving at the earliest opportunity and at almost any price. Some still think in these terms.

The middle-class Mexican who is so motivated spends beyond his means in an effort to ape the life of members of the upper class. In an effort to attain upper class "respectability," he multiplies the previously noted disdain for menial or physical labor but at the same time, in order to avoid such work, he supports servants recruited from marginal labor by working long, impossible hours at his specialty. One rather highly placed bureaucrat of my acquaintance

---

[7] In nationalistic attitudes, the Mexican of the middle class is the most violent anti-Yankee in the country. His less advanced neighbors are not aware enough of international economic or political relations to react so strongly, and most of the upper class are too cosmopolitan. Perhaps jealousy or misapprehension contribute to the pattern, but for whatever reason, it is the middle-class Mexican who continually injects into political campaigns the North American occupation of Texas, California, and the other Mexican lands during the Mexican War, or the occupation of Veracruz in 1914. Perhaps this carries back to the Díaz administration, when foreigners (including Yankees) seemed to have a preferred position over Mexicans of this class, producing ultimately the resentment that turned the middle class into the early revolutionary leadership.

who neither desires, nor is in a position, to supplement his salary
with graft, works at his government job, teaches in two separate
schools, and does outside consultant work in order to keep up appearances.

This restiveness in the middle class, which is found throughout
Latin America,[8] in my opinion is one of the early manifestations of
the process of Westernization. I believe that it comes into being
when specialization has produced a new group of individuals who
are no longer in the lower classes but because of tradition can feel
no sense of status except by identifying with the upper class. In
Latin America the feeling might be heightened by the Spanish
sense of *vergüenza*, in which the individual is haunted constantly
by the fear that he is not living up to some mythical standard
which, for want of a better one, he might equate with upper-class
mores.

It may well be that both the speed and the manner in which industrialization has come into being in the Latin American countries
have not always allowed the middle class sufficient time to evolve as
it did in some other Western-type countries. In Mexico, for example,
industrialization came quickly, imposed upon the Mexican economy
primarily by government investment, support, and direction rather
than by private and independent initiative. No gradual evolution
of a small investor, secondary management, technical and professional class with status of its own was possible. As a consequence,
those who moved into positions of leadership may have sought to
acquire status in the only way they knew how, by moving up into
the upper class. This tendency would be increased by the Mexican
version of Spanish *personalismo*, in which the personal dignity and
importance of each individual takes precedence over all other considerations. Under such circumstances, the middle-class Mexican's
tendency to advance his own position in business at any cost, or
even the frequent irresponsible acts of personal ambition by leaders
of mass functional interest associations at the expense of those who
provide the basis for their power, might find a more nearly rational
explanation.

This could explain why, during the twenties and thirties, contrary to the experience of Europe and the United States, the rapid

---

[8] See Theo R. Crevenna, *Materiales para el Estudio de la Clase Media en la
América Latina* (6 vols.; Washington, D.C., 1950-52).

growth of Mexico's middle class did not provide as stabilizing an influence as might have been expected. Throughout the early revolutionary period the members of the middle class were political to the very roots of their hair, for access to government and participation in the decision-making process were the only keys to the economic success that meant status. Government assistance and approval meant success or failure. In business it meant a supply of capital, availability of necessary machinery or raw materials, providing of vitally needed transportation facilities, relative freedom from crippling strikes or too strict an enforcement of social legislation, and even the assurance of markets. For labor or farm leaders, government support meant accomplishment of goals for the functional interest associations, whether these goals were increased salaries, winning strikes, distributing land, building dams or roads, or providing schools. Or, on the other hand, the possibility of government support gave the individual leader a bargaining point to improve his own personal position at the expense of the interest he was supposed to serve.

The gradual development of middle-class status during the later period of rapid Westernization explains why more recently, as the middle class has become larger, economically more important, and a permanent fixture in Mexican society, it finally has begun to act as a stabilizing and moderating factor in the political process. Although there is still evidence of a carry-over of the desire to move up and of the temptation to aggrandize one's position, the very size and economic importance of the middle class provide its members with both status and sufficient scope to accomplish their ambitions, without the dog-eat-dog struggles of yesteryear.

It may also be, as some observers claim, that in recent years, as urban social and economic conditions have begun to resemble those in the United States to a greater extent, the Mexican middle class has begun to model itself consciously upon the North American middle class. Certainly many North American culture concepts and values have been implanted in this segment of the Mexican people, the one that is most susceptible to change. Motion pictures, influxes of tourists, and the sending of middle-class children to the United States for advanced education and training are cases in point. Such a buttressing of middle-class values could contribute to a stronger sense of status and a consequent tendency toward social and political moderation, as the members of the middle class seek to preserve the status quo.[9]

Without much doubt, the relatively advantageous position enjoyed by the most influential interest groups within the middle class also shores up the tendency to support the status quo. The government bureaucrats, for example, are one of the strongest units in the Popular sector of the official party, and well they might be, for they receive special benefits from the government far beyond their social or economic contribution to Mexican life. Probably it would be fair to say that the low-cost housing, special commissary facilities, their own hospital and 50 per cent rebates on drugs, yearly bonuses, and all of the other special perquisites granted them, more nearly reflect their high degree of intensity of political action and consequent contribution to the strength of the revolutionary party. These qualities, rather than actual services rendered to national society or economy, are the contributions which are most highly rewarded in political life.

Between 1952 and 1958, during the first five years of the administration of President Adolfo Ruiz Cortines, Mexico's 300,000 government bureaucrats were granted special benefits in the form of raises, cost-of-living grants, and year-end bonuses equivalent to a month's salary, to the total of over 900 million pesos. This is the equivalent of 75 million dollars, if differences in exchange rate are considered, and just over three per cent of the total national budget expenditures for the period. For all of its early amorphism, then, today the urban middle class plays an important role, probably an increasingly important one, in Mexican politics.

As the Mexican economy becomes more advanced, government exercises a less preponderant influence over business, though its position still is infinitely stronger than it is in the United States. At the same time, many of the most important segments of Mexican social and economic life are now represented by institutionalized interest associations—labor unions, farm associations, professional groups, business and industrial *cámaras*, and the like. Consequently, while still important, access to and control over government no

---

[9] See Nathan L. Whetten, "The Rise of a Middle Class in Mexico," in Crevenna, *op. cit.*, Vol. 2, for a more complete discussion of the manners and mores of this group in Mexico. Another pertinent study is John J. Johnson, *Political Changes in Latin America: The Emergence of the Middle Sectors* (Stanford, 1958), especially pp. 1-44 and 128-52.

longer is the be-all and end-all in Mexican life. Business has enough internal vitality and available private capital to service itself, and most of the other factors in the social-economic process are well enough organized and firmly enough entrenched to fend for themselves with less absolute dependence upon government. As a consequence, government in Mexico has become more of an umpire or balancer of interests than a King Solomon giving life-or-death decisions, and the role of the middle-class *político* as a vender of political advantage has declined apace.

Nonetheless, the traditionally high degree of political activity by members of the middle class carries over into the present-day political system. This is true partly because, by its very nature, a moderate middle class provides a political link among all of the conflicting interest groups and associations mentioned above, a very necessary function in modern, complex Western society. Also, it is true partly because the low intensity of political initiative and ability in the masses, which results from the cultural and social limitations already suggested, naturally attracts middle-class leadership that can benefit both itself and those it serves.

This last will continue until cultural change and social advancement begin to produce leaders from the masses themselves or, as has occurred in the United States, these changes transform the masses into a part of the middle class. When and if this last happens, the middle class will become larger still, more economically important, and even more moderate as it embraces the social, economic, and political interests and attitudes of a broader and broader cross-section of the Mexican people. Meanwhile, the urban middle class will continue its present function of providing a link between all of the disparate interests participating in the political process. All the more so, because the Popular sector of the official party provides a political mechanism by which both the small town and the city member of the middle class, with their growing identity of interests and values, can work together to manipulate the process of politics.

Through the National Federation of Popular Organizations (the CNOP), a kind of holding company for all kinds of professional and civic organizations, and the government bureaucrats' union, the middle class is the mainstay of the Popular sector in the revolutionary party. Similarly, most members and many of the lower-level leaders of the few opposition parties which try to participate in national political life also are middle class in origin. In spite of its relatively small numbers, therefore, the Mexican middle class very nearly equates in political power with the mass farm and labor interests combined, particularly as most of the bureaucracy and leadership of the functional interest associations representing these interests, as well as the government bureaucracy, come from middle-class rather than working-class ranks.

Thus, even now, moderate and more nearly universal Mexican middle-class values are working in and out of the official party to aggregate interests both among and between the many competing groups which operate in rural and urban Mexico. In this sense, the existence and functioning of the middle class makes Mexico's evolving political system possible.

The peculiarly strategic role of the middle class in Mexico's political system can best be attested by pointing out that all of the country's presidents since 1920 have had their origins in this segment of society. It is hardly surprising that during the early years of the Revolution this should be so, for in essence the early revolutionary movement was a middle-class revolt against the older aristocracy. But that middle-class background, attitudes, and relationships to the major factors interacting in the political process should have become almost a conventionalized requirement for political success during the maturity of the Revolution speaks volumes for the nature of both Mexico's middle class and the revolutionary-inspired society that produces it, a point that can be demonstrated amply by considering the position and role of the country's top political leadership in the upper class.

### The Urban Upper Class

The last and least numerous subcultural type to be considered is the urban upper class. In reality it consists of two separate groups which interpenetrate but are not identical; one controls economic power and the other political power. Combined, the two include the large industrialists, big businessmen and bankers, a number of the most successful professional men, a few high-ranking military officers, the highest-echelon government officials and functional interest group leaders and, of course, other successful politicians. Another group in this class, which is a part of the economic elite in some cases but never quite participates wholly in the national political decision-making system, consists of the lineal descendants of the old landed aristocracy who managed to survive the Revolution with at least part of their status intact.

It is this last group with which we normally associate the extremes of formal, almost stereotyped, Spanish courtesy for which the Latin Americans are noted. In Mexico the social prestige of this old aristocratic clique carried over sufficiently into the revolutionary era to implant much of this formality in the habit patterns of the rising middle-class *mestizos* who rode the crest of the revolutionary wave into the upper reaches of society. If a few of the old revolutionary leaders who moved up on the strength of fighting ability or low cunning, rather than social virtues, are exceptions to the rule, their sons are not, for on the whole the Mexican upper class, no matter what its origins, is consistent in the outward manifestations of position. It is composed of a group of highly educated, well-traveled, world-conscious cosmopolitans. Those who are religious hold very orthodox Catholic tenets, but the men, at least, are more likely to be nominal than rigorously practicing members of their church.

Some of the newer members of the upper class identify to a certain degree with the ideological if not the cultural values of the West and particularly the United States, the level of whose material development represents for them a model of the new Mexico they seek to form. Those of the older aristocracy, on the other hand, tend to lean toward Spain and especially France in their thinking, as a kind of protest against the changes engendered by the Revolution. A recent increase in intermarriage among the offspring of these two upper-class factions marks the beginning of some integration between them as a more widely shared value system begins to encompass all Mexicans.

Many members of the upper class tend to think of themselves as part of an elite group, and in the sense that a less mobile class system exists in Mexico than in the United States, they are. It is not altogether surprising that such an aristocratic concept should continue to survive in postrevolutionary Mexico, for old ideas and institutionalized relationships die hard. The existence of an upper, ruling class is as old as Mexico itself and, as noted earlier, not even the social changes which accompanied the Revolution have ended a certain amount of middle-class identification of status and success with entree into the upper class.

But Mexico's present-day upper class is not so monolithic as it was in prerevolutionary days when social, economic, and political power resided in a single group. Today, neither wealth nor political power is an absolute criterion for membership, for certain members of the old aristocracy who lack both are considered to "belong." So are members of the economic elite who do not belong to the revolutionary party and, in fact, may openly support an opposition party. Conversely, some upper-level political leaders, who have a strong voice in decision-making but make no attempt to amass wealth, also are considered members of the upper class. So, too, amusingly enough, are such radicals as Vicente Lombardo Toledano and David Alfaro Siqueiros, who is noted for his lavish home and numerous expensive sports cars. Moreover, for all its tenacity in continuing to exist, Mexico's urban upper class no longer is a closed, self-perpetuating elite; middle-class penetration of the upper class group exercising political power is both possible and common. And because government still has a great deal of influence in economic affairs, entree into the group controlling the top-level decision-making process means that entree into the economically powerful group also is possible, although the overlap between the two is smaller than one might expect.

The reason that these two power-wielding upper-class groups do not coincide more fully lies partly in the nature of the political power structure that the Revolution has produced and partly in the nature of the men who hold economic power. After 1910, the leaders of the Revolution could and did take away the political power of the old ruling group, but they could not and did not take away the potential economic power and social influence that an educated and highly integrated group of citizens understanding economics, acquainted with Western technology and values, and having capital available could amass in so backward and underdeveloped a country as Mexico.

When deprived of their primary source of wealth—land—some of the members of the old ruling clique turned to other economic activities in which they had already dabbled during the Díaz regime—banking, commerce, and industry. Working with some of the status-hungry middle-class *mestizos*, who had revolutionary connections but little identification with the masses, so as to protect their new enterprises from too much government intervention, these new tycoons purchased a voice in the councils of government by including these members of the "in group" within their own councils. With Mexico's increasing industrialization and expanding economy, these new activities have prospered, benefiting both sets of partners.

It is a truism, however, that human values are a good deal less malleable than the physical conditions of technology. Despite their economic success, possibly because they mistrust it without complete political power with which to entrench it, certain members of this new class of capitalists wish a greater voice in government and even absolute control over the political process. They look back to the era of "the old general," when an integrated upper class held both economic and political control, unhampered by considerations of legal or social responsibility, except on the purely personal basis of the *patrón* system. Surprisingly enough, some highly placed revolutionary politicians tend to be caught up in this throwback to the older, aristocratic value system.

Surprising, because even the least astute *político* should recognize that a return to the prerevolutionary social and economic system presupposes undoing all of the changes which have occurred since 1910, a patent political impossibility. Among the by-products of Mexico's industrialization working on the masses (or is it the other way around?) are the other facets of Westernization—a greater sense of the nation, more social and political awareness, a higher degree of mass participation in the political process. Politically ineffectual the Mexican masses may be, but they are sufficiently aware and overwhelmingly numerous enough to preclude any hope of success in a complete sell-out of their interests to the commercial-industrial-banking economic power-elite. Any attempt by the present revolutionary leadership to do so, no matter how subtle, would cause new leaders to spring up from the middle class to mobilize the masses, who would remove the betrayers of the Revolution from authority, from the upper classes, perhaps even from life itself.

It is extremely unlikely, however, that any such attempt would be made, for despite individual relationships between the governing group exercising political power and those with economic power, they are really two quite separate groups holding different value patterns and serving different sets of interests. The business and industrial leaders who wield economic power have a much more limited and specialized set of goals than their political counterparts. While aware that they cannot accomplish all of their goals by working through friends in the official party or goading through an opposition agency such as the National Action party (the PAN), the leaders of the business community are also aware that the present political system offers them enough access to consideration in policy matters to satisfy immediate wants through such activities and also that they would lose everything in a test of power.

The leaders of the official party who exercise top-flight political power, on the other hand, have broader and more moderate values and goals. I have already suggested that most of them spring from the middle classes; they carry with them into the top political power situation middle-class values and action patterns. Many of them, in fact, refuse to use their exalted political position to force entree into the higher economic echelons. Presidents Cárdenas and Ruiz Cortines are prime examples of men who refused to enrich themselves, while Presidents Calles, Rodríguez, and Alemán were of the other sort. It is still too early to classify President López Mateos in his role as president, though his previous career and the first acts of his administration place him with the first two rather than the latter three.

Not even those political leaders who might identify more completely with economic power have been able to unite the two factions of the upper class, for the political necessity of satisfying the numerous and specialized complex of interests which make up Mexico's political system makes complete integration impossible. For all of its historical bias toward expanded industry and commerce as marks of progress, the Westernized, middle-class leadership of the Revolution could not if it wanted to, allot too large a share of the benefits of government to these activities, because the farm, labor, and allied popular interests simply would not stand for it. Even so overwhelmingly a pro-business regime as that of President Alemán had to keep a formal distinction between the official party machinery and his friends in economic activities, using the *cámaras* of commerce, industry, and the like as "advisory" links between political and economic decision-making. The economic power-elite, for its part, was quite willing to accept this arrangement because it feared that assimilation into the party might mean being swamped by the representatives of the mass functional interest associations in their interparty struggles for position.

The fact that in 1952 President Alemán could not impose a

strong pro-business candidate upon the official party to follow him in office indicates the relatively balanced power relationship between large-scale economic interests and the other interests in the Mexican political process. Alemán's successor, Lic. Adolfo Ruiz Cortines, and President López Mateos, who took office in 1958,· reflect more nearly neutral, middle-class interests which represent more effectively all of the factions in Mexican economic and political life.

This does not mean that the interests of the upper-class economic power group are not consulted by presidents such as these, or that individual political leaders within their administrations do not participate in the activities or decisions of the business community. What it does mean is that the men in these two parts of the upper class serve different and in part conflicting interests, so that for all of their social classification as members of a single class, they cannot and do not overlap completely for any appreciable length of time. It means too that those who really have decision-making power in Mexico, both political and economic, have worked out a *modus vivendi* in which the institutions of government are manipulated so as to supply reasonably responsible and satisfactory public services for most of the major factors which have to be considered if the political process is to continue operating smoothly and successfully.

### The Mexican Society

To generalize from the foregoing, for the study of national politics these six general subcultural types reduce to four broad classes: (1) unintegrated Indians who for the most part are outside of effective national life, socially, economically, and politically; (2) a lower class composed of peasants, *ejiditarios*, small farmers, and urban proletarians, who have much in common despite all of their variations in understanding of and benefits from Westernization; (3) the small town and urban middle class, including some of the larger landowners who produce commercial crops; and (4) the urban upper class.

The first class—the Indian—makes up about fifteen per cent of the population. So some four million Mexicans do not participate actively in national life and politics. The second broad class— peasant-*ejiditario* and small farmer-urban proletariat—accounts for about twenty-five million persons in the population, breaking down to about nineteen million rural and six million urban inhabitants. The middle class, both small town and urban, includes about three and a half million persons, and the upper class slightly more than 300,000. These figures are, of course, rather rough estimates, because of the difficulty in classifying certain parts of the citizenry in one or another group.

But relative numerical size of a class in the society does not tell the whole story in Mexico's politics, as this chapter must already have made abundantly clear. If class representation in the political process could be measured simply in terms of the numbers of individuals elected to public office who purport to speak for various segments in a class, election records listing the members of each sector in the official party named to office might tell the story. As a rule of thumb they would show the Popular sector names some forty per cent of the elective officers, the farmers another forty, and labor twenty. In industrial areas around Monterrey or Tampico and in districts of the capital the Labor sector might select a slightly higher proportion, just as the Farm sector would in Oaxaca or Chiapas, which are almost completely agricultural. In either case, the share of the Popular sector usually remains quite constant. In a municipal election, where small town middle-class influences can bring more effective pressure, its share actually may increase. Consider the 1957 elections for *presidentes municipales* in the state of Mexico, where the Popular sector filled sixty of the one hundred nineteen offices, the farmers fifty, and labor only nine.

The question is, can representation in the political process really be measured in terms of the number of elective posts held by individuals purporting to speak for agriculture and labor? If so, for all of the relative difference in size of sector membership, the combined total of political agents selected to represent the Farm and Labor sectors, which most nearly identify with lower-class occupational activities, scarcely allows them to hold their own in numbers with the predominantly middle-class Popular sector representatives. If not, the leadership that is supposed to represent farm and labor interests may well reflect the interests of the middle class from which so many of the leaders of all three sectors spring.

Present-day conditions or, more nearly correctly, those of the recent past suggest that the latter is the case, as demonstrated by citing class-income figures derived from the census of 1950. The economic position of the lower class relates rather closely to its lack of political awareness and consequent inability to demand full representation from those speaking for it in the policy-making process, particularly because in Mexico political decisions on farm prices, wages, and related matters are so much more vital than in a country with a more developed and independent economic system. In terms of the income of 7,569,589 gainfully employed persons out of a total population of 25,791,017 in 1950 (when one peso equalled 12.5 U.S. cents), the 85.9 per cent of the Mexican workers whom I class here as lower class received less than 300 pesos a month. The 12.5 per cent I call the middle class received from 300 to 1,000 pesos a month, and 1.4 per cent of the Mexicans in the upper class received over a thousand pesos each month.[10]

This data takes on still greater meaning in light of the fact that, during the period 1939-50, real income rose for the fourteen per cent of Mexicans not in the lower class who obtained their income from capital, salaries, etc., while it fell for the eighty-six per cent in the lower class who earned their living from rural and urban labor and services. As a corollary, Nacional Financiera, a government agency, reported that in 1955 one per cent of the gainfully employed got sixty-six per cent of the national cash income and ninety-nine per cent the remaining forty-four per cent. For all of the development of the economy, the proportionate share going to the broad mass of people was not as high as it was twenty years previously, when under President Cárdenas ninety-nine per cent of the labor force got sixty per cent of the national cash income and the one per cent the rest.

This picture, painted in broad strokes, is not as black as it appears, however, for two reasons. First, since 1950 and especially

[10] The breakdown of census figures, with my own class divisions, is as follows:

| Class Income per Month | Percentage of Work Force |
|---|---|
| Upper | |
| 1,000 or more | 1.43 |
| Middle | |
| 700-1,000 | 1.71 |
| 500-700 | 2.19 |
| 300-500 | 8.67 |
| | 12.57 |
| Lower | |
| 200-300 | 15.33 |
| 100-200 | 30. |
| 50-100 | 26.21 |
| Less than 50 | 14.38 |
| | 85.92 |

since 1952, when President Ruiz Cortines took office, attempts have been made to see that a fairer share of the benefits of Mexico's booming economy reach the masses. From personal observation, I can attest that their material well-being has improved. Secondly, figures on national cash income such as those cited ignore the fact that there is a broad range within the class. Many of the urban proletariat earn primarily from the upper level of the range and even spill into the middle class. The rural population, on the other hand, may have a lower cash income but it has improved its standard of living in ways which are not always reflected in terms of national cash income. Land distribution, improved seeds, better agricultural practices are beginning to allow the farmer to live better off the land.

Nonetheless, even taking into consideration that these figures do not present the entire picture, they do indicate one thing. Whether it is because their leaders have failed to represent them properly or because their own social limitations have hindered the members of the lower class from supporting their leaders effectively, the great mass of Mexico's population has not won nearly the share of the advantages of industrialization that its numbers warrant.

Modern, industrialized society, toward which Mexico is progressing very rapidly, always includes a large number of competitive interests which become more and more numerous as specialization of function increases; many of these interests fall behind temporarily in the race to share in its benefits. Those countries which have made a successful transition from their older system to Westernization, however, have done so because they managed to develop a broad community of shared values and the political machinery to interpret those values fairly equitably for all of the population, in spite of the immediate personal interest of a few persons and interests which have some short-term advantage.

Obviously, as Westernization has progressed in Mexico, it has had mixed effects. The passwords of progress—technology and industrial development—have brought with them the mechanization of agriculture and factory production, national markets and distribution of goods, and the beginnings of a national life. They have brought with them also the breakdown of stable local societies, the appearance of materialistic motivations and values, and the sharpening of interclass tensions where such tensions did not exist before. Mexico already has a plural society, so that the real test of revolutionary accomplishment will lie in the establishment of a value system based broadly enough to cut across geographic and/or functional differences and to contain immediate conflicts of interest. That is, a plural society but one whose members are more nearly homogeneous than heterogeneous in their understanding of and adjustment to the broad goals of government. This must mean, inevitably, a further weakening of class barriers and probably the growth of a larger middle class.

So far, considering the amount of technical change already accomplished in Mexico, the degree of social integration appears disappointing. In addition to the new, horizontal class distinctions, vertical cleavages barring any large amount of social interaction seem to have carried over even after roads are built and schools manned with teachers. Perhaps this separatism should not be so very surprising, for social attitudes tend to be more resistant to modification than do technical matters. In this case they are buttressed partly by the force of tradition, partly by the continuing existence of unsolved social and economic problems, but mostly by a lack of internal social cohesion—a lack fostered by the individual members of the society itself.

### The Composite Mexican[11]

In the village and to a great extent in the city, the average Mexican has little direct social contact outside of his immediate circle. The social function of early contacts—the extended family, close friends, fellow workers—remains the most vital in his life, though it has been disrupted to some extent first by the revolutionary upheaval and later by the inroads of other influences such as newspapers, the radio, and cinema. Organized interest associations too, perhaps a farmers' organization or a labor union, depending on the place, have begun to supply influences in competition with the more personal ones.

And yet, the growth of literacy and communications, the formation of new organizations which might seem to encourage more

---

[11] In spite of my earlier denial of the existence of a "typical" Mexican, I believe we can discuss here a kind of composite one, if care is taken to recognize the tremendous degrees of variation which are bound to occur within the country. The Mexican I describe here is nationally oriented, perhaps not quite so naïve in politics as the "peasant," but not so sophisticated as a member of the "upper class."

frequent interaction among individuals who are not in face-to-face contact, or not continuously so, have not greatly increased inter-communication and exchange of ideas among most lower-class Mexicans. It takes more than the ability to write one's name or to spell out words in a newspaper to establish two-way communication. The desire must be there, and the Mexican seldom has that desire. He does not belong to a multitude of associations or clubs which would bring him into contact with persons of different beliefs or attitudes, and which might implant conflicting interests within his mind. His social relations are much less complex.

The average Mexican tends to limit his social and even his political relations to a few persons he knows and trusts, *hombres de confianza*, as he calls them. This tendency to mistrust the outsider is not surprising in the rural villager who has had little and often unhappy contact with the wide world; the tenacity of the need in the urbanized and educated Mexican to rely upon persons he knows and trusts is more difficult to explain. It may be transmitted from an earlier and simpler non-Western way of life, perhaps in some cases by the servants so recently come from rural areas who are a fixture in many better-class Mexican homes. Or it may be part of Latin tendency, already alluded to, of identifying with a personal acquaintance with whom the individual has a mutual understanding of, and agreement upon, community of interests and goals.

This need for personal identification has political consequences, for while, like most Latins, the Mexican is highly interested in abstract theoretical concepts—a glance at his political literature proves this—in social relationships and political action the Mexican needs more. He cannot conceive of an action group in the abstract. If he is to espouse an ideology or political cause, he must identify it with a particular individual, a leader in whom the movement is personified. This tendency toward personification repeats itself in all phases of Mexican life; government, social movements, even the Church are identified not so much with principles, concepts, or morals as with some individual who may stand for them. In its institutionalized form, the Mexicans call this *personalismo*.

Thus, political parties tend to be identified popularly not so much by their grandiose legal titles as by the leader who best personifies each one. The program for which the revolutionary party stands, for example, may change in popular designation almost overnight with the inauguration of a new president, as when *alemanismo* became *ruizcortinismo* late in 1952, and the latter *lopezmateismo* six years later. In more specialized circumstances, the personal relationship between the leader of a group—say a labor union—and an individual tends to be an important motivating factor for the latter as long as the leader continues to act in such a way as to merit loyalty, insofar as the follower knows. Competing interest associations cannot easily recruit such followers, so the individual is faced with a minimum of overlapping memberships and consequent divided loyalties. For all of the proliferating number of interest associations springing up in Mexico as specialization increases, therefore, few Mexicans as yet have that sense of political ambivalence which the North American "joiner" so often feels. For the Mexican, there is only one effective group for political action, whatever it may be.

The political effects of this lack of grouping are obvious if one recalls that a number of observers have suggested that the chances for stable and democratic government are enhanced to the extent that individuals and groups of individuals within various social levels share a number of cross-cutting politically relevant affiliations. Such groups and individuals act as brokers to represent the demands of persons with whom they share some sort of group experience, even though they may not share the same political interest in a given policy-deciding situation. This reduces the intensity of political conflict and even protects the rights of political minorities.[12]

Not even the Church provides many intergroup contacts for the Mexican. In theory, religion and particularly the Catholic church is a universal agency but, as we have seen, many Mexicans do not look beyond the confines of their own district. They identify religion with the local church and the "miraculous" statue it contains, or with some variation of the cult of the saints, and even the sophisticated city-Mexican is closer by far to the "dark virgin" of Guadalupe than he is to an abstract mother of God who might intercede for him. Rome is far from Mexico, and the Mexicans who profess to be Catholic in religion are hardly catholic in their personal relations.

---

[12] See, for example, Seymour M. Lipset, "Some Social Requisites of Democracy: Economic Development and Political Legitimacy," *American Political Science Review*, LIII (March, 1959), 69-105, especially 84-85 and 96-97.

Contrary to what one might expect, the gradual evolution of a more sophisticated political system and a structured political machine in the revolutionary party has not ended the tendency toward personal identification of the rank-and-file citizen with political-functional leaders. Not many of the middle-and-upper class Mexicans look upon the president as a father-image any longer, but a very large proportion of the lower class still do. For that matter, father-image or no, the middle-class politicians crowd around the president like flies around honey, for they know well that he still is the dispenser of political favor. In this sense, *personalismo* still is a very important part of Mexico's political system.

But below the presidential level, one might have hoped that in spite of the isolation of individuals from one another, persons of different functional interests would have found a common denominator or mechanism for increased interaction in the revolutionary party. Such is not yet the case, because as now organized, the party's sector organization tends to enhance functional and economic competition, rather than to provide a tie that binds.

Under the circumstances, therefore, it is hardly surprising that a greater degree of social integration has not been accomplished. In fact, given the conditions under which social and political integration must take place in Mexico, the amount that already has occurred is an encouraging sign that, with enough time, the process will continue and an even more workable homogeneous social-political system will evolve.

CHAPTER *4*

# The Mexican Revolution

## The Revolution of 1910

Modern Mexico was born that October day almost fifty years ago on which Francisco Madero proclaimed his plan of San Luis Potosí, calling for revolt against the regime of President Díaz. His action sparked the end of one era for Mexico and the beginning of another just as sharply as did Lenin's capture of the revolution in Russia or Kemal Ataturk's reforms in Turkey. In each case, the man was a personification of changes in the political environment which extended far beyond his own part in them.

Today, after the passing of a generation, these changes continue to exert their influence, and the Revolution remains a vital force in Mexican life. Everything and everyone Mexican—even the anti-revolutionary who most loudly rails against Madero and the events of half a century—exists in an atmosphere permeated with its spirit. Every major public topic is approached, considered, accepted, or rejected in terms of what the Revolution is supposed to stand for, and no serious proponent of just about anything would dream of forgetting to claim legitimacy for his particular point of view by labeling it the authentic voice, perhaps the only authentic voice, of the Revolution. Nor would a newspaper or magazine seem quite complete without its memoir of a hero of those hectic days during which the Revolution was being formed, or its editorial exhorting Mexico to live up to the ideals for which such men fought.

Not even its most ardent enemies deny that the movement which began in 1910 was a real revolution. The first tragic decade of the new era saw bands of armed men marching across Mexico and laying waste the country at what all too often seemed to be the orders of ambitious and self-seeking politicians following one of the oldest and most often repeated traditions of Mexican politics, the taking of political power by force. Over a million people were killed or starved to death before order was restored, and the country suffered the economic consequences for years.[1] That terrible time was more than just another period of irresponsible violence in Mexico's history, however, for those first ten years of bloodshed and confusion also marked the beginnings of change—basic, permanent, and real change. This time the violence reflected the disruption of a broad range of social, economic, and political institutions which quite literally had hindered national integration and political advance for centuries. Equally important, large numbers of Mexicans accepted the concept of the possibility of change. The first, violent results of Westernization were making themselves felt.

Clearly, this was also a successful revolution, in that after the worst of the violence had abated, Mexico turned to the constructive task of building a new society and a new system of politics out of the pieces of the old, providing more effective patterns of interaction among the institutions which survived and those which were developing. New ideas and new ways of achieving older, unfulfilled goals and desires—in social thought, in economics, and in politics—emerged from the ferment of change. To the Mexicans, the values represented in this unfolding process of adjustment to changed conditions, and not the early violence, are the Revolution of 1910.

Mexico's Revolution was a popular movement, too, in the sense that if all of the factions which supported one or another concept of change or reform are considered together, their combined mem-

---

[1] The story of these perilous times is told in history books, such as Miguel Alessio Robles, *Historia Política de la Revolución* (3rd ed.; Mexico, D.F., 1946); José Vasconcelos, *Breve Historia de México* (Madrid, 1952); Herbert Priestly, *The Mexican Nation* (New York, 1938); Charles C. Cumberland, *The Mexican Revolution: Genesis under Madero* (Austin, 1952); Alberto Morales Jiménez, *Historia de la Revolución Mexicana* (Mexico, D.F., 1951). But a much more vivid account can be found in personal reminiscences such as Emilio Portes Gil's *Quince Años de Política Mexicana* (Mexico, D.F., 1941), or in some of the revolution-inspired novels, such as Mariano Azuela's *Los de Abajo* (1916), and *Los Caciques* (1917), or Martín Luis Guzmán's somewhat later *La Sombra del Caudillo* (1951).

bership makes up a very large part of the total politically aware
and active population. But the simple act of dislodging the older,
aristocratic ruling elite could not make the many revolutionary factions think as one, much less act so. If the new groups ruling Mexico
were more broadly based, during the first years of the Revolution
they were no less doctrinaire than the old dominant group. Only
time and the responsibilities of governing could turn the conglom-
erate of values held by the many revolutionary factions into a single
ideology.

### The Ideology of the Revolution

Mexico had no Marx to supply a theoretical, rational, and systematic model for its Revolution. And somehow history failed to
produce any single dominant personality who could perform this
service by centering the revolutionary doctrine in himself and his
beliefs over a long period of time. Probably the movement was too
big, too diverse, and too spontaneous to be identified with any one
program or person. Certainly during its first years Mexico's revolution was made up of acts rather than ideas, with a whole series of
attempts at one or another kind of change or reform being applied
within the context of the existing social and constitutional systems,
but with no real attempt to make the various experiments internally
consistent with one another or with the spirit or structure of the
formal governmental system.

Many of the newer and more fashionable political and economic
concepts of twentieth-century Western life were imposed upon
quite contrary thought patterns and political practices carried over
from the prerevolutionary era. Spanish personalism and authoritarianism never had blended very satisfactorily with nineteenth-
century *laissez faire* liberalism and the North American–style federal constitution. Now, suddenly, a generous sprinkling of economic
paternalism and social collectivism was added to the leaven. Top-
ping this, a number of specific doctrines evolved out of the day-to-
day experiences of the revolutionary reform movement, so that a
violent nationalism, anticlericalism, and the concept of no re-election
became part of the mixture. A little later, so did the goals of political democracy. All of these factors had to work out some sort of
relationship among themselves and to fit into a single system of
values before a full-blown ideology of the Revolution could develop.

This does not mean that the Mexican Revolution had no ideologists. The problem was that it had too many. The intellectual spokesmen of the Revolution range from one end of the political spectrum to the other, each vocally defending his own discrete interpretation of the movement. Some, such as Rafael Nieto and Luis Cabrera, were among the radical majority in the constitutional convention held at Querétaro during 1917; others, such as Graciano Sánchez and Vicente Lombardo Toledano, represent left-radical agrarian and labor emphasis in the Revolution. Still others, such as Ramón Beteta and Gilberto Loyo, reflect an identification of the movement with industrialization and economic development, while Indianists like Dr. Atl, Alfonso Caso, or Manuel Gamio identify it with a return to some of the values of the original inhabitants of the country.

Another group, which included such men as José Vasconcelos and Manuel Gómez Morín, began in the revolutionary camp, working with such middle-class leaders as Obregón and Calles, but reacted in an increasingly conservative manner to later attempts at basic social and economic change. Gómez Morín, for example, was one of the founders of the National Action Party (the PAN), which is the principal opposition party in Mexico.

Even among those commentators not so clearly identified with one or another point of view—Fernando González Roa, Alberto J. Pani, Jesús Silva Herzog, Daniel Cosío Villegas, for example—there is no single understanding of the meaning of the Revolution. Each, in contributing to the literature of the movement, sees it through his own eyes. Thus, there is no one spokesman for the ideology of the process of Westernization that is called the Revolution of 1910.

Much the same is true of the men of action, who probably shaped the Revolution more than the intellectuals. They shared no common approach to the movement they led. Madero was a political reformer of the nineteenth-century variety; Zapata cared not a whit for politics, but wanted immediate economic reform in the form of land distribution; Obregón and Calles were representative of the *norteño* clique, which could conveniently play down the reform provisions of the 1917 constitution in order to interpret personal political and financial interests as part of the revolutionary ideology. Contrast their attitude with that of Cárdenas, in whom the revolutionary myth of social reform for the farm and laboring masses became fact. Each of the earlier revolutionary leaders read his own meaning into the movement, reflecting his own values and experience, and sharing only the common rallying cry of revolutionary reform.

During the formative years of the Revolution, in the absence of a complete revolutionary philosophy of their own, some Mexicans adopted Marxian terminology. This, together with the anticapitalist, anti-Church, and xenophobic phases of the Revolution, long made the revolutionary governments more than a little suspect in the camps of the liberal democracies. Many, probably most, of these actions and attitudes were, however, more nearly negative manifestations of a positive nationalistic fervor or the reaction of rising leaders to attempts on the part of conservative institutions to limit their power than vital factors in a consistent revolutionary program. Over the years, certainly, basic Mexican values have pushed themselves relentlessly to the fore, forcing alien concepts to give way before them.

This does not suggest that there are no Communists in Mexico. There are, just as there are *sinarquistas* and others of the extreme right. It does suggest, however, that in spite of a few vociferous extremists on both ends of the political spectrum, the Revolution set at work forces that could produce a truly Mexican nation, with its own values and institutions. More important, that nation now includes a larger proportion than ever before of Mexicans who share more or less similar values. And, almost by definition, widely shared values are moderate values, especially in politics. The Revolution has succeeded finally in producing such an ideology.

It is an ideology of pragmatic experience, in which most of the more radical ideas advanced during the earlier period have been eroded by time, just as the foreign importations of European "isms" have been crushed by the strength of Mexico's own institutions. To the mass of the Mexican people, the Revolution stands simply for progress and change, which they equate with a better life for each of them. Through trial and error over the years it has come to mean integration of the Indian into the national life, improved social and economic conditions for farmer, laborer, bureaucrat, or any other Mexican and, gradually, a greater participation in the political life of the country for all of them. The Revolution also is identified with nationalism, both that true nationalism that seeks to assure all citizens a voice in national policy and some measure of control over their own destinies and the somewhat more chauvinistic nationalism that manifests itself in xenophobic attacks upon foreigners and foreign capital.

In short, with the possible exception of this very general idea of progress and change, there is no integrated and official ideology of the Mexican Revolution that is accepted by all Mexicans at all times. This is why it is useless to debate whether and when the Revolution ended, for the Revolution means everything to everybody and something different to each. For the collective land reformer, the Revolution ended with Cárdenas' term as president; for the Indianist perhaps a few years later, with the gradual lessening of the attitude that all things good in Mexico lie with that one part of the population; for other people perhaps with the advent of the business-minded administration of Alemán. For still others, the Revolution is still going on, in the gradual adjustment of all of the differing values and goals into a single, working, social, economic, and political system.

Clearly, many of the things which Mexicans once believed the Revolution to stand for were incompatible with each other, but the people's understanding of them has altered with time, so that a workable set of values is evolving. Naturally, this process has left some goals which do not fit perfectly into the broad system, and others which have had to wait their turn until time and conditions are ripe for their successful inclusion.

For all its contradictions, the spirit of the Revolution has caught and held the imaginations of most Mexicans. It has become one of those social myths through which hope in tomorrow's promise outweighs today's failures. Perhaps its very strength lies in the lack of any pre-fixed dogma, which has allowed revolutionary values and goals to be modified over the years to meet the needs of a people in flux. In any event, Zapata's cry for "Peace and Bread" long since has been translated successfully into the roar of complex machinery in an expanding economy and a developing society.

Many, though not all, of the differing goals of the Revolution are reflected in the spirit of the economic and social norms added to the new version of the Mexican constitution promulgated in 1917. At the Querétaro convention, the delegates tried to provide for suitable conditions to insure the type of good society they envisioned. To the rather traditional liberal political provisions of the Constitution of 1857 they added sections which established the responsibility of government for developing an environment in which the broad mass of citizens might be capable of exercising their civic duties. This Constitution of 1917, which still formally governs Mexico, was the first constitution in Latin America to recognize the necessity of seeking solutions to essentially nonpolitical problems as part of the search for orderly and popular government.

## The Search for Effective Government

This recognition of the relationship between social and economic environment on the one hand and political stability on the other was no little accomplishment. The Mexicans had sought to make the forms of constitutional government work during most of their independent lives, to no avail. During the century preceding the Revolution they passed law after law adopting the paraphernalia of responsible and limited government—federalism, separation of powers, electoral codes, and all the rest.[2] Without success. Historically, it seemed that even the small politically active part of the population was unable to discover a political system that could assure popular participation in government, limit constitutionally the actions of the persons who controlled the government, and at the same time provide stable administration.

So great a democrat as Juárez could achieve political stability only by means of an ironhanded rule. When his restraining influence disappeared, administrative stability degenerated into the oligarchy of the Díaz regime. This in turn led directly to the chaos of the Revolution.

Remember that the prerevolutionary *políticos* were captives of the history of their country and of the conditions which had shaped that history. Under the Spanish viceroys, loyalty to the crown and a desire to visit or return to Spain one day had been a controlling factor in the lives of the small elite making up the economically powerful and politically aware citizenry. Not since that time had Mexico been governed as a single unit. During its entire independent existence there had been no such thing as a truly national government with authority based upon common political and constitutional principles accepted throughout Mexico.

Instead, under the prerevolutionary political system each local political leader was a law unto himself. Generally he used a small clique of personally loyal followers both to dominate the great

---

[2] See Felipe Tena Ramírez, *Leyes Fundamentales de México, 1808-1957* (Mexico, D.F., 1957).

mass of uneducated and politically unaware inhabitants of the isolated region he controlled and to overawe politically active persons who might be unwilling to accept his leadership. In building his private empire, each of these *caciques*, as the local bosses were called, would use force and cunning to capture control of all the functions of political power and therefore of the formal agencies of government. If possible, he would work out some kind of an understanding with the major organized interest groups which might counterbalance his influence. These included, usually, the Church, the large landowners, and the local military leaders. Those organized interests he could not control he would attempt to crush, or at least to neutralize.

Once in power, the *cacique* might unconcernedly subvert the most basic terms of the state or national constitution. With only limited ability to exert pressure at their disposal, Díaz and his predecessors could not saturate the outlying regions of the country with military power. The problems of transportation over Mexico's terrible geographic barriers were complicated by a poorly trained and equipped national army, so that the only way the central authorities could hope to govern the entire country was to work out some compromise with the local political bosses or to dominate them completely. This was true of Díaz and of Juárez before him; it continued to be true during the first years of the Revolution. The successful president dazzled the local leaders with promises of rewards and threats of force.

Under such circumstances, the personal influence of the national leader was more effective in uniting the country than was political ideology or constitutional machinery. So long as a strong man— Santa Anna, Juárez, Díaz—dominated the situation, all remained calm, but personal control of this sort did nothing to change the system or to end the physical isolation or lack of ideological identification with the legal aims of the central government. In fact, exercise of such personalized control actually inhibited the development of loyalty to the constitutional system itself. The successful local politician was one who worked out some sort of arrangement with the national leader, rather than the man dedicated to constitutional norms. The successful national politician was the man who controlled the local *políticos*, no matter how.

With the fall of a national leader, therefore, the attempt to transfer authority to a new president almost inevitably upset the political equilibrium. Time after time, an era of peace was followed by unrest and rebellion, while ambitious politicians struggled among themselves for the presidency and its perquisites. The more evenly matched the contenders were, the longer and more bitter was the struggle; in the end the strongest or cleverest man won. Meanwhile, Mexico lost.

This is not to say that constitutionalism suffered terribly in the process, because it never really existed as a working part of Mexico's political system during the nineteenth century. Most Mexican presidents paid a certain amount of lip service to the constitution, but conditions in the country made the rule of force or cunning more meaningful than the rule of law. Given the nature of the power structure, all too often the departure from strict constitutional usage with which we tax one of these men was the only course open to him in the face of a pattern of unconstitutional acts by state or regional leaders. The real choice facing the president was not always between constitutionalism and dictatorship; more often than not it was between dictatorship and anarchy.

The same force motif that marked prerevolutionary politics recurred in the early events of the Revolution of 1910. If anything, the situation was worse, for before the fall of Díaz, the national political process had consisted of the interaction among a limited number of leaders who had to satisfy the demands of a few traditional organized interests, such as the military, landowners, and Church. Most of the politically active Mexicans belonged to the small and aristocratic ruling elite. But the Revolution occurred because the old political system was unable to accommodate the mounting pressure of demands from an increasing number of new interest groups. Many of these were willing and able to resort to force when the formal government failed to satisfy their needs.

Again, after a century of intermittent experience with forms of constitutional government, it appeared to many Mexicans that the best government was one little restrained by the norms of a constitution but which could accomplish whatever demands the individual or interest group might make upon it. For some this meant access to the process of policy-making, for others the provision of some measure of stability in the face of disturbances in the capital and peripheral areas of the country.

Most notable among the revolutionary leaders of this earlier period were the *caudillos*—political generals such as Obregón,

Calles, Cárdenas—none of whom based his position primarily upon constitutional authority or felt very much bound thereby, but who could dominate the political process and the country by the power he wielded. More legalistically inclined but less forceful presidents —not excepting Madero, the secular saint of the Revolution—may have left traditions to be respected, but they failed to provide the firm leadership and aggregation of interests in policy formation that Mexico required.

Even during the early revolutionary period, however, changing circumstances made unlikely the rise of some super-*caudillo* who could hope to succeed in providing effective government for very long. Beyond the ever-present problems of selection and of transferring power to some other strong man when the time came, the growing complexity of Mexico's society made the old-style political system inappropriate. The very forces which had produced the Revolution—increasing specialization of economic activity, the proliferation of competing interests, and all the other products of Westernization—made it increasingly difficult for even the strongest military man to rely successfully on the outmoded political mechanisms which had failed.

Personalistic control based on military force, through which policy decisions were reached in face-to-face meetings with the leader, no longer was enough, for the competing interests which had to be satisfied began to overbalance the military alone. A more viable political system had to be devised, one based on means other than physical force and through which the formal agencies of government could operate to serve the increasingly complicated demands which groups of citizens made upon the revolutionary leadership.

Of course, such a system was not accomplished at once. The complete chaos that had disrupted Mexico's political institutions during the decade after 1910 made the twenties a period of slow and painful reconstruction. The old façade of constitutionalism was continued, but a coalition of civilian political bossism and military power, rather than formal governmental machinery, was utilized to select from among the many factions and individuals who claimed the office and perquisites of governor, membership in state legislatures, and a voice in policy-making. As the country settled down, greater and greater attention had to be paid to the nonmilitary, functional interests which clamored for participation in political life. Farm and labor groups, bureaucrats, and all the other products of increasingly influential Westernization had to be considered.

But the Mexican tradition of separatism, bolstered by increasing specialization, meant that as soon as such interests began to form organizations, these split into various regional, functional, and personalistic factions. New and stronger political machinery had to be devised to channel the increased number and variety of demands and to rationalize the policy-making process. The strong-arm government of the *caudillos* could not perform this necessary political function. Yet if *caudillismo* was to be replaced by a set of mechanisms to turn the revolutionary movement into a service state, stability, the one meager advantage of personal rule, had to be retained.

To accomplish this, the revolutionary leaders used the force still at their disposal to set up a nationwide political machine through which they could impose their own interpretation of the political values upon which Mexican government should be based and at the same time exercise some measure of control over the conflicting demands of the new interest groups. The new "official party" of the Revolution provided the mechanisms for aggregation of interests in policy-making.

This was not done in any consciously rational and planned manner, for it is doubtful that Calles or even Cárdenas anticipated that the organization they established and promoted would take the institutionalized pattern it did. In many ways, the so-called official party and the political system of which it is a major part have far outstripped the ability of any individual leader to manipulate it for his own purposes.

The party and the political system that have evolved provide mechanisms to satisfy the political needs of a developing Mexico. This new political system is effective because it has developed in such a way that it reflects the needs and attitudes of the largest part of the Mexican people and is flexible enough to adjust to changes in those needs as Mexico's rapidly changing economy and social patterns so demand.

During the first years of the consolidation of revolutionary power and formation of the official party, the revolutionary leaders excluded from effective political life those persons who could not accept the Revolution and its reforms. But in order to strengthen their own positions, revolutionary leaders encouraged greater political activity by hitherto underrepresented interests—farmers, laborers, and the bureaucrats—as well as by other elements in the slowly developing middle class. Now, some thirty years after the official party was first formed, certain vital changes in Mexico's political system are becoming manifest. Not only is a greater number of rank-and-file Mexicans included on its membership roles, not only is the number and variety of formal interest associations working within the party increasing daily, but even those Mexicans who once opposed the Revolution and the semimonopolistic revolutionary party are sharing in a common value system and participating to a much greater extent in the developing political system.

Gradually, a more homogeneous political society has begun to form around the core of the revolutionary group, attracted partly by the continuing political success they demonstrate and partly by the moderating changes in the revolutionary ideology already suggested. Over the years, as transportation, communication, and education have improved, as the Mexican economy has become more diversified and more interdependent, as specialization of function has increased, as more and more of the country's inhabitants have become aware of the nation, a kind of legitimacy of revolutionary values has evolved. As the goals of the Revolution have broadened and become less radical so as to satisfy the needs of more and more of the Mexican people, a systematic adjustment between them and the most enduring of Mexico's older social and political values has occurred, producing new and more effective political institutions to replace those disrupted by the Revolution.

Because of the practical monopoly over effective force during the formative years of this new political system, resort to violence for political ends was kept to a minimum. Much of the violence during the Revolution occurred in the form of power struggles within rather than outside of the revolutionary ranks, so that as the official party has matured, improving both its organization and its rationalization of the policy-making process, wide-scale violence has virtually disappeared. In this new system of politics, dependence upon force gives way to interrelated organizational loyalties and relations, with access to representation in the policy-making process made possible for more and more interests, even including some of those still outside of the revolutionary party.

It has now become possible to transfer real policy-making power from one presidential administration to another within the revolutionary party. The new pattern that has begun to emerge in Mexican politics contains some of the personalistic elements endemic in the older system, but it also includes limitations upon the power of the individual, as might well be expected in a political system that attempts to balance a growing number of diversified interests by means of machinery dominated by a formally structured political organization. As yet, the real process of politics takes place mostly in or around the official party, which acts as a kind of auxiliary agency of government, rather than in the formal constitutional bodies such as the congress.

Nonetheless, as equilibrium has been achieved among the strongest sectors of economic and political life through the activities of the revolutionary party, political decisions are more rationalized and more predictable, as well as more nearly representative of the whole of the Mexican people, than ever before. In this sense, the government of Mexico is more nearly constitutional than it ever has been before. And more and more the formal agencies of government are being used to carry out, to some extent even to formulate, policy supported by the official party.

Between 1910 and 1920, then, Mexico's politics degenerated into pure violence. During the next twenty years or so the violence gradually diminished, but politics could scarcely be said to be formally patterned. I often think that those great sprawling murals produced during this period by Rivera and Siqueiros were indeed a product of their times. Like them, the political situation was strangely confused and out of focus, bound together only by the common theme of the Revolution. More recently, as new social and political institutions have developed in response to changing conditions, the impetus to disorder and lack of continuity has begun to lose some of its effectiveness.

With greater and greater frequency during the Cárdenas administration (1934-40), it became clear that political power lay with the official party and not with any single leader, not even so powerful a one as Cárdenas himself. This despite the fact that he is often called "the last *caudillo*." It was during this period that the last large-scale attempt at revolt against the central authorities was crushed. As a *modus vivendi* was worked out among the disparate interests represented in the revolutionary clique, the pattern of national control through official party organization became firmly established. This became abundantly clear during the presidential terms of Avila Camacho (1940-46) and Alemán (1946-52), for although in the beginning neither of them was the strong-man type found in earlier Mexican presidential tradition, their rule, supported by the official party's organization, was peaceful and even fruitful. Finally, the administration of Adolfo Ruiz Cortines (1952-58) brought Mexico many of the benefits of ordered government which would have been considered unattainable less than a quarter of a century before. This same constructive pattern continued during President López Mateos' term after 1958.

In fact, out of the terrible violence of the Revolution's early years, Mexico has managed to build a kind of government that is almost unique in Latin America. With the single exception of Uruguay, which faced considerably fewer social and material problems, no other country in the area has been able to devise a political formula by which stable government can be transferred from one national leader to another over a period of years, even decades, without direct interference by the military or the outbreak of civil strife.

Some of the Latin American countries have achieved a degree of stability, but at the expense of constitutionalism or of civilian government, or both. Witness the Praetorian Guard that dominates so many of the so-called stable governments, with generals who rule in the name of the citizens but who usually are unhampered by political responsibility or other constitutional niceties. Or consider other countries in the area which have had to defend their traditional respect for constitutional forms by force of arms, as Costa Rica did a few years ago, or work out some sort of extra-constitutional interregnum period of political adjustment, as Colombia did in 1958. Still others sacrifice constructive and orderly administration on the altar of parliamentary instability, as Chile seems to do forever. Only Mexico, so badly torn by its Revolution, seems to have faced up to its major problems of land and people and economics and to have worked out at least the beginnings of a stable political process and with it economic and social advances which can be the basis of a new society.

### Stability vs. Democracy

For all this, many thinking Mexicans are not yet satisfied with the emerging political system. They argue that stability is but the first step on the road to democratic and responsible government which they expected the Revolution to travel. While they admit the material advances of recent years, they point out that the stability on which these advances depend has been accomplished by forming a closed power bloc about a combination of special interests bearing a revolutionary label. In the name of the Revolution, they claim, this bloc excludes other competing interests from effective participation in the political process. Acting through the medium of an outwardly monolithic official party that claims to speak for the great mass of citizens, the revolutionary politicians see to it that dissident members of the opposition, or their own constituents for that matter, cannot disrupt the stability of government, but they do so by assuring that the dissident elements have no real voice in policy decisions.

Further, they cite specific failings which even the friendliest observer cannot pretend to ignore. Beyond the most obvious constitutional failure to accord the legislature and the judiciary their formal legal roles in relation to the all-powerful executive, the bill of particulars in the indictment covers a wide variety of points. Prominent among these are the record of vacillations in public policy, frequent failures in the execution of vital government functions, an ever-present graft and corruption, and a seeming inability or outright unwillingness of the revolutionary leadership to relinquish its hold on the government through the normal steps of the democratic process.

How does Mexican politics differ, the unsatisfied ones ask, from that under authoritarian dictatorships in other Latin American countries? A lack of governmental responsibility to the citizens, together with what they consider unchecked freedom of action for the official party, demonstrates to these Mexicans that ". . . Señor Madero was a dreamer, a romantic and illusory; that the opinion of the people does not even merit consideration [in revolutionary Mexico]; that democracy is an unattainable shadow in our environment."[3]

On its face, part, even much, of this indictment is quite valid. The revolutionary governments have been far from perfect in their execution of substantive policies and even less so in their political morals. Drastic shifts in agricultural and labor policies from one

---

[3] Antonio Espinosa de los Monteros, "Sufragio Efectivo o Totalitarianismo Nativo?" *El Universal,* December 29, 1950. See also the Mexico City press for reports of the analysis of the Revolution made at the Ninth National Congress of Sociology, held in Zacatecas during November, 1958, where most of the principal papers pointed up and deplored the lack of basic change in the social and economic structure since 1910, despite the Revolution.

administration to another, ill-advised public projects, costly failures of grandiose schemes—all have occurred. The function of the fixer, the more or less placid acceptance of graft, are too well known to be glossed over simply as the raving of an intemperate opposition. Much the same can be said for the difficulties of trying to dislodge the revolutionary party from its entrenched position.

But such an evaluation must be weighed in the context of the environment in which the revolutionary political system has evolved. Some of the Mexicans who find today's politics wanting are measuring the Revolution's accomplishments against very nearly impossible ideal goals rather than against the problems of the past. This is a common Latin trait picked up from Hispanic culture. Others who object to the new politics are in opposition to the Revolution as such, rather than to specific policies. Both of these groups fail to recognize the degree to which both material and political progress have affected Mexico since 1910, and the very real problems which have had to be conquered before this progress could be attained.

The revolutionary tenets and actions which are most frequently cited to demonstrate the failings of the Revolution and its leaders are indeed questionable. They must include such things as persecution of the Church, expropriation of large private land holdings to provide collective farms, government control over subsoil mineral rights, and even the expropriation of the foreign-owned petroleum operations in Mexico. But each of these actions, if considered in context, was an attempt to offset one or another counter-revolutionary influence or interest which was in itself unrepresentative of the general population or the national interest.

As the revolutionary values and the governments which represent them have consolidated their positions, the most radical applications of these acts have eased or disappeared. The beginnings of a working agreement with a less politically motivated Church, or perhaps one that no longer holds so predominant a position in the more complex society, have made their appearance. So too with secularization and democratization of education and re-establishment of privately owned but now smaller agricultural holdings. More recently, a formula has been worked out between government and private interests for exploitation of mineral resources, and foreign capital once again is being courted, though this time under more controlled conditions.

If opposition to the revolutionary party exists—and it does—it is more opposition to the individuals who control the party than to the Revolution itself. The fundamental question of revolutionary reform long since has been resolved by irremedial fact, so that now the struggle is over who shall administer the Revolution and how. The oldest and most consistent opposition party—the PAN—for example, has a picture of that "dreamer," Sr. Madero, hanging in its principal public meeting room in the nation's capital.

Moreover, it is no longer valid, as once it certainly was, to say that the revolutionary clique excludes representatives of major interests from participation in the political process. On the contrary, the very stability to which the accusers of the Revolution allude grows out of the fact that the present-day power structure recognizes the newer interests engendered by Westernization, and the political process translates their conflicting goals into workable governmental policy. The objectors, even those who speak in complete good faith, fall into the age-old trap of measuring the accomplishments of the Revolution by yesterday's experiences rather than today's events.

## The Dilemma of the Revolution

One reason that the political goals of the Revolution have not been won as speedily as might have been desired is that Madero set into motion a spontaneous reaction to a number of very different problems which in turn produced what might be called two separate revolutions, happening simultaneously. One, a social and economic revolution, inevitably involved upheaval, class conflict, and dissension as it attempted to curb the vested interests of the old ruling elite to serve the more general mass of citizens. The second, a political revolution, just as inevitably sought moderation and national unity upon which to base the development of permanent institutions of responsible government. Both sets of aspirations were true reflections of desires felt by large sectors of the population, but it was impossible to carry out the two revolutions at the same time.

Probably priority on the revolutionary calendar had to fall where it did—on economic and social development. Justo Sierra pointed out just before the storm broke in 1910 that the Díaz regime had sacrificed political development to other aspects of social evolution.[4] And yet the very length and excesses of the violent phase of

---

[4] *Evolución Política del Pueblo Mexicano* (Mexico, D.F., 1940), p. 455.

the Revolution demonstrated only too clearly that social development itself had not progressed notably under the old general. Until at least a minimum of education and social integration, together with some sense of economic security, could penetrate the mass mind, no political revolution accepting the concept of "one man, one vote" could hope to succeed.

The political goals which Mexicans seek from their Revolution are the end-product of a particular kind of society. They evolve slowly out of systematic adjustment of values inherent in widespread literacy, a high level of general education and knowledge, a rising standard of living for most of the population, improved communications and ease of movement from place to place through the country. The resultant expansion of political awareness, of individual independence and acceptance of personal responsibility for civil improvement, of the sense of the nation, are basic requirements for democratic political life. Without this preparation in the citizens, the foundations of responsible and representative government are built on sand, as Díaz proved at such a price to Mexico.

Of necessity, therefore, during the early part of the Revolution most of the programs, plans, and catchwords of the movement dealt in specific terms with the more pressing material problems—land distribution, economic reform and expansion, in general with the dreams of a better life. Meanwhile, the yearning for political advances, which was no less strong, was much more difficult to satisfy. In practice, change in the social and economic factors of life prevailed over the search for honesty and political responsibility.

Given the semifeudal conditions from which it sprang, the need to integrate large numbers of formerly apolitical persons, together with the slow growth of systematic and complementary habit patterns, for most Mexicans the surprising thing is that the Revolution has carried the country as far as it has on the road to political stability and productive national life. They have learned to live with its moral failings and to look on politics with a kind of good-natured cynicism that would be the despair of some Anglo-Saxon good government organizations. They enjoy mightily such stories as that of the large numbers of ex-cabinet ministers and retired generals who live in Cuernavaca on what has been nicknamed Ali Baba and the Forty Thieves Street. Each politician claims that he is Ali Baba and that his neighbors are the forty thieves.

At this juncture in Mexican history the really vital question is not whether the achievements of the Revolution to date have resulted in the kind of responsible and effective government that we normally associate with democracy, important as this may be. It is, rather, whether the reforms already accomplished and the things for which Mexico's revolution stand can in time be expected to evolve into such a system of government.

CHAPTER *5*

# Development of an Official Party

## The Three Stages of the Revolutionary Party

The dynamics of transfer from government dominated by force and individual personality to government by political organization are difficult to capture. One can account for a good part of these dynamics by considering them as a consequence of the very real changes brought about by expanding Westernization, encouraged by the revolutionary program—extending education, developing the national economy, and moving toward a more mature society in Mexico. Similarly, when Westernization is coupled with a forceful revolution, one can construct a sort of logic of institutional change on a basis of enforced application of the values of the successful revolutionary faction and the weakened position of those who defend the older system. But neither Westernization itself nor the forced adherence to new values explains the precise evolutionary process by which the new political system takes form or the reason it assumes the particular form that it does.

Given the conditions described previously, the difficulty in achieving central government at all had much to do with the development of a political system based on a single effective party that could concentrate its efforts on that pressing problem. Perhaps the most logical explanation of successful transfer of political authority to that party and its allied functional interest associations lies in the monopoly of political power it enjoyed during its early days, and the manner in which it has managed to maintain and even to extend that monopoly as the political system has become more complex.

Just as the party itself resulted from the conditions which obtained as the new political system began to evolve, the structural form of the revolutionary party organization also grew out of the nature of the interests participating in its activities, and the interaction among them within the party.

We can trace the evolution of the official party and the political system it controls through three successive stages. Each stage is marked by a decrease in the influence of localized personalistic militarism and a corresponding increase in the role of the party apparatus in controlling the factors of the political system. As a corollary, almost in exact proportion as the party expanded its influence over nominations, elections, and other forms of selecting government officers, a growing observance of the outward forms of constitutional government appeared.

The first stage of the revolutionary party's evolution covers the period of formation, the early development and gradual implementation of the party monopoly over effective political power. During this period the party was little more than a coalition of semi-independent local organizations dominated by individual military or civilian bosses. The binding tie was found in the prestige of General Calles, who dominated the coalition and its leaders, but in so doing enabled the revolutionary party to defeat all other political movements opposing it.

With an increasing number and complexity of organized interests operating in the party as a result of the growing specialization of function engendered by Westernization, the next stage was marked by centralization of authority in the associational hierarchy and the party bureaucracy, which overlapped to some extent. At this stage, the President of the Republic became the single most powerful leader in the party and the country. Using the party machinery, including the bureaucracy of the allied functional associations, he acted as a court of last resort in settling the inevitable clashes of conflicting interest which occurred so frequently in a speedily changing social and economic environment. His word was law, and woe betide the interest group leader who disputed it, no matter how irrational or unfair the decision might be. By this time, opposition parties had little or no chance to defeat the official party's political machine, by either ballots or bullets.

In the third stage, through which the party now is passing, relationships among all of the principal interests both in and outside of the official party's ranks have become somewhat more institutionalized. The greater degree of adjustment among them, as each fits into its relative place in the political system, permits a less rigid domination of the political system by the party machinery and the president. In fact, although the needs of the country still require strong central control over policy and politics, new political tendencies have begun to assert themselves. Multiplication and specialization of interests, together with diversification of interest within the older functional interest associations, have weakened the old monolithic structure of the party sector apparatus and changed the role of its leader. The president's function as party chief and political master of the country now consists of balancing interests, of adjusting conflicts so as to avoid disruption of economic and social development, and of encouraging participation in the national political system by as many Mexicans as possible, in order to reduce still further the possibility of interruptions in the peaceful operation of the political system. Moreover, it has become fashionable to encourage the existence of opposition parties, so long as they do not become too strong.

Quite obviously, changes in the revolutionary party and the political system have not been so sharply defined that a specific date can be assigned to the three stages listed above. Instead, each has evolved slowly out of its predecessor, with some of the earlier characteristics carrying over. Consequently, tempting as it might be to equate one stage with each of the three names the official party has worn, this would be both misleading and incorrect.[1] Probably the clearest way to differentiate among the three stages is to review some of the events which influenced the evolution of the revolutionary party from its inception to the present.

## Postrevolutionary Politics[2]

The chaos of the first years of the Revolution had the effect—for

---

[1] The revolutionary party was called the National Revolutionary party (*Partido Nacional Revolucionario,* or PNR) from 1929 to 1937. From that year until 1945 it was the Party of the Mexican Revolution (*Partido de la Revolución Mexicana,* or PRM). Since then it has been the Institutional Revolutionary party (*Partido Revolucionario Institucional,* or PRI).

good or evil—of eliminating most organized political activity as it had existed under Díaz. Until 1917, only the military factions surrounding the various revolutionary *caudillos* seemed to be politically active or, at any rate, politically effective. With the gradual return to some semblance of order following the emergence of Venustiano Carranza in 1917 as *Primer Jefe* of the Revolution, many of these military factions took on civil political trappings. The leader of each exercised political domination over the area he controlled, sometimes with the title of state governor, sometimes as military zone commander, or sometimes simply as the local strong man.

Certain labor union chiefs and a few farm leaders also had taken their organized followers into politics, forming coalitions with ambitious military chieftains. Both the civilian and the military politicians hoped in this way to extend their own influence. Even before 1920, therefore, incipient interest groups and associations had become active ingredients in the political situation.

Several attempts were made to form national class or interest parties about this time, but despite their functional interest façade, most of them were personalistic in nature, and so-called national parties often were local in influence and transitory in nature. This was particularly true of those parties which did not enjoy alignment with a powerful and successful *caudillo,* for no party seemed able to prosper without some measure of support from the group of military leaders who surrounded Carranza in the national capital. In the final analysis it was not the popular will or ballots, but recognition of electoral victory by the central authorities that decided the outcome of all elections, national or local.

Nonetheless, these civilian parties were important to the military politicians for two reasons. First, they offered a convenient means of supplying civilian support that increased the respectability of the military governments. Secondly, for all their weakness, these civilian parties were the nearest thing, other than the military itself, to organized power groups in the revolutionary movement. In a situation where the military force at the disposal of two competing *caudillos* was substantially equal, support of an individual by such a civilian party well might spell the difference between political success or failure.

---

[2] Sources describing the political events of this period have already been cited in footnote 1, Chapter IV.

All in all, this lack of broadly based and effective civilian parties produced an extremely unstable political situation, as coalitions formed and dissolved in response to the shifting ambitions of their various members. The speed with which the many factions rose and fell betrays their lack of institutional basis, for although each claimed to represent the Revolution, or some phase of it, behind every party lurked a personalistic leader. Each leader was willing to work with others when expedient, but he constantly was seeking his own ends. If in order to achieve those ends it became necessary to reverse allegiance from allies to enemies overnight, he was usually ready to do so. Similarly, if it became necessary to betray the interests of his rank-and-file followers for his own benefit, this sort of leader all too often was equally prepared to do this.

The political maneuvers following the downfall of *Primer Jefe* Carranza and his Constitutionalist party in 1920 offer convincing illustration of just how lacking was the basis of an institutionalized party system. The three-general *junta* of Alvaro Obregón, Plutarco Calles, and Adolfo de la Huerta—the triumvirate of Agua Prieta— who had united to oust their former chief when he tried to impose a hand-picked candidate to succeed himself was a shaky affair at best. As "acting president," de la Huerta saw to it that Obregón's Liberal Constitutionalist party won the presidential election of September 5, 1920, but soon afterward disagreements between the new president and other party leaders led to withdrawal of Obregón's support of the party. The Liberal Constitutionalist party disintegrated, but two other parties came into prominence.

For a short time many smaller and less well-connected factions were forced to stand aside while the Labor party (*Partido Nacional Laborista*) and the Cooperatist party (*Partido Nacional Cooperatista*), a farm group, struggled to win the essential support of the president. Finally, in 1922, it appeared that the second party had won out. President Obregón forced the *laboristas*, who were really the political arm of Luis Morones' Mexican Regional Federation of Labor, the CROM, to withdraw from the municipal elections in Mexico City. Within the year, however, Jorge Prieto Laurens, the leader of the *cooperatistas*, threw away his advantage when he supported the abortive revolt of General de la Huerta against an attempt to impose General Calles instead of himself in the 1924 presidential election. This left the *laboristas* as the only nationally organized political party.

President Obregón was too wise a politician to leave such concentrated power in the hands of an ambitious man like Morones, especially when he was about to deliver the presidency to Calles. Before the end of his administration in 1924, Obregón's compensating policy had become quite pronounced. As a counterbalance to the political ambitions of Morones he turned to the Agrarian party (*Partido Nacional Agrarista*), which also had supported him during the de la Huerta revolt. Not unexpectedly, the marked preference for agrarian interests shown during the last year of Obregón's term diverted Labor party support away from him and into the arms of General Calles, who welcomed the party as a prop for his new administration.

Even though Obregón had been Calles' close friend and had supported him rather than de la Huerta for the presidency, Calles was ambitious, so he promptly accepted Morones and the *laboristas* because he knew that he could not capture support of the agrarian groups from the former president. As chief executive, Calles saw to it that the Labor party was well cared for in government positions and in influence. Morones became a cabinet minister and the unions in his labor federation found it difficult indeed to lose a strike. Both prospered accordingly.

Outside of the presidency General Obregón continued to wield a great deal of political influence because of his close ties to the military and to agrarian interests, an influence that Calles could not counteract by favoring his labor collaborators who, for all their discipline, simply were not numerous enough. Near the end of Calles' four-year term, the division into *agrarista* and *laborista* camps became increasingly hostile. It is indicative of the lack of national integration at this time that the struggle for control of Mexico did not take place within the national administration but rather in the hinterland, where the two factions fought to win the support of local *caudillos* in order to capture the state governments. Both factions also tried to organize the farmers on the newly formed *ejidos* but without many positive results. The time was not yet ripe. Such a contest could end in only one of two ways; either open warfare would break out, or one of the two leaders would capitulate to the other.

In the final analysis, President Calles was the weaker of the two and he knew it. Rather than risk an open break, he swung the government's support back to Obregón, though in doing so he abandoned the revolutionary principle of "no re-election." By forcing adoption of constitutional amendments permitting a second presidential term, Calles made possible Obregón's re-election. In the 1928 election campaign, therefore, General Obregón was supported by a coalition of parties headed by the *agraristas* and including the unwilling *laboristas*. He was opposed by an anti-reelectionist faction that rebelled when it became obvious that Obregón would win. So, once again, the army cast the deciding ballot in the contest by putting down the revolt, after which there could be no question of the result. General Obregón was elected president, but before he could assume office he was assassinated by a religious fanatic. This left President Calles as the strongest *caudillo* in the country, but it also left a political vacuum.

## The Official Party—PNR

President Calles was faced with a dilemma. His term in office was running out, and not even Obregón had attempted to impose himself for a second term immediately. The amended constitution still required that a full term elapse before a president returned to office. The only solution seemed to be a resort to *continuismo*— to impose a weaker politician in the presidency while Calles himself remained the power behind the throne. To do this, he had to convince his fellow *caudillos* of the necessity for such an imposition; to do it successfully, he had to consolidate his power so that he could control the new president.

Calles managed to surmount the first major obstacle by convincing the other military leaders that the balance of power was so evenly distributed among them that any attempt to choose an army candidate would result in deadlock or civil war. Emilio Portes Gil, the civilian political boss of the state of Tamaulipas, thereupon was selected and duly elected Provisional President of Mexico by unanimous vote of the national congress. Portes Gil was particularly well-suited for Calles' purpose because he had neither the *agraristas* nor the *laboristas* as personalistic followers.

President Calles took the next great step in his plan on September 1, 1928, the occasion of his last annual message to Congress. Announcing his retirement from public life, he called on all dissident elements to unite in forming a single "Revolutionary" party, one that, in his words, would represent the people, end the domination by *caudillos,* and limit the narrow partisanship of class interest.

During March of 1929, in the historic city of Querétaro, where the Constitution of 1917 had been written, the *Partido Nacional Revolucionario* was set up as the accepted agency of the Revolution. Unlike its official successors, the original PNR was not highly centralized; instead it was an amalgam of local political machines and of various agricultural, labor, and other interest associations, backed by the silent but ever-present force of the military. Included were the organizations of the military *caudillos*—Rodríguez in Sonora, Cárdenas in Michoacán, Cedillo in San Luis Potosí, Maximino Avila Camacho in Puebla—and those of the civilian *caciques*—Portes Gil in Tamaulipas, Adelberto Tejeda in Veracruz, and the party of the recently deceased Felipe Carrillo Puerto of Yucatán. Each component in the coalition was to retain its organizational identity but act under the mandate of a National Executive Committee.

To be sure, in making this concession to Calles, the generals had no intention of giving up any of the power they exercised. Their cooperation was, to them, no more than a temporary expedient to carry them through a somewhat clouded political situation. A few local political leaders refused to enter Calles' coalition but in time their political strength withered away, for local machines could not oppose the combined might that the PNR could bring to bear.

The attitude of the leadership of the functional interest associations toward the PNR was no less devious than that of their military brethren. They had no wish to lose control over their followers. Having been in opposition to Calles, the Agrarian party was an especially hard nut to crack. Nevertheless, with the aid of one of its less intransigent leaders, Aaron Sáenz, and by spending plenty of government money, Calles managed to split the farm party's organization, purge his opponents, and add the *agraristas* to his coalition.

Ironically, Morones' Labor party, which previously had supported Calles, remained outside of the official fold. Partly because of suspicion of the strong man's motives, partly through lack of encouragement from Calles because public opinion somehow connected the *laboristas* with Obregón's death, Morones did not join the PNR. He and his labor organization have been trying ever since to regain their lost prominence, with little success. Other labor groups of course now flocked to the new party, but they gained few immediate advantages. For the time being, the power factor represented by organized labor, as compared with other factions in the party, was not strong enough to warrant major concessions. Presidents Portes Gil, Ortiz Rubio, and Rodríguez, all of whom served at one period or another during the next presidential term, were not particularly dependent upon labor.

Neither was Calles. Although he had relinquished the office of president, as *jefe máximo* of the revolutionary party he exercised an almost complete control over the increasingly centralized political organization. He continued to think in the personalistic tradition, however, not recognizing that the existence of the PNR had changed the nature of his relationship with his followers. In 1931, for example, Calles put his son Alfredo, who was not yet old enough to hold office legally, into the state legislature of Tamaulipas. He also tried to force amendment of the state constitution of Tamaulipas to reduce the minimum age for gubernatorial candidates, so that he could consolidate his position in the state by imposing Alfredo as governor. Emilio Portes Gil was particularly outraged by this, because Tamaulipas was his own stamping ground. As he put it a few years later, "General Calles was not satisfied that his sons Rodolfo and Plutarco governed Sonora and Nuevo León. He also wanted Tamaulipas under the thumb of the family." [3]

During the early years of its existence, ex-President Calles was successful in manipulating the apparatus of the PNR and in dominating the men who held the office of president. Consider what happened in 1930. Calles concluded that the allotment of farm land to unprepared peasants should be speedily brought to a halt. He therefore made the kind of offhand decision in momentous matters that is so characteristic of the charismatic-type leader. Small groups of state governors were called to Mexico City, where Calles gave them their orders. Eleven states promptly adopted legislation to end the land program, and by 1932 total land distribution fell to one-third that of 1929. Three governors who refused to comply with Calles' commands were quickly and effectively disciplined. Their particular candidates to succeed them as governor were rejected by the official party in all three states. All of this occurred after Calles had left the presidency. Little wonder that Mexicans call this the period of *callismo*.

---

[3] *Quince Años de Política Mexicana*, p. 460.

It was obvious that the central organization of the revolutionary party was growing stronger and that in the beginning, at least, Calles controlled it. Each of the semi-independent forces which combined in 1929 had given up a little authority to form the coalition. Now the party gradually was eating away at their remaining independence and at the same time building up its own resources. Almost immediately after the PNR was formed, for example, President Portes Gil had issued an administrative order requiring every national employee to contribute seven days pay each year to the party. This allowed the party to develop and support its own bureaucracy. Similarly, government expenditures were used to expand the prestige and power of the official party, often at the expense of the heads of local political machines and the leadership of functional interest organizations which were its principal components.

At Aguascalientes in 1932, the inevitable happened. A party convention changed the structure of the PNR, abolishing the confederation of regional and local parties and establishing a hierarchy of municipal, state, and national conventions which were to decide policy and select candidates. The principal concession to the functional organization was the retaining of "fraternal" relationships between farm organizations and labor unions whose political branches had been absorbed into the party.

The improvement in party discipline made for an efficient machine, one that quickly realized certain other decisions reached at the Aguascalientes convention. The PNR decided to reaffirm the revolutionary concept of "no re-election" that had been weakened to permit General Obregón to seek a second term in 1928. Despite a rather complicated process for amending the Mexican constitution, the eight necessary amendments had been proposed by the party, voted on by both houses of Congress, ratified by the required majority of states, and promulgated by the national government by March of 1933, within a space of five months. Ease of constitutional reform is characteristic of Mexico, but the existence of a national party whose leader's word was law both in Mexico City and in the state capitals greatly facilitated the process.

Quite obviously, most national and local political chieftains were not happy to see their own authority diminishing or that of Calles growing. If the strong man grew more powerful during the era of *callismo*, however, neither he nor the other leaders could have realized that he was presiding over the ultimate derogation of his own ability to exercise that power. In setting up the official party organization, he had motivated forces which he could not control. During the 1928-34 presidential term, Calles managed to remain the power behind the three men who held office, but all through this period and during the first years of the following administration, changing conditions altered the relationship between the bureaucracy and leadership of the official party and the president, or more correctly the presidency, which was growing stronger, until the channels of control became institutionalized.

## Expanding Presidential Power

Authority gradually had been centering in the presidency because the increasingly complicated environment made impossible the previous situation, in which political favors flowed from the national capital at the whim of a leader who based his actions on personal relations with each petitioner. Slowly, as new and competing interests had to be satisfied and compromise achieved, a more complex manner of reaching policy decisions evolved.

The chief executive, no matter who, controlled the bureaucratic machinery carrying on the detailed, day-to-day work of government. This machinery decided which road, which school, which irrigation dam should be built; this machinery determined which strike was legal and which was not; to a very great extent, this machinery accepted or rejected rival claims of state or national electoral success.

Not even a power-hungry strong man such as General Calles could apply himself to every detail, so most of these matters were left to government agencies or the bureaucracy of the functional interest organizations allied with the revolutionary party. This whole decision-making apparatus centered in the president, so that acting both in his constitutional and in his political capacity the chief executive exercised continually expanding influence over the leaders of subordinate interest organizations and governmental units.

This is not to discount the continuing importance of General Calles or the tenacity of the personalistic tradition. The old loyalty to the *jefe máximo* continued to play an important role in politics at the beginning of the Cárdenas administration. They tell the story of General Matías Ramos, who ignored a call one day from the president because he had gone down to Cuernavaca to see Calles. When asked by Cárdenas why he had failed to obey his commander-in-chief, the Constitutional President of the Republic, General Ramos is reported to have replied, "I'm telling the President of the Republic that I went to see my chief, General Calles."[4]

If President Cárdenas had possessed a weaker personality, there is no telling how much longer Calles might have dominated Mexican political life, even though sooner or later the seeds of change already planted undoubtedly would have borne fruit because of the growing concentration of authority in the presidency. But Cárdenas was a strong leader in his own right and, at the same time, disagreed with much of Calles' interpretation and implementation of the Mexican Revolution.

For all that he had been hand-picked for the presidency by the *jefe máximo*, Cárdenas was very popular himself, as a soldier, as a politician, and as an individual. He had been a successful governor in Michoacán; he had been president of the National Executive Committee of the PNR; he had served as Secretary of War and Marine, and as Secretary of *Gobernación*. In spite of the excellent political relations he had established with the principal politicians—the king-makers—as a candidate Cárdenas traveled throughout the entire country, campaigning in every town and village he could reach. Not only politicians, then, but many of the common people knew, respected, and trusted him.

Cárdenas' popularity resulted from two related factors. First, the politically awakening masses knew and identified with him because he had taken the trouble to come to them. After he took office, popular support grew because it became clear that he, in turn, could identify with the masses. Cárdenas was more nearly a "national" president than any of his revolutionary predecessors because, unlike Obregón, Calles, and the others, he was no member of that old-style, middle-class, *norteño* clique that sought to use politics and the office of president to move from the middle to the upper class.

Instead, Cárdenas represented, in fact in many ways was, the prototype of the new Mexican middle class. By representing effectively a much larger proportion of Mexico's proliferating interests, Cárdenas and those like him provided a link to bind together all facets of national life. This, rather than any administrative ability, was the secret of his strength and his popularity. It still is, for the Mexican masses seem instinctively to recognize this quality in him.

---

[4] Quoted in *Hoy*, February 28, 1953, p. 4.

The corollary second factor of his popularity lay in the fact that in Cárdenas the myth of the Mexican Revolution came to life. By the very token that he identified with the people and their problems, the young president sought to turn the phrases of revolutionary reform into facts, and the public soon learned that it could measure his sincerity not simply in words but in deeds. Undoubtedly it was his zeal to accomplish the goals of the Revolution speedily, together with his patriotic nationalism, that earned Cárdenas the reputation of a radical. Land distribution and oil expropriation may seem the acts of an angry man, but only if taken out of the context in which they occurred. These, like so many other of Cárdenas' works, were attempts to redress lopsided conditions. In fact, in almost everything he did, Cárdenas was more nearly a moderate than a radical; the very real moderation with which Cárdenas attempted to solve the problem of church-state relations is a case in point. The difficulty was that he was operating in a social and political system that had listed to the right for so long that it developed a permanent bias, so that whatever he did seemed to lean to the left.

During the first years of his term, President Cárdenas' left-liberal policies were in strong contrast to the growing evidences of conservatism (or, perhaps, of self-aggrandizement) displayed by General Calles. Before he could hope to assert his own attitudes fully, however, the president had to reorganize the political power structure in his own favor. For two years, therefore, Cárdenas realigned the principal functional power groups participating in national politics and particularly in the PNR. Where previously its permanent membership had been composed primarily of government employees and office-holders, the party now sought workers and peasants on the basis of alliance with their trade unions and the inclusion of members of *ejido* communities. By 1936, the revolutionary party could boast of a membership of almost a million members.

In rebuilding the power structure of the PNR, Cárdenas was careful not to arouse the enmity of existing interests. He appeased the bureaucrats by supporting legislation establishing the theory of a permanent civil service and recognizing the right of government employees to strike, as well as by granting them economic benefits. He attempted to impose as many national and state officers who were personally loyal to him as possible, but he carefully avoided open conflict with General Calles' adherents, at least until he could organize the mass bases of his strength. In doing this, the president had all of the advantage on his side, for General Calles had long since lost sight of the interests and needs of labor and agrarians, as well as direct contact with lower-rank politicians. As chief executive, on the other hand, Cárdenas had all of the legal and extra-legal resources of government to win their support, and both groups were ripe for organization.

No new, dynamic labor organization had risen during the years of the puppet presidents to replace Luis Morones' Regional Federation of Labor (CROM) after it had lost official support, together with most of its national political importance, first during the election campaign of 1928 and later with the formation of the PNR. Similarly, the integration of the politically active part of the old *agrarista* party into the PNR had left the rank-and-file agricultural worker with few independent farm organizations and less leadership. President Cárdenas had merely to offer a minimum of government support to a clever organizer and these potentially important sources of political power would speedily rally to his standard. He found the man for his purpose in an ambitious young leftist intellectual, Vicente Lombardo Toledano.

Lombardo Toledano had been one of Morones' more able aides in the CROM, but when the CROM fell from favor he left it in order to organize his own group, the General Confederation of Mexican Workers and Farmers (CGOCM). Under his able leadership, conveniently coupled with the friendly influence of the 1931 federal Labor Code, the CGOCM grew until it could act as the nucleus for a new and more inclusive labor and farm organization. This new agency came into being in 1935 as the Mexican Federation of Laborers (CTM). From the very first the CTM flourished, for widespread knowledge and evidence that it enjoyed presidential favor attracted previously independent unions and encouraged individuals to join the new unions its organizers set up. Its membership, which included both industrial and agricultural workers, soon became the single largest organized group in Mexico.

Despite the friendly assistance Cárdenas had offered Lombardo Toledano, the president had no intention of putting a monopoly over the massive political power represented by a combination of labor and agriculture into the hands of a possible rival. Nor did he want these newly awakened interests to overbalance the other factors of the revolutionary power structure. Consequently, Cárdenas set the official party organization to work establishing separate Peasant Leagues in each state, "with the help of the federal personnel of the executive dependencies . . . , principally the Agrarian Affairs Department and the Secretariat of Public Education," as one PNR publication puts it. These state Leagues were then united in a National Farmers' Federation (CNC), to which some of the previously organized CTM agricultural groups were then attached.

Quite naturally, the leaders of the CTM objected to depletion of the group's membership by taking from the parent organization the farmers it had organized. Only the strength of the president's personality convinced Lombardo Toledano that he should give up the farm groups he had formed, and then he did so with the understanding that the component members of the newly independent CNC Peasant Leagues should have the right to consult with the CTM on matters of mutual interest.

By the beginning of 1936, as a result of these organizing activities, the major organized interest groups, with the exception of the army, were led by individuals personally loyal to President Cárdenas. The old Mexican game of playing one political force against another in order to balance out possible rivals finally had worked against General Calles; he had not kept up with the growth of the new political forces. Only the military remained to be won over or kept neutral, and if the generals had personalistic ties to the older general they also liked the younger general. President Cárdenas held most of the trumps in his hand.

The climax came when General Calles made his first overt attack on the administration's liberal policy of permitting industrial strikes, together with a thinly veiled threat against the president himself. A so-called Proletarian Defense Committee rallied to the side of President Cárdenas immediately. This show of organized strength, backed by the bureaucrats, together with the obvious intention of the army to remain neutral, was sufficient to decide the great mass of politicians. In April, 1936, General Calles was forced to leave Mexico, demonstrating graphically to anyone who might need further convincing that President Cárdenas was master of the political situation.

Once his undisputed leadership had been established, the president cast about for means of formalizing relationships among the various organizations and interests, both in and outside of the PNR, which had supported his administration. For a time he seemed to favor formation of a Popular Front similar to those in France and Spain at the time. Early in 1937, the CTM sent out feelers on the matter to the PNR, to the farmers' organizations, and to the Communist party, although the Labor Code at that time specifically forbade political action by unions.

Nothing ever came of the plan, however, for various reasons. The army completely rejected any coalition including the Communists. Moreover, the chance of any coalition of leftists succeeding had diminished markedly about this time, for the arrival of Leon Trotsky in Mexico had split them wide open. The Communists would never enter a government accepting the presence of the exiled Russian, but he could not be expelled without alienating other important leftist leaders. On this issue, Vicente Lombardo Toledano, following the Communist party line, came into almost open conflict with General Francisco Múgica, who accepted Trotsky. This disagreement may have cost either Múgica or Lombardo Toledano the nomination at the next presidential election, for they had been the two most likely heirs apparent. Certainly it weakened the position of the leftists, resulting in the nomination of Manuel Avila Camacho, a middle-of-the-roader. Diego Rivera, too, accepted Trotsky, suffering a long excommunication from the Communist party as a result. A few years later he recanted his heresy, but it was only a short while before his death in 1957 that he managed to win readmittance to the party.

Most important, the concept of a Popular Front simply did not fit the needs of Mexican political conditions. It had developed as a political device in countries where an institutionalized multiparty system already existed. Rather than a device of this sort, which would turn interest groups into competitive hard-core class parties, during this period Mexico required some sort of political mechanism that could channel the activities of the developing specialized interests into a constructive and integrated political system. As a consequence, President Cárdenas gave the projected Popular Front the *coup de grace* when, in December, 1937, he called for dissolution of the PNR and formation of a new revolutionary party.

### The PRM—Corporate Centralism

The new Party of the Mexican Revolution took as its organizational basis a corporate structure embracing the diverse interests which supported President Cárdenas' version of the Revolution. Although no attempt was made to change the conventional system of geographically designated electoral districts established by the Constitution of 1917, the PRM abandoned the classical concept of nominations on the basis of popular primaries.

The party's corporate structure divided organized political activity into four functionally based "sectors"—agricultural, labor, popular, and military. Where once candidates had been selected by the entire party membership, voting in national, state, or local primaries, the revolutionary party's candidates now were to be apportioned among the several sectors. Before each state or national election, the sector organizations, meeting jointly, determined how many and which candidacies, except the presidential one, were to be allotted to each sector.

The sector organization or, in actual practice, the sector's leadership, then named individual candidates for the offices allotted to it. The individuals so nominated then were supported in the campaign and at the polls by the combined efforts of all four sectors. The only exception to this practice was that the military sector did not nominate or participate in local and state-level elections. Not unexpectedly, considering that members of the same party manned the electoral machinery and counted the votes, the candidates so nominated enjoyed amazingly uniform success at the polls.

Presidential nominations also reflected a corporative tendency. Selection of the revolutionary party's candidate at the national nominating convention required the support of a majority of the sectors, at first three of the four and later, when the military sector had been dissolved, two of the three sectors.

Taking their cue from President Cárdenas' speech calling for formation of the new party, official apologists stressed two points. The PRM was a genuine national organization, in that both popular participation and the sources of financial support had been broadened considerably. Second, they pointed out, at long last the military had been brought openly into politics, obviating the need for its constant illegal intervention in political affairs.

As to the validity of these points, it certainly is true that the PRM represented a broader scope of interests than had its predecessor, and that temporarily at least the military did participate formally in politics. Moreover, the new sector organization represented rather faithfully the structure of power that Cárdenas already had developed in the old PNR during the last few years of its existence.

Most of the interest groups and functional organizations in existence at this time which could or would work with the new, more active revolutionary leadership were included in one of the four sectors.

The basic unit in three of the four sectors was the local organization—the Peasant League, the labor union (or confederation of local unions), or the political association. These in turn were grouped in a statewide federation of other similar functional units, according to sector. The state federation then represented the organizations in the state affiliated with the sector in a nationwide sector organization. The only sector not so organized was the military, which employed the regular army subdivisions as its units.

The *Confederación Nacional Campesina*, with its paper membership of two million (every *ejido* farmer was enrolled automatically), became the farmers' sector of the new party. Although its effective membership undoubtedly was a good deal smaller than was claimed, the CNC broadened the base of members in the party and strengthened its dominant role in Mexican politics, for the isolated and politically naïve farmers were easily manipulated by their leaders. The announced aims of the farm sector were to hasten land distribution, to combat local officials who obstructed land reform or other activities beneficial to the farmer, to carry grievances to the national capital, and in general to aid peasants in solving their problems. In practice, a fair start was made in achieving these goals, for the CNC was at that time the only agency formally representing agriculture in the official party, so that its leaders had an enormous influence over the president in all phases of policy-making for the farmer. This was especially true while Cárdenas was president, for he identified Mexican progress and fulfillment of the revolutionary goals with agricultural development to a greater extent than have any of his successors.

The Labor sector also had a mass membership but, unlike the farmers, even in 1937 no single agency represented the organized workers. The Mexican Federation of Labor (CTM), at that time still led by Vicente Lombardo Toledano, dominated the sector and took the lion's share of patronage, but other labor organizations participated in its activities. Among these were two federations, the *Confederación General de Trabajadores* (CGT) and the Treviño CROM, which had split from the Morones CROM, together with the independent electricians and miners unions. Because most labor organization was concentrated in a few urban centers, the smaller membership and divided representation of the Labor sector were compensated in some measure by disciplined action and unity of interest.

The third sector of the PRM, the so-called Popular sector, included a membership as functionally heterogeneous as those of the Labor and Farmers sectors were homogeneous. The real strength of the organization lay in the Federation of Government Employees' Unions, the FSTSE, representing both state and national bureaucrats. They were included here because President Cárdenas felt they should not have any directly shared political interest with nongovernmental organized labor. Certain nonindustrial unions, organizations of professional persons, youth groups, cooperative societies, and a number of miscellaneous organizations also acted through the Popular sector, which was divided into ten functional branches. In a sense it served as a catchall for any of the party's supporters who did not fit into another sector. As such, with the exception of the leadership of the other sectors, the Popular sector included virtually all of the former members of the old PNR.

It is hardly surprising that so diverse a membership had difficulty in organizing for action. Not until 1943 was it possible for a constituent convention to meet to set up the National Federation of Popular Organizations, the CNOP, which was to act as the formal mechanism uniting the member agencies. Even with the CNOP to act as a coordinating device, some of the components of the Popular sector have been restive. The FSTSE, for example, has sought a stronger role in the sector. Indeed, in 1946 and several times during the 1950's the government unions bid unsuccessfully for a sector of their own.

Considering its amorphous membership, the Popular sector was remarkably successful in obtaining patronage and in influencing policy. Undoubtedly this can be attributed to the nature of its membership for, as we know, in Mexico, the middle-class, professionally trained person represents a much higher degree of intensity of political action than does the less well-educated farmer or laborer. In the PRM as then constituted, and in the official party today for that matter, this group has political importance all out of proportion to its numbers.

Establishing a Military sector in the PRM touched off a tremendous furor. It was argued that the army had never acted officially in national politics, and that the precedent should be retained. In reply it was suggested that as the real power in Mexican politics, or at least the strongest single factor of power, the military's political activities should be brought out in the open where it could be held accountable for such activities. And it was true that at that time army officers held well over half of the more important positions in the government service, elective or appointive.

The military itself seems to have had little desire to be placed in the arena of politics. In December of 1940, after less than three years of existence, the Military sector was dissolved, with most of the officers holding elective offices passing to the Popular sector. This does not mean that the army divorced itself from politics. On the contrary, having returned to its old position behind the throne, the military's role in Mexican politics has remained strong and partisan. Acting through the Popular sector, although in recent years its activities have been somewhat less obvious than formerly, the military continues to wield a very important influence in policy-making.

### The Consolidation of Power in the Revolutionary Party

In bringing together the most active interest groupings under the mantle of the revolutionary party, where they could be dominated by national-level sector organizations, Cárdenas took a giant step toward centralizing political control in the national capital. Internal policy concerning each sector's interests was made and implemented by means of the pyramidal sector organization but, given the realities of the political and social environment, rather than moving from the grass roots up, policy decisions usually emanated from the bureaucracy and leadership of the sector, filtering down through the hierarchy to the rank and file.

Decisions of the central sector authorities were, of course, always subject to the approval of the president. In practice, conflicts among the sectors—or even within a sector, if the question was serious enough—were settled by the PRM's National Executive Committee, which usually meant by the president himself. These mechanisms for reaching decisions or selecting candidates may not always have represented perfectly the needs or desires of the mass membership, but on the whole they did reflect the relative political pressures which the most active interest groups could bring to bear upon the national leadership, including the president. In Mexico, as anywhere else, the basis of political decision-making was not so much moral responsibility as the degree to which various elements in the political situation were willing and able to act in order to enhance their own position and to protect their own interests.

The corporative nature of the PRM had the effect of sounding a death-knell for the political machines of the once all-powerful local *caudillos*. What little political independence had been left to the states by the PNR now was divided between the state government and the sector organizations. At the local and state levels the sector leadership was supposed to act jointly with each other and with the state officials, but the competing functional interests inherent in each sector tended to separate it from the state party organization and the elected officials, and to make it dependent upon the national leadership of its own functional interest organizations. Access to the president, who controlled political decision-making affecting the very lives of local functional units was, to a great extent, through the sector leaders rather than through the elective officials of the state administration. Remember, too, that because of the poly-functional nature of political leadership and the control by the sectors over nomination of state officers, most state government officials represented a particular sector's functional interest rather than some more general welfare of the state at large, so that resort to a state official not named by the sector concerned could offer little hope of satisfaction.

The PRM's corporate structure also added to the financial strength of the central party organization at the expense of the local machines. To the old check-off of contributions from national government employees, now made "voluntarily," the national machine could add equally "voluntary" contributions collected by the sector organizations from organized laborers and farmers. Furthermore, the state machines, once well oiled by money collected from the state's public servants, soon discovered that much of this money was being diverted to the national capital by the leadership of the Popular sector. This was coupled with the ever-increasing financial dependence of the formal state governments upon the central authorities, because just as the growing complexities of social and economic life called for greater expenditures by governmental agencies, the national government was busily pre-empting most of the major sources of tax revenue for itself. This forced the local officers to go to Mexico City, hat in hand, seeking grants from the national government to satisfy the demands of their constituents.

One great compensation for the loss of local independence and initiative came in the form of electoral success. On the local as well as the national level, the increased number of disciplined interest associations and the greater degree of integrated political activity, not to mention the growing availability of public and private funds, reduced the chance of any opposition party winning elective posts almost to the point of nonexistence.

During this period the PRM overlapped almost completely with the more formal agencies of government; as a consequence it picked up the popular designation of "the official party." The president of the party's National Executive Committee met with the president's cabinet as a matter of course, and quite frequently the party actually initiated official actions. Starting with Cárdenas' administration, for example, Six-Year Plans for economic and social development were prepared by the PRM, "with the government collaborating," as one of the plans describes the process.

Identification of the official party with the state became so confused in the minds of the party bosses that the Supreme Court was forced to remind them in one case that "the PRM is not a dependency of the federal executive power; . . . it does not constitute an official service . . . so its thirty per cent discount [on telephone service] cannot be enforced by legal means."[5] Such reasoning is hard to drive home. As late as 1950, President Alemán issued an executive decree assigning "the property known as the ex-chapel of La Milagrosa in Guadalajara, Jalisco, to the service of the state, to install the offices of the PRI."[6] (The PRI is the present version of the official party.)

As the official party constantly grew stronger, the president of Mexico who headed it grew stronger still. The full party apparatus worked to build the public personality of the chief executive as a figurehead of the revolutionary movement with whom the Mexican people could identify. In his pre-election campaign, Cárdenas had set the style for future presidential candidates, who utilized cars and planes, motion pictures and radio to bring their faces and their voices to more people more often than even the local *políticos* had ever succeeded in doing. Once he was elected, the entire administra-

[5] *Informe Rendido . . . a la Suprema Corte de Justicia de la Nación . . . 1942*, "Informe de la Presidencia," pp. 77-78.

[6] *Diario Oficial*, May 8, 1950.

tive program was identified with the president. Roads and schools and dams and all the rest were the product of *cardenismo, avila-camachismo,* or *alemanismo,* not the normal functioning of an abstract and lifeless government. Thus the chief executive gained an aura of authority as spokesman for the Revolution while at the same time he represented the revolutionary party and the interests which composed it. In a very real sense he tied the whole system together, making possible the party's very existence.

To this end the president used his power to enforce discipline within and among the functional sectors in much the same way as he did to control the state politicians. By granting periodic concessions or withholding them, as the situation seemed to warrant, or by making or breaking individual leaders, as their loyalty deserved, he controlled local as well as national politics to a remarkable extent. With this control he could dictate nominations, elections, appointments, and removals at all levels of government. And, for all practical purposes, he could appoint or remove the leaders of the functional interest associations making up the sector organizations.

It was the president who balanced the competing demands of the many interests for which the sectors stood. It was he who saw that they did not dissipate their strength in senseless factionalism. In 1940, for example, each of the three sector blocs in the Chamber of Deputies claimed the right to provide a majority of the fifteen members to be appointed to the Permanent Committee of the Congress. The president, working through the Secretary of *Gobernación,* who has responsibility for control of Mexico's internal politics, forced a compromise by selecting the membership himself.

During the 1940's, the official party continued to consolidate its position, gradually perfecting a smoothly running national political machine. With his ability to manipulate the sector organizations, the incumbent president was able each time to build an organization politically loyal to and dependent upon him. The first political act of a new president was to impose governmental officers at all levels satisfactory to himself and then to use his power to keep them obedient to his dictates.

Before the revolutionary party's lines of control over the political system became institutionalized, the president sometimes found it necessary to remove recalcitrant state officers by means of constitutional article 76, which allows the national Senate to declare that legal powers in a state have disappeared.[7] More recently, however, the president's position in relation both to the party and to the organs of government has become so well established that he no longer needs to resort to this form of discipline. Instead, he reserves article 76 for the infrequent occasions when he must throw a political supporter to the wolves in order to placate public outrage. No matter how he does it, the chief executive is in a splendid position to punish speedily any politician who fails to submit himself to the authority of the Revolution, as personified in the president.

Note how the governor of the sovereign state of Guanajuato addressed himself to President Avila Camacho: "Mr. President, I have been in charge of the government for two years now. Within the limits of my competence I have tried in every sense to do nothing but second the work that you as President of the Republic are carrying on to unite the Mexican nation and to intensify its productive force. Nonetheless, if for reasons unknown to me you find my activities in governing Guanajuato unsatisfactory please tell me so frankly, for I do not wish to be other than a factor of loyal and full cooperation within your regime."[8]

Despite these flattering words the governor found himself removed from office a short time later, because rigged municipal elections in the city of León had resulted in a riot during which troops fired on protesting citizens, killing a large number. If the president knew how to impose a governor, he also knew how to remove him as a sop to public opinion.

As a consequence of the successes of the revolutionary party, as well as their dependence upon presidential rather than popular favor, many political leaders lost all respect for even the pretense of legal elections, relying instead upon the twin pillars of organization and force to keep them in power. In accepting the nomination of the official party as governor of Durango, for instance, General Elpidio Velázquez is reported to have joked, "Here I am to be sworn in. In Durango it is the people who are swearing."[9]

Despite the excesses of some of the revolutionary politicians, the centralization of authority effected by the official party was not

---

[7] See my "Some Aspects of Mexican Federalism, 1917-1948," especially Chapter II.

[8] Ernesto Hidalgo, *El Caso de Guanajuato ante la Conciencia de la Nación,* (Gráficas Guanajuato, Mexico, D.F., 1946), pp. 76-77.

[9] *"Aquí vengo a protestar yo. En Durango él que protesta es el pueblo."* Quoted in *Hoy,* May 4, 1940, p. 13.

entirely bad for Mexico. The virtual monopoly over meaningful political action held by the PRM made very unlikely the appearance of any strong or lasting opposition to upset the country, while the president's control function over the most active interest groups within the party kept internal friction to a minimum. A corresponding political stability resulted. Mexico finally got a chance to settle down, to consolidate some of the gains already made under the Revolution, just as the central government began to amass sufficient resources to enable it to take advantage of the political calm to advance the reform program it supported. At long last, the country found some of the time required to expand its economy and to build a more integrated national society, so that the process of Westernization proceeded more rapidly than ever.

### The Problem of Popular Participation

Certain social and nonmaterial effects of Westernization began to make themselves felt politically as early as the middle 1940's, near the end of the administration of President Avila Camacho. Almost inevitably, as popular awareness increased and as specialization of function became more marked, the corporatively structured party began to feel pressure for change. By the very fact that the PRM included specific functional interest associations within its sectors, it excluded others, as well as individuals whose integration into national life tended to throw them together as interest groups which had not yet crystallized into formal associations. At the same time, the old functional organizations that made up the sectors no longer could satisfy the increasingly diverse interests which were subsumed within them.

Inside the party itself, some degree of sentiment for changing its structure became manifest, primarily because the machinery then provided by the sector system could not satisfy all of the interests pressing for recognition. Emilio Portes Gil, who often speaks for the professional politicians, as opposed to functional farm or labor leadership, suggested abolishment of the sector system entirely. He claimed that while President Cárdenas had altered the structure of the old PNR in order to correct certain vices, the PRM had acquired its own set of evils because the leaders of the functional sectors were dominated in their activities by motives of gain and self-aggrandizement.[10] As already noted, the unsuccessful attempt

---

[10] *Quince Años de Política Mexicana*, p. 227.

on the part of the government bureaucrats to set up their own sector indicated a certain lack of satisfaction with the representation afforded them in the Popular sector.

At the same time, a growing number of party leaders recognized that the PRM's system of functional organizations could not provide sufficient access for the ever-growing number of politically aware Mexicans outside of the member associations. Attempts had been made to broaden the basis of the Popular sector so as to resolve this problem, but by far the largest proportion of the Mexican people still could not participate in the real governmental policy-making agency—the revolutionary party that controlled the nomination and election of Mexico's constitutional rulers.

By 1946, as Avila Camacho's term was drawing to a close, the need for party reorganization seemed clearer than ever. Mexico's participation in World War II had placed a high value on the forms of democracy, just as more and more citizens were becoming alert to the importance of politics. These factors, coupled with almost crude impositions of municipal governments during 1945, set off a wave of protests which spread throughout the country. Serious disturbances were reported in at least five cities, culminating in the clash between civilians and military forces in the city of León, which led to the removal of the governor of Guanajuato mentioned previously.

With a presidential campaign in the offing, the proponents of reform managed to convince President Avila Camacho and a majority of the party leaders that at least some change in the outward structure of the party ought to be made. Consequently, the same national party convention that nominated Miguel Alemán for the next presidential term, using the old sector method to do so, changed both the name and the internal structure of the party. It became the *Partido Revolucionario Institucional,* or the PRI, and the political role of the sectors was supposed to be changed drastically.

Like the old PRM, the new PRI kept the three sectors as basic organizational divisions of the party, but the new rules sought to strip them of their corporative political functions. Each of the three sectors was to remain autonomous in social and economic action, but the central organization of the party would carry on all political and electoral activities.

In attempting to assure the end of sector political power, the all-important nominating system was changed. For all elective positions save that of President of the Republic, across-the-board primaries rather than sector designation of candidates was to be the rule. For presidential nominations, the party's national convention was to be composed of ten delegates from each election district; each delegate was to cast ballots proportionate to the number of party members he represented, with a majority vote of total party members assuring nomination.

Quite obviously, this nominating system would have reduced the influence of the national leadership of the sectors in local elections and even, to some extent, that of the local leaders. It also would have reduced the proportionate role played by the functional interest associations formally affiliated with the revolutionary party, as opposed to those emerging interest groups which had not yet been able to win a place for themselves in the sector organization. Not unexpectedly, therefore, a certain degree of dissatisfaction over the change was heard.

By far the loudest objection came from the Labor sector, the power of which was concentrated in a few areas rather than spread throughout the country. In the past, labor's well-disciplined organization had compensated both for smaller numbers and geographic concentration of power, permitting its leadership to claim a reasonably high proportion of elective offices and to play a strong role in nominating the president. Now, it seemed logical to suppose, labor would lose out to agriculture, with its mass supporters all over the country, and to the Popular sector leadership, with its broad following among the general public.

Vicente Lombardo Toledano, who at that time still was influential with the CTM, although he was no longer its Secretary-General, having been "kicked upstairs" in 1940 as head of the Latin American Federation of Labor (CTAL), undoubtedly suspected that the move was the opening shot in a battle to deprive the labor leadership of the advantages it had enjoyed and to bring the party back into the hands of the professional politicians. Being a Marxist, he probably also suspected that it was an attempt on the part of the capitalists who controlled Mexico's growing industrial machine to weaken the voice of the worker in government councils. At the nominating convention for the 1946 election, however, over the protests of Lombardo Toledano the corporative structure of the party was abandoned. Soon after President Alemán took office, Lombardo's worst fears seemed to have been realized. The new president used troops to break an oil strike. Within a short time, the labor leader left the official party to start an opposition party of his own, followed by a few union leaders and other elements dissatisfied with conditions in the PRI.

For once, Lombardo miscalculated. Despite the nominating convention's action, the time for ending the political functions of the sectors had not yet arrived. The revolutionary party still was not bound together strongly enough by loyalty to general principles to enable it to operate within the give-and-take atmosphere of primary elections. At the same time, the leaders of the functional associations found it difficult to give up entirely the special status they had enjoyed under the corporative system. During Alemán's term, the situation remained up in the air, but before the 1952 presidential campaign began, dangerous public demonstrations of internal party conflict took place, especially in terms of congressional nominations.

Of necessity, therefore, at a meeting held in Cuernavaca in 1950, the older sector system of nominations was revived, so that the alternative method never was tested in a presidential election. For all of its defects, the sector system provides a means of preserving party solidarity by keeping power struggles within the organization. As previously, the party bureaucracy and the sector hierarchy can reach the necessary decisions, with the inevitable disputes going, ultimately, to the president for determination.

Nonetheless, the conditions which had given rise to change in the party structure continued to exert pressure for some adjustment in the political system. For the most part, the revolutionary party has attempted to satisfy the pressures of a larger politically aware population and a growing number of specialized and competing interests, not by changing its corporative structure, but by broadening and expanding it, and by providing alternative means of access to the decision-making process by interests not included in any of the party's sectors. In doing so, the relative role of formal governmental agencies in decision-making has grown, and that of the party machinery has become more attuned to the constitutional machinery.

The number of formally organized interest associations belonging to the sector organizations is greater now than ever in the party's history and it is now possible for individuals to participate in party activities through membership in the Popular sector. Equally important, the consultative process whereby important factors in

Mexico's society and economy which are not part of the sector organizations can participate in political decisions affecting their status has been institutionalized to a very great extent. The means by which such interests as the Roman Catholic church or the trade and industrial confederations can be sure of a voice in policy will be detailed in our consideration of the political-administrative function of the presidency.

In changing back to the sector system, the party made every effort to include as many interests as possible under its protective and dominating wing, a process made easier by the lack of any single ideology of the Revolution or identification with a single functional interest. While the PRM had recognized the class struggle and had sought to prepare the Mexican people for a "workers democracy and socialist regime," the PRI in addition was declared "the organizer and control over the middle class, as well as the defender of the *municipio*, of agrarian reform, of the rights of women, of youth and Indians, of morality in citizens and in government officials, of civic education, of economic intervention of the state and of protection of public interests, without by this limiting the opportunities of private enterprise for its development."[11] If they missed anything, one can scarcely blame the party leaders; they tried to include every interest.

The only direct concession that the PRI has made to the growing pressures upon it for greater popular participation in the selection of candidates has been at the state, local, or *municipio* level. In an experiment first tried in the elections of *ayuntamientos* for the state of Baja California (Norte) held in April, 1959, a new procedure for choosing the party's nominees was adopted. Any group of 200 or more dues-paying members of the party could submit an election slate to the local PRI Municipal Committee, together with substantiating discussions of each candidate. The Municipal Committee would then send copies of these slates, together with its comments, to the state-level party committee and to the Central Executive Committee in Mexico City. This last, after considering the comments of both local and state-level committees would narrow the number of slates to two, one of which would be selected by the local PRI nominating convention. The nominating convention, however, would be composed of the usual 60 delegates, with 20 coming from each of the three party sectors.

---

[11] *Tiempo*, February 17, 1950, p. 7.

As the experiment worked in Baja California, the party regulars contributed the vast majority of slates, the Central Executive Committee in Mexico City saw to it that no outright "mavericks" were included in the slates returned to the local committees, and the nominating conventions at the *municipio* level tended to select those lists which most nearly reflected the power status in the area. Nonetheless, the experiment did work in Baja California and also in the states of San Luis Potosí and Zacatecas, later in the year. At a meeting of state and district leaders held in May, 1959, this system of nominating the PRI's local and state candidates was extended to all state organizations in the country.

Limited to local elections as it may be, this evidence of the effectiveness of increasing popular pressures upon the official party suggests that within the foreseeable future mass participation in the political process is both possible and probable. This should be the next stage in the evolution of the revolutionary party.

CHAPTER *6*

# Mexico's Party System

## The Single Dominant Party

One can as correctly say that today Mexico has a single-party system as say that the United States has a two-party system. In both countries, the success of the major party or parties overshadows the very existence of minor parties that represent specialized political viewpoints and seldom capture more than a token representation in local or national government. Size of membership and electoral success, however, are but the end-product of the evolutionary process that produces broadly based, nationally oriented, and pragmatically inclined parties attracting larger numbers of supporters and wielding greater political influence than their more narrowly conceived minor counterparts.

Just as the Democrats and Republicans evolved into such parties in response to the social and political needs of the United States, so the revolutionary party in Mexico has taken upon itself the performance of a wider political function demanded by the Westernization of the country. In its new political role, the PRI acts as a kind of auxiliary constitutional mechanism that makes possible limited and responsible national government. By providing a structured and internally disciplined political agency, the party forces a certain amount of adjustment and balance among the demands of the interests represented by associations belonging to its sector organizations. At the same time, it supplies a hard core of support to

145

the formal governmental agencies regulating those interests outside of the party's machinery and discipline. Despite weaknesses in Mexico's recently evolved political system and in the older constitutional system, therefore, the multiplying interests which must be accommodated in the decision-making process can be both represented and controlled through the good offices of the revolutionary party.

Unless some such aggregating mechanism had evolved, Mexico might have been forced to continue relying upon *caudillismo* for political integration, as the only alternative to the dividing tendencies embodied in the doctrinaire and personalistic factions which had controlled early revolutionary politics. Why this national, pragmatic, aggregating mechanism took the form of a single party, closely identified with the state, rather than that of an independent, two-party system as in some other countries, was explained in the previous chapter. So was the reason for Mexico's functional interest associations generally being closely related to, rather than separate from, that single major party. Again, we saw why, during the present relatively unstable transitional stage in the development of systematic relations among interest associations, the revolutionary party uses the device of sector organizations to provide a control mechanism for manipulating these specialized interests as they interact within the party and the political system.

This chapter further develops the theme of a political system based upon the operations of a single dominant party. To do so, it takes into account the nature of the relationships among the interests subsumed within each of the three sectors of the revolutionary party, as well as the relationships among the sectors themselves. It further considers the role of other parties in the political system, whether these minor parties align themselves with or stand in opposition to the all-powerful and very nearly all-embracing official party. It does not, however, carry the description beyond the party system, leaving consideration of other aspects of the political system to later chapters.

Certainly there can be no question that at this stage of Mexico's political evolution a preponderance of power resides in the government party. For years now, all twenty-nine state governors, together with the local administrations they dominate, have been in its hands. So have all or nearly all of the seats in both chambers of the Congress of the Union. Needless to say, the President of the

Republic too has had a double function, on the one hand as a constitutional officer and on the other as undisputed chief of the revolutionary party and master of the entire political system.

During the presidential campaigns of 1952 and 1958, several of the minor parties allied themselves with the PRI rather than place their own leaders in competition with the official standard-bearer. Not even those opposition parties which did run presidential candidates were able to put up nominees to contend for every seat at stake in the congressional election held at the same time, for only the revolutionary party has effectively operating political organizations in all states and territories. In by-elections the imbalance is even more pronounced. During the 1955 congressional campaign, for example, the PRI put up candidates in all 162 districts, the PAN in 89, the Popular party (PP) in 66, and the Nationalist party (PNM) in only 40. At that, only a half-dozen minor party hopefuls managed to win seats in the Chamber of Deputies. For 1958, the PRI again nominated candidates for all of the 162 deputies' and 60 senators' posts; respectively, the PAN named only 140 and 50, the PP 69 and 21, the PARM 13 and 46, and the PNM 51 and 9. In many state-level elections none of the other parties bothers to nominate persons for state office at all, so that the posts go by default to the PRI's *candidatos únicos.*

Party membership is no less one-sided, with the revolutionary party reporting five to seven times the combined membership of all other parties legally recognized in the country. During 1954, a non-election year, for example, the PRI reported 3.5 million members, the PP 191,000, the PNM 182,929, and the PAN 100,000. Obviously, the automatic inclusion of members of the functional interest associations affiliated with one or another of the government party's three sectors swells its membership totals, sometimes even with persons who might be active in other political parties. Nonetheless, the proportionate size of the official party, as compared with the others, is overwhelming.

## The Legal Status of Parties

Not surprisingly, considering its domination of politics and government, those sections of the national election law dealing with political parties go far to enhance the position of the revolutionary party. In the name of establishing a system of permanent and responsible national parties, the law describes parties as ". . . associations for electoral purposes and political orientation, by law made up only of Mexican citizens in full exercise of their civil rights. . . . [These associations] are agents of the electoral agencies and share with them responsibility for the enforcement of constitutional provisions concerning election matters."[1]

On the face of it these are worth-while goals, as are many of the specific provisions of the law, but all of them are difficult to achieve under the best of circumstances. And the best of circumstances are not always available, for the provisions of the law are administered by the central government's *Secretaría de Gobernación*, which quite naturally reflects a certain degree of bias toward the desires and attitudes of the official party. Some of its actions, both in recognizing and in withdrawing recognition of political parties, have suggested political rather than strictly administrative motivation.

This places a potent weapon in the hands of the government, for only those parties registered with *Gobernación* are considered legally constituted and therefore entitled to nominate candidates for national office. Moreover, no party may participate in a national election until it has been recognized as a national party for a minimum of one year. Given the natural apathy of most Mexicans in political affairs, it is difficult enough at any time for a new political party to meet the standards imposed by the election law, much less a year before the heat of a political campaign generates interest.

In order to obtain registration as a national party, the political group requesting recognition must demonstrate that it meets certain minimum standards, which were increased sharply by amendments to the election law adopted in 1953. *Gobernación* determines whether these standards have been met. During the precampaign skirmishing before the 1958 presidential election, recognition was granted to one party—the PARM[2]—of very doubtful ability to meet the law's membership requirements, and denied to another— the Communist party—which was much stronger and more completely organized. Ignoring the relative political merits of the two groups, it was quite obvious that the decision was made on quite different bases than those established by the Election Law:

---

[1] *Ley Electoral Federal, Diario Oficial,* January 7, 1954. Although the law was passed in 1951, it was amended extensively by the 1953 session of Congress. See Chapter III of the law for portions dealing with political parties.

[2] The *Partido Auténtico de la Revolución Mexicana,* a creation of several older revolutionary leaders, will be discussed below.

   I To have at least 2,500 members in each of no less than two-thirds of the country's states and territories and, in any case, a minimum of 75,000 members;

   II To pledge obedience to legal and constitutional provisions, to prohibit subordination of the party to foreign political parties or international organizations, and to engage to participate only in peaceful political activities;

   III To hold in at least two-thirds of the federal entities a meeting to select delegates to a national constituting convention of the party. At both the state-level and the national meetings, a notary must attend, in order to attest to the legal number of members and to the fact that decisions were reached by vote of a majority of delegates;

   IV To adopt a statement of party principles and, as required by the national constitution, a distinctive name that does not allude to race or religion.

Parties which do not meet these requirements or which, for whatever reason, are not granted official registration by *Gobernación*, may not appear on the ballot or participate in the meetings and discussions of national electoral agencies. The only hope of the nonrecognized party or the independent, nonaffiliated candidate lies in the write-in, which is permitted. This is a very weak hope indeed, as the nonrecognized Communist party discovered during the 1958 campaign. Not even Vicente Lombardo Toledano's fellow-traveling Popular party (PP) supported the Communist candidate. Of 7,485,403 presidential ballots counted, only 10,346 were for nonregistered candidates and not all went to the Red candidate.

*Gobernación* determines when a party has complied with these legal requirements for registration, announcing its decision in the *Diario Oficial* and informing the government electoral agencies concerned at the same time. The recognized party thereafter may send an accredited observer to the meetings of these government bodies, but this person may not be a member of the national or state executive or judicial branches of government, or on active duty as a military or police officer. Parties legally may form permanent or temporary confederations or a coalition to support a single candidate; if they do so, they must register the fact with *Gobernación*, and the coalition may send only one representative to functions of electoral agencies.

As the election law operates in practice, sending observers to sit in on meetings of electoral agencies seems a somewhat hollow rite. The principal agency administering elections, the Federal Election Commission, for example, is composed of the Secretary of *Goberna-*

*ción,* one senator, one deputy, and three representatives of legally recognized national parties. According to article 11 of the law, if the parties cannot agree upon which three of them shall select members of the Commission, the public members will do so, "taking care that the three parties selected be the most important in the country and of differing ideology or program."

What happened before the 1958 election is typical. The five nationally recognized parties could not agree, so the representatives of the executive and legislative branches selected the PRI, the PAN, and the PP, much to the chagrin of the PNM and the PARM. But this meant that the PRI really had four of the six members—three public and one party—while of the remaining two only the representative of the PAN opposed the candidacy of Lic. López Mateos, for the PP attempted to ally itself with the official party's presidential candidate. Observers from the minor parties, with or without a vote, scarcely can hope to influence the administrative decisions of so unbalanced an agency.

The domination by the government party is no less pronounced in the cancellation of a national party's registration. If, through its own initiative or as a result of complaints lodged by some other political party, the *Secretaría de Gobernación* finds that the terms of the election law are being violated, the guilty political party may find its registration cancelled, permanently or temporarily, after an administrative hearing during which spokesmen for the offending party may defend its position. Temporary cancellation of registration generally is imposed to force compliance with the law's provisions on party structure or educational activities, permanent cancellation for unconstitutional acts or resort to force in political acts.

No appeal to the courts can reverse decisions of *Gobernación* in these matters because the only available procedural legal recourse, the writ of *amparo,* is not operative in political questions. During 1949, under a similar provision of a previous law, the registration of the right-wing *Partido de la Fuerza Popular* was withdrawn at the request of the PRI because a group of *sinarquistas* had insulted the statue and memory of Juárez. The courts refused to intervene in the matter.[3] Similarly, early in 1954 under the present law, the registration of the Federation of Mexican Peoples' Parties, which

---

[3] See *Excelsior,* January 29, 30, 1949; *Tiempo,* March 9, 1950, p. 8. Precedent for the court's refusal to act is located in the *Seminario Judicial de la Federación,* apendice a Tomo XCVII, p. 335.

had supported General Henríquez Guzmán in the 1952 presidential campaign, was cancelled for alleged illegal resort to force.[4] And, as already mentioned, several times since 1950 the government has refused to grant recognition to political groups seeking registration.[5]

In addition to minimum numbers of members and nationwide state organizations, the election law requires that both before and after registration has been accorded a national political party, its party organization adhere to a common structural pattern. Each national party must be governed by a National Assembly, meeting periodically, and a permanently established National Executive Committee. Furthermore, in each state or territory where the party has more than 2,500 members, the state organization must be headed by a state Executive Committee. This pattern seems logical, considering Mexico's federal system, but some other might be equally logical and this one is strangely like that of the revolutionary party. In truth, the original draft of this election law was sponsored officially by the PRI.

Once organized and recognized, each national party must issue a monthly publication, have permanent offices, and provide cultural and civic centers in which its members may meet. This is part of an announced attempt to raise the political and social level of the citizenry, but despite the provision that adherence to these requirements be proved biennially to the satisfaction of *Gobernación*, very little party action can be noted in any party headquarters between elections. One Mexico City publication went so far as to celebrate the first anniversary of the 1952 presidential election by publishing pictures of the obviously empty and unused meeting rooms in the imposing national headquarters of the PRI itself.[6]

This extensive national legislation, so unlike the limited, diverse, and primarily state-level regulation of party organization and activities in the United States, points up dramatically the differences in the political environment of the two countries. It also underlines the fact that some of the political problems endemic in Mexican culture have not yet been solved, despite the new political system that is evolving.

---

[4] See the Mexico City press of February, 1954, for accounts of the situation leading to the decision.

[5] See, for example, the *Informe Rendido . . . a la Suprema Corte de Justicia . . . 1950*, "Informe de la Segunda Sala," pp. 63-64, or *Tiempo*, July 27, 1951, p. 5.

[6] *Hoy*, "El Mausoleo de la Democracia," July 11, 1953, pp. 8-11.

The high degree of centralization built into the party system by concentrating administrative authority in the *Secretaría de Gobernación* reflects the revolutionary government's determination to hasten the advent of an institutionalized political system based upon permanent, nationwide, and responsible parties, but it also reflects the paucity of spontaneous grass-roots movements in that direction by private citizens. The temptation, to which the revolutionary leadership has succumbed, is to attempt to legislate such a party system into existence by establishing extremely high standards of party size, activity, and the like.

Unless conditions suitable for such a system exist, however, attempts to legislate party responsibility and intraparty democratic relationships between leaders and followers are foredoomed to failure. Enforcement of high-sounding legal provisions will be spotty at best, and the law itself may be incomplete because it grows out of wishful thinking rather than pragmatic experience. We have already seen that the portions of the election law dealing with party registration sometimes are interpreted by *Gobernación* in a less than objective manner.

Another case in point, demonstrating that the election law is somewhat contradictory concerning internal party relations, lies in its positive requirement that political parties encourage informed and mature political activity on the part of their members, which very nearly is negated by the neglect to provide the general membership with adequate legal means of holding the party leadership responsible for executing the will of the rank and file.

Article 30 of the law, for example, requires that some predetermined system for selecting electoral candidates be adopted by each party, but specifically prohibits "public acts similar to constitutional elections," effectively barring a direct primary system, even if administered by the party itself. This tends to throw control of nominations into the hands of the professional politicians and keep it away from the rank and file. Not even the 1959 liberalization of the PRI's state and local nominating procedures described at the end of Chapter V has affected the location of this important source of political power substantially.

Much the same is true in terms of individual political responsibility. On the one hand, the law specifically requires adoption of party sanctions applicable to members who fail to meet the "moral or political principles" of their party, but on the other it provides no corresponding sanctions to be invoked by individuals against party functionaries. The only legal norm to which party heads are held states that they shall be criminally and civilly responsible for their official acts. Generally, however, this provision applies in terms of the party's external relations—with government agencies, for example—rather than as a means of assuring internal responsibility. In such cases, initiative is apt to lie with the public authorities rather than with private citizens.

Just as the election law tends to centralize the whole party system in *Gobernación,* so it also tends to concentrate power in the leadership of individual parties, to the detriment of individual rank-and-file initiative. This failure to encourage greater respect for responsible internal party relations is an unfortunate but hardly unexpected oversight, for it reflects the pattern of Mexican politics. The low intensity of mass political participation makes it doubtful that at this juncture in Mexico's political evolution the omission is very significant, except as an indication that little or no popular pressure for such control devices exists.

Even if party members had both the desire and the legal mechanisms to hold their party officers more responsible, given the present political situation, in which power is centered in the leadership of the official party, chances are that any legal decision would be colored by political bias. Whether the matter should involve the PRI or one of the minor parties, both the executive officers in *Gobernación* and the judicial officers who must hear legal cases are apt to reflect the attitudes and desires of the official party leadership, with little likelihood that fear of popular reaction will deter them from basing decisions on political expediency.

Consequently, until such time as a higher proportion of Mexico's citizens are prepared to take the political initiative, no amount of legal norms will build a more democratic party system, because political rather than legal or administrative pressures are the real answer to political party irresponsibility. As yet, the average Mexican is not ready to assume the role of an active political party member. Until recently, this has been even more true of the mass membership of the PRI, which could attain its most immediate goals through sector organization support, than it is of the individuals in minor parties.

This does not mean that party leadership—PRI or other—can ignore completely the interests of the average member of his party, for if Juan Diego does not attend party meetings, except as he is turned out to meet a visiting dignitary, or if Fulano de Tal does not contribute to his party,[7] he still has a role to play. In general, the individual allows the party to act for him, but he retains a kind of negative influence in the form of support for or opposition to a given leader in the frequent internecine struggles that are part of Mexican party life. His attitude is determined, of course, by whether he is satisfied with what the leader has done to represent his interests, as he sees those interests, or whether he believes the promises of the person attempting to supplant that leader. Unlike the Mexican Indian, once he becomes aware of his potential political power, there is in the *mestizo* little of that "damned wantlessness" of the Russian peasant that so irritated Lenin.

Within these negative boundaries, however, the party leaders are left with a great deal of independence of action, and the degree of demand for immediate responsible interest representation is much lower in Mexico than in some other political cultures. The high degree of centralization in the PRI and the concentration of authority in its organizational hierarchy, including that of the sectors, demonstrates this rather clearly.

## The Party Structure

The structure of the revolutionary party is complex, one might almost say cumbersome. But, as we have seen, its present form is a direct result of efforts to supply the mechanisms needed to make a national system of politics possible in Mexico's highly pluralistic society. As a relatively simple coalition of local political machines, labor unions, and farm organizations bound together by the personality and power of President Calles, the PNR had little need for complicated machinery. Over the years, however, the revolutionary party has developed into a highly centralized national political

---

[7] In financing the revolutionary party, for example, with the exception of more or less forced levies from government employees and, less regularly, from members of functional interest associations, contributions come from only three to five per cent of the party membership. Most of this non-check-off type of contribution stems from high elective and appointive officials and ambitious officers of farm groups, labor unions, and the like. The average member is not sufficiently interested in participating in party affairs to spend money in this way. One portion of the 1959 changes in the PRI's nominating techniques relates to this problem. Only dues-paying members of the local organization are entitled to initiate or sign petitions suggesting slates of candidates for nomination by the party.

organization that tries to balance an ever-increasing number of interests represented in its membership. The inevitable result is today's *Partido Revolucionario Institucional,* which claims almost forty per cent of the registered voters in Mexico—some three and a half million members (or more, if some claims are recognized).[8]

At the national level, the PRI is governed by three interdependent bodies, a National Assembly, a Permanent Commission (*Gran Comisión*), and a Central Executive Committee. Of the three, the Central Committee and its president are by far the most influential, partly because the party's statutes give them a high degree of strategic control over other party organs, partly because the Committee's membership represents functional interest associations which are the principal sources of political power, and partly because it is through this agency that the President of the Republic wields his concentrated authority.

According to the party statutes, the National Assembly is the "supreme organ of the party." It meets every three years, and in special session on call of the Central Executive Committee. The composition of the National Assembly is determined by the convocation announcement, also issued by the Central Committee. In the past, such party meetings usually have consisted of about a thousand delegates, divided equally among the three sectors of the party and representing the several component functional interest associations making up each sector. The duties of the National Assembly include review of the activities of the other national-level organs of the party, evaluation of the political and administrative policies of the government in light of the party program, changing the principles, program, and statutes of the party, and electing the Central Executive Committee. Unlike the national conventions of major parties in the United States, this party business usually is not combined with presidential nominations; a separate nominating convention is held.

Almost without exception, the meetings of the National Assembly of the official party have been manipulated by the leadership of the party and of the sector organizations which send the

---

[8] The best recent discussion of the organization of the revolutionary party is Frank R. Brandenburg, "Mexico: An Experiment in One Party Democracy," unpublished Ph.D. thesis, University of Pennsylvania, 1956. The formal statement of PRI organization can be found in its *Declaración de Principios, Programa de Acción y Estatutos,* Mexico, 1957.

delegates. The party bureaucracy, working closely with the office of the chief executive, prepares the agenda for the meeting and sees to it that the proper persons speak, that acceptable candidates are selected for party office, and that the desired decisions are reached. Certainly all of these matters are forecast quite accurately in the newspapers days and even weeks before the National Assembly meets. In plain words, though the party statutes call it the "supreme organ of the party," it is not here that political power resides in Mexico.

The second national agency of the PRI is the *Gran Comisión*, to which the so-called supreme power of the party is delegated between sessions of the National Assembly. It is composed of thirty members, each sector electing ten during the meeting of the National Assembly. These members normally remain in office until the Assembly meets again. The duties of the *Gran Comisión* include receiving the annual report of the Central Executive Committee, acting as a final review board on sanctions applied by the Central Committee against party members, and ending such sanctions. Its duties also entail naming a new President or Secretary-General of the Central Executive Committee if either must be replaced for any reason, as well as agreeing to recommendations by the Central Executive Committee for convocation of the National Assembly and national nominating conventions. To fulfill these duties, the *Gran Comisión* meets at the call of the Central Executive Committee; once convoked, it may deal only with the matters listed on the agenda with which it is provided.

The real power of the national organization of the PRI lies in the Central Executive Committee, which "represents the party throughout the country." It is composed of seven members; a President, a Secretary-General, one Secretary each for Agrarian, Labor, and Popular Activities, and two Secretaries for Political Activities—one a senator and the other a national deputy. The President and the Secretary-General of the PRI are elected by its National Assembly (which really ratifies the national president's choice), the three functional secretaries by their respective national sector organizations, and the senator and the deputy by caucus of the party members in their legislative chambers. The Secretary for Popular Activities is aided by two Subsecretaries, in order to provide better representation for the diverse groups which make up the Popular sector.

The powers of the Central Executive Committee are extensive; they comprise direction of all national functions of the party as well as control over most of its state and local activities. Its composition enables the Committee to reach both the formal agencies of the party and the functional organizations in the sectors as well. More specifically, its authority extends over enforcement of observance of the party program and statutes, including decisions of the National Assembly. The CEC has responsibility for day-to-day direction of party activities, appointment of committees and delegates to control and orient party activities, enforcement of internal party discipline, convocation of "regional conventions" to form the state-level party organizations, removal for cause of members of the state and municipal party committees, naming temporary officers of the state-level committees when the old officers are separated permanently. It also convokes the National Assembly and the *Gran Comisión* and exercises broad control over the selection of party officers and nomination of party candidates at all levels including, since 1959, review of slates of state and local party nominees. Finally, the Central Executive Committee establishes and enforces regulations concerning the organization and functioning of the municipal-level committees. In short, it is the apex of the hierarchical pyramid organization that controls the entire party.

For binding action, at least five members of the Committee must be present at its meetings. In every case one of these must be the President of the Committee or his designate. In practice, most of the power of the Committee is exercised by and through this officer. He calls meetings, presides, carries out decisions; he also prepares the party budget and controls the expenditures under it. In "urgent cases" he may act solely for the Central Executive Committee. Obviously this is a very important political post, one which carries with it in the popular mind the designation President of the revolutionary party. The party bureaucracy and the treasurer are specifically responsible to the President of the Committee, as are Offices of Feminine and Youth Activities and the Institute for Political, Economic, and Social Studies.

The broad powers of the President of the Committee have developed easily and naturally over the years, for the holder of this position really represents the national president in the deliberations of the official party. Portes Gil held the post after being president, Cárdenas before taking office. Most of the men who have been

## The Organization of the PRI

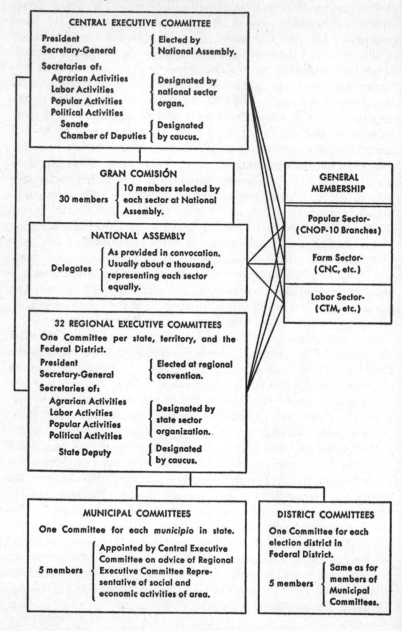

**CENTRAL EXECUTIVE COMMITTEE**

President
Secretary-General } Elected by National Assembly.

Secretaries of:
Agrarian Activities
Labor Activities
Popular Activities
Political Activities } Designated by national sector organ.

Senate
Chamber of Deputies } Designated by caucus.

**GRAN COMISIÓN**

30 members } 10 members selected by each sector at National Assembly.

**NATIONAL ASSEMBLY**

Delegates } As provided in convocation. Usually about a thousand, representing each sector equally.

**32 REGIONAL EXECUTIVE COMMITTEES**

One Committee per state, territory, and the Federal District.

President
Secretary-General } Elected at regional convention.

Secretaries of:
Agrarian Activities
Labor Activities
Popular Activities
Political Activities } Designated by state sector organization.

State Deputy } Designated by caucus.

**GENERAL MEMBERSHIP**

Popular Sector- (CNOP-10 Branches)

Farm Sector- (CNC, etc.)

Labor Sector- (CTM, etc.)

**MUNICIPAL COMMITTEES**

One Committee for each *municipio* in state.

5 members } Appointed by Central Executive Committee on advice of Regional Executive Committee Representative of social and economic activities of area.

**DISTRICT COMMITTEES**

One Committee for each election district in Federal District.

5 members } Same as for members of Municipal Committees.

President of the Central Executive Committee (or its equivalent in the older versions of the party) have gone on to high elective or appointive office, usually as a painless means of easing them out of this strategic role in the party organization so that an incoming president can appoint a new party boss in whom he has personal confidence.

In the period between organization of the PNR in 1929 and the changes made by incoming President López Mateos in 1958, sixteen men have held this office, several more than once, for a total of nineteen separate terms. Of the sixteen, nine were military politicians (eight generals, one colonel) and seven civilians. Recently, as the political situation has become more stable, the rate of turnover has dropped; between 1940 and 1959, only six men have been President of the Executive Committee. The last four have been generals.

The Secretary-General of the Central Executive Committee is an administrator who heads the party secretariat. Adolfo López Mateos, the PRI's candidate for president in 1958, was Secretary-General during the 1952 presidential race, when he acted as campaign manager for Adolfo Ruiz Cortines. From his party position Lic. López Mateos entered the cabinet as Secretary of Labor and Public Welfare.

Below these national-level party agencies are thirty-two Regional Executive Committees which function in the Federal District and the two national territories as well as in the twenty-nine states. Each Regional Committee has six members—a President, a Secretary-General, Secretaries for Agrarian, Labor, and Popular Activities, and a Secretary for Political Activities, who is selected by caucus of party members in the unicameral state legislatures.

The Regional Executive Committee is elected at a regional convention of the Presidents of each state's Municipal Committees; this state-level meeting is called by the Central Executive Committee and presided over by its delegate. The convention elects the President and the Secretary-General of the Regional Committee by majority vote; the other members are selected by the state sector organizations they represent. The President and Secretary-General hold office until the next convention, which must be called by the Central Executive Committee in Mexico City. If one or both of these state-level officers should become unavailable, the Central Committee appoints their temporary substitutes.

The functions of the Regional Executive Committees consist of carrying on all party activities in the entity; this includes aiding in solving differences among the sectors and individual party members, creating the local political study centers required by law, and, with authorization of the Central Committee, convoking and regulating *municipio* and state-level nominating conventions, as well as attesting their decisions. The Regional Committee also hears the formal acceptances of candidates for posts in the municipal *ayuntamientos* (city offices), as well as for state legislative and judicial offices.

Four of the six members, including its President or his designate, must attend every meeting of the Committee, where decisions are made by majority vote. The President of the Regional Executive Committee has much the same centralizing power at the state level as does the head of the Central Committee at the national. Usually, if the governor of the state is acceptable to the President of the Republic, the Regional President represents the state executive in party matters; if the governor is not acceptable, the post may be used to restrict the political power of the governor.

At the local government level, in the *municipios*, the PRI party machine is represented by a Municipal Committee or by a District Committee (in the Federal District only). It is composed of five members, who must live in the *municipio*; they are appointed by the Central Executive Committee in the capital on proposal of the Regional Executive Committee. The five municipal committeemen are supposed to be representative of the economic and social interests in the area they serve. If and where all three sectors of the official party have functional organizations at this municipal level, they name the Committee members jointly; otherwise, those sectors which do have local organizations select them. In the Federal District, where there are as many District Committees as election districts, they serve as a kind of ward committee, with the same composition, organization, and duties as their nonurban counterparts.

Each local Committee elects its President and Secretary-General from among its five members. The President calls sessions when he deems necessary, presiding and directing debate, as well as seeing that decisions are put into effect. He also controls the Committee's funds and represents it formally in party or public activities. According to the party statutes, decisions at Municipal Committee meetings are reached by majority vote; sometimes, however, it is obvious that the vote was prearranged in earlier private sessions.

Beyond carrying on the program and plans of the party at this local level, the Municipal Committee prepares and keeps up to date the roster of local party members, sending copies to the party organization in the state and national capital. During the 1958 presidential campaign, the Municipal Committees worked closely with the sector organizations in an all-out effort to encourage badly lagging voter registration.

From the foregoing, it must be obvious that a high degree of authority over the revolutionary party's affairs lodges in its hierarchy, centering in the Central Executive Committee in Mexico City. Note how almost all party activities and appointments pass through its hands.

The *Gran Comisión* approves convocation of the PRI's National Assembly, but it is the CEC that calls the Commission's meetings and fixes its agenda. Similarly, the CEC calls meetings of Presidents of Municipal Committees to compose the statewide regional conventions; it also names the presiding officer. Later, after the Regional Committee is organized, a representative of the CEC must attend all meetings and, as we already know, not only does the Central Executive Committee designate the five members of the Municipal Committees, on recommendation of the state-level Regional Committee, but for cause also may remove the officers of the latter and name new ones, who act until the next regional convention. Again, the CEC participates in and must approve internal nominating procedures for the party's candidates, as well as reviewing the application of sanctions against individual members. Finally, the CEC, with approval of the Permanent Commission, calls the presidential nominating convention.

Without going into detail, long observation demonstrates that the Central Executive Committee uses this authority to good purpose in translating the wishes of the President of the Republic into political reality. It is one of several weapons he keeps in his arsenal of political power; the very fact that he has such weapons and can use them means that he seldom has to. In the next chapter, however, we shall see one example of how control over the date of the presidential nominating convention can enhance the authority of the chief executive.

## The PRI's Sector Organizations

The three basic sectors—Farm, Labor, and Popular—upon which first the PRM and then the PRI were built, have remained the major units for interest representation in the revolutionary party since 1940, when the Military sector was dissolved. If increasing specialization has multiplied the number of competing interests to be satisfied and, therefore, the number of functional interest associations in each sector, it has been possible until now to contain their struggles within the sector organizations and the mechanisms of the official party.

Regarding the relationship of the average member of the party with his sector, the expansion of technology and the increase .of production accompanying Westernization so far have offset to some extent the pressures which might result from greater social and economic desires and even from growing political awareness. So long as immediate material demands can be satisfied, the members' lack of interest in political participation allows the leaders of functional interest associations relatively wide latitude in their own political activities. Recently, pressures upon functional leaders have begun to mount, however, because revolutionary reforms are producing ever-larger numbers of politically aware Mexicans demanding greater social and economic benefits just as the first spurt of industrial and agricultural production is beginning to level off.

These pressures inevitably produce a greater degree of inter-action within each sector as well as contention among the three, for the heads of the functional interest associations seek to solve their problems by increasing the share of benefits flowing to their own followers. Up to the present, these struggles have been kept within bounds because, for all of the proliferation of interests, in each of the three sectors one larger association or combination of interest groups has held dominant power, while the authority of the President of the Republic has balanced the demands among the three sectors.

On the surface at least, the Farm sector has kept the greatest appearance of homogeneity, with the *Confederación Nacional Campesina* retaining its position as the principal spokesman for *ejido* interests in particular and farm interests in general. Through its local Leagues of Agrarian Communities, the CNC represents over two and a half million *ejiditarios*. A few other agricultural interest associations also participate in the sector's activities, some as integral and permanent parts of the sector and others on a temporary basis. The *Sociedad Agronómica Mexicana,* for example, was added to the sector permanently during the 1952 presidential campaign, so that professional agronomists might be represented formally in this part of the revolutionary party's organization. On the other hand, local or specialized farm interest groups such as the *Frente Zapatista de la República,* may ally themselves with the Farm sector temporarily for electoral purposes.

Despite this appearance of homogeneity, Westernizing influences have been at work producing a spate of more specialized farm interests which the CNC seems unable or unwilling to represent, because they run counter to the collective ejidal system. As a consequence, some of these interests have found places in the other sectors, where primary goals are not so rigidly identified with this particular type of farming interest. Some of the farm population, say the owners of private farm property or members of farm-produce marketing cooperatives, can be found in various sections of the Popular sector's CNOP; others, who work on the land for day-wages or who drive farm trucks, belong to one or another union attached to the Labor sector.

Not unexpectedly, the tendency toward specialization of function has progressed even further among those Mexicans engaged in urban, industrial activities who make up the Labor sector.[9] Here, however, the divisive tendencies of competing interests are further heightened by ideological and personalistic differences, which split the sector not only into numerous functional organizations but also into two antagonistic political factions.

The Mexican Workers' Federation (CTM) remains the largest and most important single labor organization, though its claims of two million members probably are exaggerated. Now that Vicente Lombardo Toledano has left both it and the PRI, the CTM is led by Fidel Velázquez, who abandoned his former radicalism to attack leftist labor elements, thereby gaining the support of the president then in office—Miguel Alemán—and capturing control of the federa-

---

[9] See the following books for recent discussion of various aspects of Mexico's labor movement and its role in politics: Alfonso López Aparicio, *El Movimiento Obrero en México* (Mexico, D.F., 1952); Rosendo Salazar, *Líderes y Sindicatos* (Mexico, D.F., 1953), *Historia de las Luchas Proletarias de México* (Mexico, D.F., 1956), and *La CTM:Su Historia, Su Significado* (Mexico, D.F., 1956).

tion. The CTM provides leadership and a core of strength about which cluster the more moderate labor organizations; collectively they are known as the *Bloque de Unidad Obrera,* or BUO, and comprise some 85 per cent of the popular membership of the Labor sector.

Within the sector, but opposing the BUO, is a second group of labor organizations, oriented toward the left. Its largest member, the second most numerous labor group in Mexico, is the *Confederación Revolucionaria de Obreros y Campesinos* (CROC), formed in 1952 by combining several leftist organizations, some of which had abandoned the official party to help form Vicente Lombardo Toledano's Popular party, only to return when the PP failed to gain enough political momentum to protect their interests.

During his administration, President Ruiz Cortines seemed to be playing the CROC off against the CTM, permitting the former to organize in direct competition with already existing CTM unions and even allowing its leaders to make public attacks charging the CTM hierarchy with having betrayed labor's interests and with having lined their own pockets at the expense of the workingman.

As we shall see presently in our discussion of the political situation leading up to the 1958 presidential election, this unusually permissive attitude in the chief executive may have resulted because certain of the leaders of the CTM and the other labor unions making up the BUO tended to lean toward the rightist (*alemanista*) political faction in the PRI that sought to restrict Ruiz Cortines' reformist activities, so he may have turned to the opposing unionists to contain these pressure tactics. The attempts of the anti-BUO leaders to capture control were made more effective by the legitimate feeling that the established leadership, especially in the CTM, seemed more interested in winning personal political influence than in representing the economic interests of the rank-and-file workers caught in an inflationary trap.

The struggle within the Labor sector carried over into national politics, both during the 1958 presidential campaign and afterward, providing a source of acute embarrassment both for outgoing President Ruiz Cortines and for newly inaugurated President López Mateos after he took office in December, 1958. Although the BUO, working in cooperation with the bureaucrats union in the Popular sector, assumed primary responsibility for coordinating labor support for candidate López Mateos, he did his best to provide a degree of recognition for the dissidents also. In fact, one of the first labor speeches made by the revolutionary party's presidential candidate was to a rally sponsored by the anti-BUO faction, despite the fact that the rivalry between the two labor camps weakened the effectiveness of the PRI's campaigning. On one occasion, for example, when the CROC tried to hold a mass meeting in Santa María del Río to whip up support for López Mateos, the CTM did everything in its power to prevent a large turnout, even resorting to threats from the public authorities to discourage attendance. Anti-BUO labor leaders retaliated in kind at other rallies, impairing the over-all effect of the official party's campaign.

Labor infighting was not confined to these two factions, however, for Antonio C. Rivas, Secretary-General of the CGT, which ostensibly is a member of the BUO group, circularized his member unions just before the election, recommending that their members vote for Adolfo López Mateos but instructing them not to support congressional candidates named by the CTM. This move, aimed primarily at Fidel Velázquez, who ran as a PRI senatorial candidate from the Federal District, lowered the total votes cast for certain labor candidates, but it did not change the outcome of the election in any district. Nor did it have any effect upon the candidacy of Abelardo de la Torre Grajales, then Secretary-General of the FSTSE, who was the Popular sector's candidate for the second senatorial seat.

Far more important than election bickering was the series of wildcat strikes which occurred during and after the campaign, especially those of government unions sparked by ambitious leftist leaders who sought to take advantage of the change-over of administrations to enhance their power. Before the election on July 6, 1958, the telegraphers went out, in February, followed in May by the left-wing members of the primary-school teachers in the Federal District, who tried to force their own leaders into control of the union. After the election, the teachers struck again, imposing Otón Salazar as their leader in the capital; they were followed by several important locals of the petroleum workers. At the National University in Mexico City and in Monterrey the students struck against increased bus fares, impounding the buses and bringing public transport to a halt. Again, at the Polytechnic Institute in the capital the students struck against an unpopular director. All of these student movements were strongly supported by the leftist, anti-BUO faction, who sought to turn the students' actions to their own benefit in

## THE SECTOR ORGANIZATION OF THE PRI

**Farm Sector**

1. Confederación Nacional Campesina
   A. 2,332,914 ejido families on 18,564 ejidos
      (1956 agricultural census) — 2,500,000
   B. Sindicatos Campesinos (organization of wage-
      laborers on private lands, affiliated with the
      CNC) — 150,000
2. Sociedad Agronómica Mexicana — 10,000

Total in Farm Sector — 2,660,000

**Labor Sector**

1. Affiliated with BUO
   A. Confederación de Trabajadores Mexicanos
      (CTM) — 1,500,000
   B. Confederación Regional de Obreros Mexicanos
      (CROM) — 35,000
   C. Confederación General de Trabajadores
      (CGT) — 25,000[a]
   D. Railroad Workers Union (STFRM) — 102,000[a]
   E. Mining and Metal Workers Union
      (STMMSRM) — 90,000
   F. Petroleum Workers Union (STPRM) — 85,000[a]
   G. Telephone Workers Union (STRM) — 10,000
   H. Motion Picture Workers Union (STPCRM) — 6,000
   I. Other independent unions (FNRT, FTDF,
      FNUT, FAO, ANDA, ATA, etc.) — 20,000

   1,873,000

2. Anti-BUO Affiliates
   A. Confederación Revolucionaria de Obreros y
      Campesinos (CROC) — 150,000
   B. Confederación Revolucionaria de Trabajadores
      (CRT) — 25,000
   C. Electrical Workers Unions (3 unions) — 50,000[a]
   D. Other independent unions — 15,000
   E. Sindicato de Trabajadores Agrícolas
      (in formation)

   240,000

Total in Labor Sector — 2,113,000

**Popular Sector—CNOP**

1. Civil Servants
   A. Bureaucrats Unions (FSTSE) — 300,000
   B. Teachers (SNTE) — 55,000[a]
2. Cooperatives
   A. National Federation of Cooperatives — 275,000
   B. National Cooperative League — 3,000

3. Small Farm Proprietors
   A. Confederación Nacional de la Pequeña
      Propiedad Agrícola ............................................ 850,000
   B. Asociación Nacional de Cosecheros ........................ 15,000
4. Small Merchants ⎫ These overlap
5. Small Industrialists ⎭ ............................................ 40,000
6. Professionals—Intellectuals ...................................... 55,000
7. Youth Groups
   A. Confederación de Jóvenes Mexicanos .................... 75,000
8. Artisans (nonsalaried service employees) ................ 70,000
9. Women's Organizations
   A. Sociedad de Técnicas y Profesionales .................. 25,000
   B. Others (Mujeres Revolucionarias, Mujeres en
      Marcha, etc.) ................................................ 10,000
10. Diversified Persons (a catchall for all kinds of
    otherwise unaffiliated Mexicans) .......................... 75,000
    
    Total in Popular Sector ................ 1,848,000
    Grand Total in Three PRI Sectors .... 6,621,000

ᵃ The mere fact that a union or labor confederation is listed as affiliated with the BUO or against it does not always mean that it collectively or all of its locals or individual members support the position irrevocably. The railroad workers and the petroleum workers in the Labor sector, and the Federal District's primary-school teachers in the Popular sector, nominally support the BUO, but in actuality, until the government's crackdown precipitated by the railroad strike of March-April, 1959, they cooperated with the anti-BUO forces. At the same time, the electrical workers, who belong to the anti-BUO faction, broke off their cooperation with the leftist railroad leaders after the same strike. Similarly, although the CGT nominally is part of the BUO, the Secretary-General of the federation instructed his followers not to support the candidates for congressional office put up by the CTM during the 1958 political campaign. On the other hand, although the bureaucrats union (FSTSE) operates out of the Popular sector, it considers itself a part of and works with the BUO.

the internal struggle in Mexican labor. In the case of several of these strikes and student movements, the president was forced to resort to military force to restore order.

By far the most disruptive labor activity after the election was the series of strikes on Mexico's rail lines called by Demetrio Vallejo, who had managed to capture control of the railroad workers union in 1958. Within a few months after President López Mateos' inauguration, it became obvious that Vallejo was more interested in fomenting trouble than in resolving labor disputes; after a particularly disturbing strike crisis during Holy Week, 1959, in which thousands of persons on vacation were left stranded, the courts declared the strike illegal and the government arrested Vallejo and several hundred of his followers. In the process, the headquarters of the railroad union were raided and the Attorney-General announced that evidence had been discovered linking Vallejo and several of his cronies to the Soviet embassy. The direct result of this announcement was the ousting of two Russian diplomats from the country, the replacing of the left-tinged officers of the railroad workers union with a more moderate set of leaders, and the breaking of the strike by the use of soldiers on the trains.

The firm action of the president and the affront to Mexican nationalism implied in the Soviet intervention resulted in at least a temporary cessation in the most obvious activities of the left wing of Mexican labor. President López Mateos has made it clear that the ungrateful reaction of the leftist labor leaders to his conciliatory gestures during the 1958 election campaign leaves him little choice but to demand a greater sense of responsibility from the chiefs of organized labor during the remainder of his administration.

So far, the struggle between the right and left wings of Mexican labor has tended to weaken the Labor sector's relative position in the national structure of power, but because of the preponderant strength of the CTM behind the BUO, coupled with the government's crackdown on leftist unions after the 1959 strikes, the battle has been too one-sided to threaten disintegration of the sector itself. If, however, the revolutionary government continues allowing the CROC and its allies to build their relative power, a crisis could occur when the two factions more nearly equate in influence. The seeds of such a crisis were planted in February, 1958, when a member-organization of the anti-BUO bloc—the National Sugar Cane Workers Union—initiated attempts to organize Mexico's two million day-wage rural workers into a farm laborers union. If these organizing attempts should prove successful, the anti-BUO labor group could surpass the BUO in total membership. Even though the farm laborers may not be so politically effective as their numbers seem to indicate, because of their less sophisticated background and rural location, the Labor sector of the PRI might split wide open. At any rate, more labor energy and influence may be wasted on internecine battles than applied to the broader function of influencing the national policy-making process.

Given the nature of its composition, it is hardly surprising that the Popular sector continues to represent by far the most diverse number and type of interest associations of the three basic divisions of the PRI. On the face of it, the National Federation of Popular

Organizations (CNOP) is a single functional association; in actuality it is a composite of a very large number of such groups, multiplying daily. Almost every one of its ten branches is really a holding company for more different conflicting interests than one would expect to find in an entire sector, so that the surprising thing is not so much that it enjoys marked political success as that the sector has been able to avoid bursting into pieces.

Perhaps the best illustration of the diversity of CNOP membership would be to review its activities within a fixed place and time. During March of 1954, a delegate of the CNOP worked at restructuring the Municipal Leagues making up the state organization of the Popular sector in Sinaloa. In the *municipio* of Concordia he set up a league including the government workers union, small farm proprietors, small businessmen, a women's group, a youth group, and an association of *diversos* (unclassified persons). In the *municipio* of Rosario, the league established included all of the above, plus a small-industry section and a cooperative group; in Sinaloa de Leyva an organization of artisans was added to the others, and in Guasava, a *Unión de Profesionistas Intelectuales*.

Later that same month, a state congress of the CNOP was held in the capital of Sinaloa; it was opened by the President of the Central Executive Committee of the PRI with a eulogy of Juárez on his birthday and of Cárdenas on the anniversary of the expropriation of foreign-owned oil properties. During the work sessions, the meeting discussed problems of literacy, cost of living, social aid, and reforestation in the state. Then, following consideration of the work being done by the local units of the National Committee for Moral, Material and Civic Improvement, the CNOP congress turned to the question of organizing newly enfranchised Mexican women for political, social, and economic action, as well as to discussion of methods of cooperation by the Popular sector in the campaign to halt the exodus of *braceros* to the United States.

If, in spite of its diversity, the Popular sector and the CNOP have managed to remain a single working unit, it is because the members of the sector's organizations have had a measure of success in obtaining material and social desires appropriate to their middle-class political astuteness, far more success than the other two sectors. Part of this success is due to the hard core of strength given to the CNOP by the relatively large size (300,000) and strategic position in policy-making enjoyed by the Government Employees Union.

But the other interests in the CNOP must pay a price for the role played by the bureaucrats.

We saw in an earlier chapter that the FSTSE several times has sought to form its own sector but that instead the government workers have been dissuaded by granting them extra benefits far beyond those enjoyed by most other Mexicans in comparable positions.

There are those who question whether the Popular sector can be kept intact by continuing to favor the bureaucracy. They point out that, regardless of all their benefits, the government workers continue to feel restive in the sector, and that other interests in the CNOP are not entirely satisfied with the present arrangement. For one thing, although the Popular sector now gets a lion's share of government benefits and elective offices, a high proportion of both go to the FSTSE. Second, as specialization progresses and social maturity develops, not even the ten branches of the CNOP are diverse enough to satisfy all interests involved in the organization. Early in 1958, for just one example, many of the small shopkeepers in the capital complained about being compelled to join and support the Federation of Small Businessmen, saying that the larger *comerciantes,* who controlled the body, collected their dues but never consulted the small store-owners, much less rendered them any real service. Finally, it is noted, repeated suggestions have been heard seeking establishment of a large-scale business and heavy industrial sector. If this should be done, the existing balance of relationships in the Popular sector could be upset.

The problems inherent in rapid growth both of size and complexity of interest representation are not limited to any one sector of the official party, for they are a part of the Westernization of Mexico. As a corollary to rapid expansion of numbers, occasioned by increasing participation in national social and economic life, by entry into the PRI of individuals and organizations formerly in the opposition, as well as by the enfranchisement of Mexican women, functional specialization has developed apace in all walks of life, multiplying the number and types of interests participating in each sector.

Competition, both in terms of representation of mass members of functional interest associations and as a means of personal aggrandizement of their leaders, continues to expand throughout each of the sectors. Not even the existence of a dominant stabilizing agency such as the CNC, the CTM, or the FSTSE that dictates the division of the sector's political spoils entirely resolves the problem, for each of these itself is a kind of omnibus holding company for inherently competitive interests, collective or individual.

The CTM, for example, has a very hard time satisfying its component unions, although it takes some seventy-five per cent of the elective posts assigned to labor and otherwise favors its members' interests. Well it might have difficulty, for in its Federation of Laborers of the Federal District alone, comprising mainly service employees, food producers, and the like, the CTM has more than 500 unions, representing 246,000 workers. This is a large number of pieces into which to slice the pie. Moreover, for all of the influence wielded by the CTM, it does not have absolute power over the unions making it up, as was demonstrated in 1957 when Fidel Velázquez complained at a national meeting that only some 20 per cent of the member organizations, representing only 10 per cent of the total membership, had paid their quotas to the CTM central organization.

The rigidity of the CNC in representing ejidal interests, on the other hand, has driven large and influential agricultural interests out of the Farm sector and into the other two. Even the government bureaucrats union, which long was noted for its high degree of internal integration, very nearly split over the claims of rival cliques to name the new Secretary-General elected in March, 1959. Only the influence of President López Mateos averted an open break between them.

Because of the rapidly changing factors of sector membership, coupled with the beginnings of overlapping individual interests and consequent multiple memberships in functional interest associations belonging to one or more sectors of the PRI, it is almost impossible to estimate accurately the relative influence of the sectors or their component parts in the decision-making process. Even the total membership of the revolutionary party is open to serious dispute.

During the 1958 presidential campaign, for example, General Olachea, then head of the PRI's Central Executive Committee, stated that about three and a half million party membership cards were out, just as leaders of the CNOP claimed three million members, a third of them women, for the Popular sector alone. At the same time, official estimates of the members of the functional interest associations affiliated with one or another of the three sectors gave the revolutionary party a total paper membership of over six million, as can be seen in the breakdown presented previously.

Some of these discrepancies in judging the party's numbers can be explained in terms of overlapping memberships, as in the case of almost a million small farm proprietors listed both by the CNC because they have *ejido* land grants and by the small farmer section of the Popular sector because they belong to the Small Farm Property Federation, or of the thousands of schoolteachers who belong both to the Intellectuals' section and to the Feminist section of the Popular sector. Similarly, most of the 250,000 members of the National Cooperative Federation in the Popular sector participate there because they belong to a very small consumers, producers, or service cooperative, but their principal allegiance is to an organization in the Farm or Labor sector. Another explanation lies in the quarter million or so persons who belong to opposition parties despite nominal membership in the PRI sector associations. But by far the most valid explanation of differences in membership totals is that the revolutionary party leaders just do not know how many members their component associations have, for the functional leadership is prone to exaggerate wildly in order to build its own influence in political affairs.

Given these uncertainties, efforts to measure the relative political influence of each sector (much less its basic component units) are not likely to be very fruitful. Some indication of sector influence has already been given in discussing the social and economic position of the classes belonging to the several sectors. Further indications will appear in our discussions of nominations, elections, and presidential influence over the decision-making process in subsequent chapters. One aspect of PRI sector relationships is worthy of note here, however. If factionalism exists, and it does, it is "coordinate factionalism," for in spite of the obvious growth of pressures upon the party machinery because of the changing power factors, that machinery has managed to continue providing a workable system for satisfying (or at least controlling) the demands of the interest associations participating in Mexican politics. It does so because of the marked institutionalization of political relationships that has taken place in the revolutionary party during the past two decades, as a result of the stabilizing effect of the sector machinery.

## Some Comments on the PRI Organization

In every system of government one of the really difficult problems to solve is that of representation. Most countries have adopted a district system in which the district represents more or less equal shares of the population, or particular political subdivisions, or a combination of the two. No one denies that under the district system inequities can and do occur, because of the way in which boundaries are drawn, because of the existence of minorities which do not accept the views of the majority, or because of accidents of location of one interest group with greater effectiveness of organization than others. Nevertheless, if the population of a country is sufficiently homogeneous, the district system seems to be the best yet devised for purposes of representative government. A few countries have devised special systems to assure some representation of minorities, but on the whole, proportional representation or reserving a stated share of legislative seats for the opposition are nothing more than refinements on the more general district system.

Considering that Mexico based its constitutional system on a North American model, it is not surprising that the district system is the legal basis for representation. But we know that Mexico is not yet as completely homogeneous and Westernized a nation as the United States. Is it not natural, therefore, that the country's real political system, the operation of which is formalized through the revolutionary party, should provide an auxiliary system of representation more nearly in accord with the realities of Mexican political life?

No one, I suppose, really believes that the sector system of selecting and supporting candidates and representing interests is a perfect or permanent solution to Mexico's political problems, but for the time being it seems the only way to assure a stable national government. At the very least, the sector system shows a tenacity in the official party organization indicating that for the time being the nature of Mexican society requires this type of hierarchical relationship, for it results not simply from the slow growth of general agreement on political values, but also from the continuing weakness of internal cohesion in Mexican social life. The absence of any high degree of overlapping membership in groups of divergent interests which might provide a bridge from one political concept to another still requires this extra machinery to close the gap, if a national political system is to exist.

To many politically aware Mexicans, membership in a farm organization, a labor union, or a "popular" organization is tantamount to membership in the revolutionary party that governs the country; for most, this is a satisfactory solution to the problem of political action. Particularly, it avoids the problem of primacy, as several groups might assert competitive claims on an individual and reduce his over-all effectiveness in politics.

True, in some instances the Mexican may find a conflict between loyalty to his "revolutionary" organization and to other institutionalized bodies. For example, until recently, Church membership and revolutionary political activity were very nearly incompatible. His Church called upon the Mexican Catholic to protest against lay education, as exemplified in article 3 of the constitution, and to seek restitution of its traditional rights, temporal and spiritual—the very antithesis of what the Revolution stood for. In recent years, however, both Church and State have begun to learn to moderate their demands. The Church no longer openly demands acts incompatible with the citizens' activities in other, nonreligious areas of interest, and the leadership of the party has accommodated some of the pressures brought on it, easing the most stringent controls over the Church and permitting it a freer action in nonpolitical matters. Pope John XXIII's consecration of the Bishop of Guadalajara as Mexico's first cardinal and the public prayers for God's blessing upon President López Mateos' administration led by the Auxiliary Bishop of Mexico, both late in 1958, indicate the degree of rapport that has evolved of late.

More to the point, with regard to party organization, while the CNC and the CTM may work long and hard together to achieve a particular political aim, they must work through the machinery and within the framework of the official party. In the case of both Church-state relations and the competing functional interests of the two mass-membership sectors, the shared interests implied in the PRI outweigh the divergent interests, insofar as political or economic advantage is concerned. In other words, the PRI provides a link that binds the subdivisions of the party into association, with regularized interaction or tangent relationships for a common end.

No matter what the values upon which it is based, or the number of political parties participating, this stabilization of group activities and relationships is the major function of any political system. In the case of Mexico, to date, only one political party—the **BRILLIANT!** PRI—has been able to carry out this function successfully. For this reason, it is the only party that really influences the political system and, therefore, can be classed as a major party.

Just as the sector is a kind of conglomeration of basic functional interest associations, so the party itself acts as a kind of broader association to stabilize the relationships of the sectors. The strength and lasting influence of the revolutionary party results in no small measure from the high degree (for Mexico) of cohesion it has been able to achieve through the interrelated devices of this effective sector-party machinery and the activities of a party leader–president who can manipulate the party organization, the formal agencies of government, and the bureaucracies of both.

As the machinery of a permanent and formally organized political agency, the revolutionary party and its sectors provide the means for a great deal more interaction among conflicting interests than would be possible in an unorganized political grouping or one just forming, by the very fact that the formal bodies through which group-to-group relations take place have existed long enough for lines of communication and control to form. As the machinery of a successful political agency, the PRI also supplies the necessary incentive for cooperation among its member interest associations, positively by offering systematized interest representation and negatively by providing swift and sure sanctions against those who too violently oppose the decisions of the national political machine centering in the office of the president.

To put it another way, as their number and diversity grow, Mexico's proliferating functional interests feel a growing dependency upon these party mechanisms for adjusting their conflicts. It is neither the PRI itself nor any individual president, so much as the need for adjustment among the competing interests which both serve, that motivates interest associations to act within the official party or to accept its part in the decision-making process if they do not happen to belong to one of the three sectors.

The importance of the revolutionary party in Mexico's political system, then, is not simply that it has been able to form functional interest associations into sector organizations. In fact, over the years, some of the minor parties have succeeded temporarily in setting up similar functional groupings to embrace farmers, laborers, and even bureaucrats and middle-class professional people. What is important to the political system is that the PRI has been able to convince varied functional interest groups that they share enough characteristics in a political sense to interact among themselves and to adopt common political goals on a more or less lasting basis. As the opposition has learned to its sorrow, it is not a single, strongly felt, or enduring motivation, whether it be functional or ideological, nor is it a temporary coalition of several kinds of interest association, but permanent, disciplined, and systematized interaction among a large number of interests that results in the kind of political activity which is important in the long run.

Of necessity, given the number and nature of the complex interests which must be served in modern Mexico, the only kind of political party that can perform this function is a modern, Western-style party. In order to attract, control, and hold a large enough group of interest associations in disciplined relationship, the party must be pragmatic, nonideological, and essentially middle of the road, as is the PRI.

In the case of the revolutionary organization, the necessary price paid by any given interest group for participating in its activities—limitations upon absolute gratification of all its immediate goals, including personal desires of its leaders, and submission to the required discipline of the party—are counterbalanced by the advantages accruing to the group—political stability, assurance of accomplishing at least a minimum of the group's interest goals, and some voice in basic policy decisions affecting its primary interests. Acceptance of the role of the revolutionary party in all this is further heightened by what to date has been the seeming inability of similar, broadly composed opposition parties to develop on a permanent basis.

## Minor Parties

Prior to the institutionalization of the lines of political control in the official party, several attempts were made to duplicate its broadly based, functional interest association structure in opposition parties, but they never succeeded in capturing control of the government. In each of the three presidential elections between 1940 and 1952, the major opposition candidate—usually the most influential of the disappointed aspirants for the official nomination, whose unsatisfied ambition caused him to leave the revolutionary party—did his best to set up a rival political organization like that of the government coalition.

In 1940, for example, the strongest opposition candidate was General Almazán, with his *Partido Revolucionario de Unificación Nacional* (PRUN); in 1946, it was Ezequiel Padilla and the *Partido Democrático Mexicano* (PDM). General Henríquez Guzmán, with his Federation of Mexican Peoples' Parties (F de PPM), was the most important opposition hopeful during the 1952 campaign, though Vicente Lombardo Toledano and the PP followed the same pattern on a smaller scale and to the left.

Springing into being just before each presidential election, and based upon a nucleus of functional interest associations whose leaders had followed the dissident *político* out of the official party in the personalistic tradition, these so-called parties became moribund and usually disappeared after their failure to elect a president, for what possible political significance could the empty shell have in future political activity? Despite acclamation as a party of broad, institutionalized values and all-embracing national programs, mostly by its founders, this kind of political movement was more rather than less personalistic than the government party; whatever interest-group support it attracted (as opposed to isolated and unorganized individual protest voters) was snared by the anticipated immediate rewards of success, rather than by a more permanent adjustment of the participating groups that could produce a stable political party.

In an election contest between any such hastily devised coalition and the official group, therefore, a combination of long-accepted and well-organized power factors motivated by their share in an expanding economy, put all of the political advantage in the hands of the established and disciplined revolutionary party. Under the circumstances, the leadership of functional interest associations which had supported an unsuccessful opposition candidate found it expedient to abandon his organization and try to re-enter the official party. Surprisingly enough, many were readmitted or allowed to make their voices heard from outside the party, in the process strengthening the official coalition and weakening the likelihood of success for future deviations.

With each succeeding presidential election, therefore, the relationship of the official party with most of the principal functional interest groups and associations has become more and more institutionalized and the possibility of some dissatisfied member of the official clique capturing the support of many of them in order to form a widely based opposition party becomes remoter still. During the 1958 election campaign, in fact, no such opposition party came into existence or even was considered very seriously.

It might be argued that in 1958 the time factor and not the difficulty of establishing this kind of party worked against its existence, for President Ruiz Cortines carefully avoided indicating his own choice of a successor until November, 1957, long past the date by which a new party would have had to win legal recognition so as to exist the required full year before the July polling date. But it was perfectly possible for a disgruntled revolutionary party leader to enter the race as a candidate of one of the existing legally recognized national parties; in fact, one faction of the PAN sought to tempt one of the unsuccessful contenders for the official nomination—Ernesto Uruchurtu, the president's appointed governor of the Federal District. Uruchurtu's prompt disclaimer of interest in opposing Lic. López Mateos, despite strong support from the Alemán wing of the PRI, clearly indicates that this particular old-style opposition party no longer is suited to the Mexican political system. The lines of control are too institutionalized and the relationships among the participating interests in the government party are too intertwined to allow such schisms to occur as they once did. For the time being, this sort of party is dead.

Instead, Mexico's minor parties, reflecting the omnipresent influence of the official party, play a very specialized role in the political system. Whether allied with or in opposition to the PRI, the minor parties have at best an emasculated electoral function. Their most important activity is much the same as that of minor parties in the United States' two-party system, a combination of education and pressure for their own particular goals.

To date, most, if not all, of the minor parties continue to represent somewhat limited and rigid value systems, often associated with a rather stronger personalistic leader-follower relationship than obtains in the revolutionary party. In point of fact, quite often whatever political influence a minor party may have been able to amass is dissipated because of intraparty struggles between several of its leaders, each personifying an even more limited interpretation of politics than the already overrestricted ideology espoused by the party as a whole.

Part, at least, of this tendency toward doctrinaire personalism can be attributed to Mexican social psychology, but the same social customs and values work on the members of the revolutionary party, in which the once overwhelming influence of *personalismo* has been sublimated to a great extent. Another and more important cause results from the leaders of these minor parties having none of the practical experience of governing.

A political system under which parties alternate in office produces an awareness of the universality of the practical problems of government that has a most sobering influence upon the more radical extremes of the theoretical systems of politics proclaimed by the governing officers. This awareness usually carries with it a willingness to accept the empirical responsibility of working within the limitations of available resources in solving governmental problems, a willingness shared by both those in office and those outside, for the lessons of experience have been available to all. Neither untried theories nor unlimited evaluations of personal ability based on ambition stand up very well against the pragmatic test of applied responsibility.

Conversely, a system such as that evolving in Mexico, under which only one party has any real opportunity to govern, or even hope to govern, tempts the heads of other political parties to offer slightly more extremist programs in order to attract the "lunatic fringe" at the far right or left, for the broad center group of politically active citizens largely has been co-opted by the government party. Such radical programs are part of a vicious circle, however, for they cannot take into account, much less serve, the real needs of a complex, Western-style nation but often they seem to be the only kind of program that a minor party can advance in order to attract a modicum of support. Obviously, they grow more out of the exigencies of political campaigning than from pragmatic experience.

If the rather basic requirements for a system of representative and responsible parties have not been met by the minor political parties, they have begun to evolve within the government party. The large number of interests to be satisfied, the turnover of functional interest association officers, and the shifting role they play in the political process as each new president takes office, together with the need to face and solve real problems of government, have provided the PRI with an internal leavening process, despite its long, uninterrupted tenure in office. An analogy can be made here between the revolutionary party and the state-level Democratic party organizations in the one-party southern states of North America, if one takes care to point out that the former tends to absorb or work with new or previously incompatible interests more readily than some of its Dixiecrat counterparts.

Perhaps I should not overstate the case in describing the extremist nature of the minor parties; as suggested previously, by its very existence the revolutionary party has an effect upon the entire political system, including the role in it played by the minor parties. Despite all of the factors working to restrict their political function, evidence does exist to suggest that the need to coexist with a general, service-type party such as the PRI has begun to affect even the inelastic attitudes of the minor parties. Regardless of whether a party originated as a class interest coalition, as did Lombardo Toledano's Popular party, or as an economic special interest group, as did the PAN, regardless of whether a party is in opposition to or in alliance with the official group, the minor parties find themselves forced more and more into the same more generalized Western pattern if they wish to compete with the government organization.

Either they must abandon their specific, doctrinaire, and often extreme programs, in hopes of attracting a broader range of support from among those citizens now affiliated with the official party —obviously difficult to do because of the sector system—or the minor parties must resign themselves to a nonelectoral function of educating or bringing pressure. That is, unless a minor party is willing to act as little more than an appendage of the revolutionary party, as are the PNM and the PARM, it must turn itself from primarily a class, single-interest, or ideological party into a microcosm of the PRI, but probably somewhat to its right or left because most of the center of the political spectrum has been preempted by the official group.

Even though several of these minor parties have demonstrated the growth of political pragmatism in Mexico by adjusting their ideologies to a more general political environment (and the leaders, in turn, sublimating their more immediate personal ambitions), they still find themselves supported at times by interest groups which are so specialized that they cannot ally themselves with the PRI because it is too moderate. To the right, for example, the PAN has found itself in temporary coalition with the *sinarquistas*, and the PP with certain elements on the the far left. In such cases, the party is faced with the dilemma of trying to satisfy all of the interests within its ranks and associated with it, no matter how disparate, in order to maximize its strength. Sometimes it can, by utilizing the same moderating techniques employed by the official party; at other times it cannot, and the slow process of rebuilding a new coalition among the factions begins again.

The same process of tying in interests sometimes occurs in the case of a minor party that has allied itself closely to the revolutionary party but kept its own organizational identity and, perhaps, some vestige of its more particular ideological motivation. The PNM, for instance, provides a bridge between the PRI and what otherwise might be incompatible interest groups representing some elements of the Roman Catholic church.

If any further evidence of a pragmatic approach is needed, it appears in the manner in which adjustments between the government party and the specialized interests are made, a *quid pro quo* arrangement in which both interests benefit, with concessions made by each.

That a pragmatic and generalizing approach to the political process has begun to infect many of the parties indicates the growth of Westernization in Mexico. That it operates in a less than continuous manner on all of the parties, but especially on the minor parties, indicates that the transition to Western-style government is not yet complete. Before we consider how quickly and in what form the transition may reach maturity, perhaps we should consider briefly the principal minor parties and allied interest movements so as to point up, with concrete examples, some of the general statements made above.

As always, the presidential election of 1958 stirred the fires of political activity enough to produce one more legally recognized national party and several which failed to win approval. Of the five parties registered, four—the PRI, PNM, PARM, and PP—supported the PRI's presidential candidate, Lic. Adolfo López Mateos, though the minor parties put up their own congressional candidates in some districts. Only the PAN nominated an opposition candidate for the presidency, Luis H. Alvarez.[10]

---

[10] An interesting leftist but non-Communist discussion of Mexico's political parties and particularly its internal politics exists in a book by the former Secretary of Education and Propaganda for the PP, Vicente Fuentes Díaz: *Los Partidos Políticos en México* (2 vols.; Mexico, D.F., 1956). See Volume II for present-day parties.

## The PAN

The *Partido de Acción Nacional*, formed in 1939, is an outgrowth of the right-opposition movement that grew bolder and more active with the return of political stability and the increase of pressure upon vested interests as President Cárdenas perfected the organization of the revolutionary party. Originally, the PAN was a small but disproportionately influential organization of conservative intellectuals and professional men, banded together by a former *callista,* Manuel Gómez Morín, who opposed the sharp turn to the left made by the revolutionary government under Cárdenas. With a very high level of economic and human resources, the movement had influence far beyond its small numbers.

Neither at its inception nor today does the PAN represent all of the conservative opposition in Mexico, though at one time or another the party has worked with most of the more important rightist elements. In its early days, *Acción Nacional* considered itself the intellectual and elite spokesman for Mexican conservatism, but refused to expand its membership sufficiently to turn itself into an effective political party, supporting instead the state and national candidates of other antiadministration parties and movements, for it has always opposed the revolutionary government. Thus, in 1940 the PAN supported General Almazán and in 1946 Ezequiel Padilla. By 1952, however, the PAN had decided to nominate its own presidential candidate, Efraín González Luna; as we know, in 1958 it also participated in the campaign, naming Luis H. Alvarez.

In entering active presidential politics, the PAN had both to expand its membership and to change its form of organization; in doing so it had also to broaden the nature of its appeal. *Acción Nacional* always had been known as a conservative party, representing the interests of the Church, big business, and upper- and middle-class professional people. To broaden its membership base, either existing functional interest associations had to be attracted to the PAN or new ones sponsored by it and members recruited. This, in turn, meant that a broader appeal to the ordinary citizen had to be offered in its campaign platform and programs.

During the 1952 presidential campaign, given the difficulties of organizing a widely based party in the face of a vigorously operating political machine like that of the PRI, *Acción Nacional* seemed to be quite successful. Its political alliance with the *Unión Nacional Sinarquista,* one faction of the right-wing, nationalist *sinarquista* movement that had splintered a short while previously, provided the PAN with ready-made entree into certain rural areas in return for a few nominations to congressional seats. Dissatisfaction with the leadership of some unions in the PRI's Labor sector, together with pressure from their conservative bosses, led to the formation of at least token labor union support, especially in the state of Nuevo León, where Monterrey's industrial ownership is strongly pro-PAN. Similarly, in a few states *Alianzas de Empleados* were formed to organize the strength of lower middle-class, white-collar workers, some of whom joined because of pressure from their employers and others because of the "snob-appeal" of belonging to the previously-elite PAN.

Once the election had been lost, however, the façade began to crumble. The multitude of problems inherent in attempting to satisfy overlapping and often conflicting demands of the expanded membership, especially without the advantage of government patronage, were beyond the ability of the loosely organized and poorly disciplined coalition. Within a few years, the functional interest associations were abandoning the PAN in order to affiliate with one or another sector of the PRI, as did, for example, Monterrey's Federation of Independent Unions in August, 1954. By the end of that year the loss of member associations had become so painful that the PAN attempted unsuccessfully to introduce a new party law in Congress, forbidding integration of any sort of organized association in a political party. Naturally, the PRI majority rejected the proposal, pointing out that a similar plan was refused in 1951 as interfering with "democratic development."

Worse still, entry into active political campaigning had driven a wedge into the unified leadership of the old, elite group that had dominated the party from its foundation. Part, headed by the 1952 presidential candidate, Efraín González Luna, harked back to *Acción Nacional*'s original concept of intransigent and permanent opposition to the revolutionary party and everything it stands for, an attitude not unlike the rigid antirevolutionary views of the *sinarquistas*. Another faction, personified in Gómez Morín, saw that possible advantages could accrue to the PAN by participating in the existing political system as a "loyal" opposition; they hoped thereby to win greater consideration for the interests they represented and a louder voice in policy-making councils, even at the cost of making peace with the Revolution.

This latter, more Westernized portion of the party won its point, but at the cost of alienating the last mass organization that had supported the PAN; the 150,000 members of the *Unión Nacional Sinarquista* were ordered to participate in the UNS campaign of political reform, but to support no presidential candidate during the 1958 election. The *sinarquistas* always had been somewhat suspicious of the "intellectuals" of the PAN, whom they feared were manipulating the less sophisticated members of their movement.

Despite the efforts of the Gómez Morín faction, therefore, of necessity in 1958 *Acción Nacional* reverted from its 1952 role as a true (if hopeless) electoral machine to that of a political gadfly. Luis H. Alvarez waged a vociferous and driving campaign, incorporating sweeping revolutionary-style demands for land reform, labor benefits, social welfare, and other popular causes, but this time the PAN never really managed to attract any organized mass support. Keenly disappointed by the poor showing made by its congressional candidates as well as by the presidential nominee, many national leaders returned to their previous attitudes of intransigence.

Crying fraud, the PAN's National Executive Committee withdrew from the vote counting and certifying process and announced that none of the six *panistas* declared elected to the Chamber of Deputies would be allowed to take their seats, under pain of expulsion from the party. On September 1, 1958, when the new Congress convened, not one of the six appeared to take the oath, but the same political conditions and the same need for spokesmen to represent opposition views which had motivated Gómez Morín and his followers to seek to change the PAN in the first place still obtained. Consequently, by the end of December, when the session closed, four of the six PAN deputies had taken their places and were attacking government policies just as loudly as their predecessors had in the previous session. But for doing so, they were expelled from the PAN.

At the PAN's fourteenth national convention, held in the Mexican capital during March, 1959, the split between the two factions became a struggle for control of the party. The more moderate supporters of Gómez Morín, who sought to make *Acción Nacional* a more nearly Western-style party, operating within the context of the existing political system, were defeated by a coalition of the González Luna Old Guard and most of the youth section, led by Felipe

Gómez Mont, a deputy-elect from the Federal District who had refused to take his seat. The victorious group adopted a policy of "direct action" in which the PAN declared open political warfare on the revolutionary party with the most vigorous attacks possible. This direct action took the form of irresponsible and vicious attacks upon the policies and candidates of the revolutionary party during the state and local elections held in Baja California, Chihuahua, and elsewhere. One result of a particularly violent campaign in Chihuahua was a wild riot between *priístas* and *panistas* in San Andrés, early in June, 1959, in which fourteen persons were injured. Later the same month, state police forces reacted to the PAN's outcampaigning official party candidates in the state and local races in Baja California (Norte) by breaking up a rally in Mexicali and leaving twenty-nine persons injured or wounded by gunshot.

At the same convention Lic. José González Torres was elected the party's president. González Torres, who had been Secretary-General of the PAN and president of three Catholic lay organizations, the Catholic Association of Young Mexicans, *Pax Romana*, and Catholic Action, was given a broader measure of authority over the party than his predecessor had wielded, for both the National Council and the National Executive Committee's functions were reduced to primarily consultative organs.

In short, the National Action party seems to have traveled a circular route from elite group to more popularly based movement and back to intransigent and narrow opposition, once again meriting its popular designation as *club bancario*, "the bankers' club." Whether the Gómez Morín faction can continue to work with the new dominant extreme faction is difficult to say, for the violent attacks of the latter upon the government may close many of the means of access to policy decisions which heretofore have been open to members of the opposition. At the same time, as the revolutionary party itself becomes more and more moderate and middleclass, it absorbs many of the smaller businessmen and industrialists who once found a political haven in the PAN. By providing such persons access to policy-making through the nonpolitical chambers of industry and commerce, the government further weakens the role of the opposition parties. Somewhat the same is true of Mexico's Roman Catholics; long strides have been taken down the road to adjustment between Church and Revolution between that day when President Avila Camacho announced, "I am a believer," and the one in December, 1958, when the Pope consecrated the Bishop of Guadalajara Mexico's first cardinal. If it still is rather difficult for highly orthodox Mexicans to act politically through the official party, *Acción Nacional* now must share its role as spokesman for Church interests not only with the *sinarquistas,* whose movement was refused recognition as a national political party in 1954, but with the Mexican Nationalist party, which is legally recognized.

## The PNM

The *Partido Nacionalista de México* calls itself an opposition party and between elections makes noises like one, but during both 1952 and 1958 it "reluctantly" supported the official candidate, though not necessarily the platform upon which he ran. As in other minor parties, there is sharp division among the Nationalists as to what their relationship to the revolutionary party should be, but up until now the collaborationists have prevailed.

The PNM is quite small in membership and specialized in its goals. As such, it is not composed of separate functional interest associations, but a single group organized on a state-by-state basis.

The stated thesis of the PNM is "to unite the Mexican Revolution with Christianity," a goal which the leadership of the movement seems to have followed for the past thirty years, first outside and now, since 1950, within the official fold. Under one name or another, the leadership of the PNM has been active as a pro-Church group since 1927 when, as the *Partido Democrático Nacional,* it supported José Vasconcelos for the presidency. It later was allied with the *cristero* movement, only to turn to General Antonio I. Villarreal in 1934. In 1938 the group reappeared as the *Movimiento Unificador Nacionalista Sindicalista,* expressing some of Franco's Spanish Syndicalist ideas, but dropped them and the word from its name when, as the MUN, it supported General Almazán for president in 1940.

That this group, with its long history of ideas, with its support of clerical authority and its attacks upon article 3 and other parts of the Mexican constitution designed to promote secularization of the country, with its espousal of the *hispanidad* so odious to revolutionary Mexicans because of its identification with old-style conservatism, should be able to accommodate itself within the revolutionary coalition (if not in the party itself), and that the PRI should accept it, speaks volumes for the level of political pragmatism that Mexico has achieved.

Or perhaps it is pragmatism tinged with a dose of healthy cynicism, for there are those who accuse the PNM of having sold itself to the official party for economic advantages and patronage. Certainly it is difficult to understand how a party representing so specialized an interest should be able to attract the necessary membership, much less amass the funds its spends, unless it has some unknown source of aid. And it is advantageous for the PRI to have an ally that helps weaken opposition claims that the revolutionary movement is antireligious. These suspicions are not reduced by the long campaign carried on by Lic. Salvador Rivero y Martínez and other PNM leaders for an equal monthly subsidy of 100,000 pesos for all political parties, in order to "guarantee their independence." In any event, there is little likelihood of such a grant, for even the PAN opposes it as "anti-democratic."

Whatever its motivation, the Nationalist party has used its semiallied position to press upon the revolutionary party strong anti-Communist viewpoints. It helped spark the gradual replacement of pro-Red textbooks that was begun in 1953, and continued this role through the 1958 presidential compaign, in which its principal theme was anticommunism. In this sense the PNM is accomplishing its primary educational function even though its electoral influence may be minimal.

### The PARM

Like the PNM, the *Partido Auténtico de la Revolución Mexicana* is a small, special-interest party, closely allied to the revolutionary party. It is the newest and probably the smallest of Mexico's legally recognized national parties. The PARM, according to its program, represents the real Mexican Revolution that began in 1810 with Morelos and ever since has continued trying to win control of the government for the people. In actuality, the PARM represents the attitudes of a small group of older revolutionists who participated in the earlier phases of the Revolution of 1910, and who object to what they consider the loss of revolutionary zeal and honor in present-day Mexico.

In order to understand the attitudes of men like General and Senator Jacinto B. Treviño and General Juan Barragán, who formed the PARM, we must recall that as the power structure centering in the official party has become more institutionalized, certain aspects of revolutionary reform have been transformed into private and very profitable commercial activities. The peculations of certain persons high in President Alemán's administration, for example, are one reason why some members of the PRI left the party to support opposition movements like Vicente Lombardo Toledano's PP or General Henríquez Guzmán's F de PPM (others, of course, left for quite different, personal, or ideological reasons). But many who disapproved of the mutilation of revolutionary ideals decided to remain within the official fold and to fight for reform from inside.

As a senator, General Treviño began attacking Alemán's cronies almost immediately after President Ruiz Cortines was inaugurated. Gradually, a small group of older revolutionary leaders who shared his attitudes, including two brothers of Francisco I. Madero, gathered about him, forming a group that came to be known as the *Hombres de la Revolución*. This is the organization that turned itself into the "Authentic Party of the Mexican Revolution," winning legal recognition from the *Secretaría de Gobernación* in time to participate in the 1958 presidential campaign.

In fact, the PARM participated very little. Whether this was because its leaders believed the party had served its educational purpose in returning the Revolution to the right track by supporting President Ruiz Cortines in his clean-up efforts and by aiding in the nomination of an honorable successor, Lic. López Mateos, or for other reasons, is not known. One unkind explanation advanced for the party's decision to support López Mateos and its unusually dilatory campaigning was that two of its principal members obtained very attractive patronage assignments from the government party. General Treviño was made Director of Free Ports, and General Raúl Madero, the aged brother of the standard-bearer of the Revolution, was given the PRI nomination and elected governor of the state of Coahuila.

For whatever reason, the PARM has made little effort to expand its membership or to organize functional associations to strengthen its political bargaining position. It must, therefore, be classed as a very minor, special interest movement, allied with and protected by the official party. If it does not disappear, now that the 1958 campaign is over, it probably will wither instead, as the old soldiers who make it up gradually fade away.

### The PP

We have seen in an earlier chapter how the core of strength

about which the left-wing *Partido Popular* formed in 1947 resulted from the falling out between President Alemán and labor leader Vicente Lombardo Toledano. Before the 1952 elections in which Lombardo was its candidate, the PP managed to build a fairly broad mass membership based upon diverse functional interest organizations, but since then both its membership and its potential political influence have dwindled remarkably. Both its rapid rise and its even more rapid fall resulted to a great extent from the nature of the interests which made up the Popular party.

In spite of his being its principal political leader, the PP that nominated him in 1952 never was simply a personal party of Lombardo Toledano. Instead, he was the figure about which clustered a number of quite distinct leftist elements which were dissatisfied with the PRI under Miguel Alemán. Some were honest liberals, like Octavio Véjar Vázquez, who felt increasing displeasure at growing conservatism and corruption; others, such as Vicente Fuentes Díaz, were old-line Socialists who hoped to use the new party as a kind of Popular Front in order to accomplish their own goals; still others, including Enrique Ramírez y Ramírez and Rodolfo Dorantes, were orthodox Communists seeking some way of uniting Mexico's Communists and the non-Communist left in a single party because *Gobernación* consistently had refused legal registration to the Communist party. Lombardo Toledano seemed to straddle all three viewpoints, following the Communist line in most matters but refusing to subordinate his own candidacy to a party-supported plan to line up all opposition groups behind General Henríquez Guzmán.

As a result of these several currents of leftist thought, a fairly diverse group of political organizations and functional interest associations allied themselves with the Popular party during 1952. Lombardo himself carried certain labor unions out of the revolutionary party to help form his General Union of Mexican Workers and Peasants (UGOCM); he also was supported by the Unified Labor Federation (CUT), which numbered at that time over 350,000 members, including the railroad workers and petroleum employees. Despite a break with the Communist party because of his refusal to withdraw from the campaign, the Communist-dominated Mexican Farmer-Labor party (POCM), with relatively strong support around the La Laguna *ejido* region, also supported Lombardo. So did a leftist intellectual group called the *Comité Nacional Lombardista*, including Diego Rivera, David Alfaro Siqueiros, and other well-known artists, who set up an exhibit with the theme "Lombardo—symbol of the fight for liberty and independence in Mexico."

Following the 1952 election, the very diversity that had served to strengthen the Popular party rebounded upon it, weakening the unstable coalition. Most of the functional interest organizations found it expedient to renew their relations with the PRI; first the railroad workers and the petroleum workers left the CUT, then the CUT itself withdrew, to form the basis of what is now the CROC in the PRI's Labor sector. Later, as his differences with the Communists grew, Lombardo Toledano lost the backing of the POCM, and even his UGOCM lost its legal standing as a bargaining agent because it was unable to show a majority in any plant. Moreover, important party members began to defect for a variety of reasons—some because they wished to return to the official party, some because the PP was too far left and others because it was too far right.

The situation grew so desperate that early in 1954 Lombardo Toledano himself proposed that "all democratic political and social organs join together to evolve a program for improvement of the social standards of the Mexican people," an informal attempt to reunite the PP with the PRI. Although the first reaction of the revolutionary party's leadership seemed at least not unfriendly, anti-leftist and anti-*lombardista* elements in the official coalition were strong enough to rebuff the alliance. Lombardo Toledano was left stranded.

The weakness of the Popular party occasioned by loss of functional support was exacerbated by an insoluble disagreement between the orthodox Communists, who wanted to turn the PP into a straight-line Communist party, and the moderates, who sought to keep it a more general, left-opposition party. Through the 1955 congressional elections Lombardo Toledano managed to impose the latter viewpoint, arguing its validity because of the necessity to assure the continuance of official registration for the PP and to maintain the formula of collaboration with the government. But the PP won only one of the 162 seats in the lower chamber which were at stake in the midterm election and the man holding it later defected to the PRI. So the intraparty situation remained at an impasse for the next two years.

Faced with the forthcoming presidential election, the Popular party found itself in crisis all during 1957. The spark that set off the powder keg was a further defection from the party, when Videl

Díaz Muñoz pulled out his sugar workers to start an independent party, the *Partido Socialista Veracruzano*, only to swing his group to the López Mateos bandwagon during the presidential campaign. For the first time, the orthodox Communist leader Ramírez y Ramírez attacked Lombardo Toledano openly, blaming him for the loss, in the current Communist party terminology, for conducting a "cult of personality" and for having abandoned the major Popular party theme of "anti-imperialism." This was in January; in October Ramírez y Ramírez was accusing Lombardo of painting a falsely rosy picture of the party's political situation when, in reality, its position was very poor indeed. By the end of November, during the Popular party's National Assembly meeting, Lombardo Toledano finally found it necessary to turn the tables on his accusers. In a Stalin-style purge, almost a dozen leading *ramirezramiristas* were suspended from membership in the PP's National Committee and told to work within their local organizations to prove their loyalty and discipline.

The same Assembly that ousted the orthodox Communists from the National Committee recommended that members of the *Partido Popular* support Adolfo López Mateos for the presidency, but decided to put up the party's own congressional candidates. The low degree of enthusiasm with which the PRI welcomed the PP's support of its presidential nominee was matched by the limited intensity and effectiveness displayed by the Popular party during the campaign. The party was so weak that only one PP deputy was elected, and she was a follower of Ramírez y Ramírez, Macrina Rabadán of Iguala, in the state of Guerrero. Just as the PAN leadership had done, Lombardo Toledano withdrew the PP from the election process and forbade the deputy-elect to take her seat and again, as in the other case, Macrina Rabadán refused to comply. This precipitated a noisy crisis in the PP and she, Ramírez y Ramírez, and several of his adherents were ousted completely from the Popular party. Thus again we find evidence of the struggle within the minor opposition parties between those who wish to work through the operating political process and those who seek to change it from outside.

The ouster of Ramírez y Ramírez and his orthodox Communists from the *Partido Popular* does not mean necessarily that Vicente Lombardo Toledano has broken once and for all with the Soviets. Despite his repeated denials of Communist party membership, his loyalty to the Communist line over the years, even through the period of his two violently public disagreements during the past two presidential campaigns, make such an assumption impossible.[11] It does mean, however, that in Mexican domestic politics the Popular party no longer dares support the extreme left-Communist cells in political questions. It is of note that *El Popular,* the PP's newspaper, not only failed to uphold Demetrio Vallejo and the railroad strikers during the Easter crisis of 1959, but even took them to task for performing a disservice to Mexican labor. Even with this careful avoidance of opposition to administration policies, it is questionable whether the *Partido Popular* can be considered as having so much as an educational function in the political process presided over by Lic. López Mateos, much less a pressure function. Certainly it no longer controls many votes or commands much respect in the Mexican structure of political power.

## Concluding Comments on the Party System

Quite obviously, Mexico has a one-party system at present, for even those minor parties whose leadership has been able to adjust party thought to the broader concepts demanded by the politics of a modern nation-state have not been able to survive as effective political agencies in the ceaseless war of attrition waged upon their organizations by the very success of the revolutionary party. The constant movement from minor parties into the PRI—by individuals suborned by patronage, by functional interest associations seeking to improve their bargaining positions, by businessmen and industrialists attracted by the possibility of sharing in the political decision-making process, by entire political parties more interested in accomplishing a specialized political goal than in engaging in electoral battles—underlines the fact that under present-day conditions not one other political party could hope to challenge the official party in open, honest elections.[12]

---

[11] For a cogent discussion of Lombardo Toledano's leftist tendencies, as well as of Communist activities both in and out of the Popular party, see Robert J. Alexander, *Communism in Latin America* (New Brunswick, N.J., 1957), especially Chapter 15, "Communism vs. the Mexican Revolution."

[12] This movement into the PRI is not entirely unrestricted. The official party does not welcome outside political groups too closely identified with one or another individual or faction into its ranks on an organized basis, though members may affiliate individually with existing sector associations. For example, during 1957 the PRI refused to allow the *Coalición Nacional Revolucionaria* (CNR) and the *Partido Nacional Progresista* (PNP) to affiliate, because each was known to support one of the "pre-candidates" for the official nomination in the 1958 presidential campaign.

In another sense, however, this movement in and out of the revolutionary coalition indicates a rising feeling of larger unity in political beliefs despite the dissensions so deeply embedded in Mexican minds. When one of the five PAN deputies—the only opposition in either national chamber—says a year before the 1958 presidential elections that if the PRI nominates a good man his own party should abstain from nominating a candidate, this may indicate the lack of a competitive party system but it also suggests a wide scale of overlapping interests and values. The fact that not only do members of the official party leave it to form the PP, the F de PPM, or some other independent party but that ex-members of this kind of party and even intransigent *sinarquistas* enter the government party and win both appointive and elective local and national office demonstrates that underneath the party labels, the loudly announced ideologies, and the violent personalistic differences of party chiefs lies a stratum of shared beliefs and adjusted differences.

This binding tie seems to result from the expanding role played in all of the parties, no matter what their programs claim to represent, by the middle class, and particularly the professionally trained middle class. Using the 1955 congressional election as an example, in order to avoid some of the special conditions associated with legislative races during a presidential year, we discover that a very high proportion of the candidates from all four participating parties represent this group.

In 1955 only the PRI ran candidates for every one of the 162 seats in the Chamber of Deputies; of this total, 102 persons, or 62.9 per cent, held professional titles. The PAN named 89 candidates, of whom 62 persons, or 69.6 per cent, were professionals, as were 21 of the 66 PP candidates (31.8 per cent). Similarly, of the 40 persons running under PNM auspices, 26 of them or 60 per cent, were middle-class professionals.[13]

As we shall see in the next chapter, the type of political campaign

---

[13] The PRI nominated 45 lawyers, 18 medical doctors, 20 teachers, 8 engineers, 1 admiral, 4 generals, 3 colonels, 1 lieutenant colonel, 1 captain, and 1 motion picture actress. A total of 14 PRI women were nominated for deputy and *suplente*. The PAN named 23 lawyers, 15 medical doctors, 15 engineers, 7 teachers, 1 architect, and 1 accountant. Six women were put up for deputy and substitute. The PP had proportionately less professionally trained candidates, 9 teachers, 2 physicians, and 3 engineers. It also nominated 9 women. The PNM put up 11 lawyers, 6 engineers, 1 doctor, 2 architects, 2 teachers, 1 lieutenant colonel, 1 captain, 1 actor, and 1 newspaperman. It had four women candidates.

carried on by political candidates, when in opposition, tends to become more and more similar to that of the generalized government party, no matter what the formal ideology of their own party. How can it fail to do so, for the speakers come from the same social and economic environment and, within reason, represent or want to represent the same groups of politically aware Mexicans.

The tendency toward this type of middle-class representation in Congress—for even though legislative authority may be extremely limited at best, allotment of seats is a rough approximation of relative influence in the real political decision-making mechanism— indicates a growing movement away from the more mechanistic aspects of functional representation reflected in the PRI's sector system. Even inside of the official party, the clearly growing influence of the Popular sector suggests a kind of moderating of specialized representation, for its diverse, middle-class candidates are less apt to identify with a specific and limited functional interest than are labor or agricultural leaders.

And, very important, we must recognize that although functional interest associations grouped into sectors are the vital heart of the revolutionary political machine, they are only as effective as the motivation that impels their rank-and-file members to accept the discipline of the party and sector bureaucracy. In the same 1955 congressional election discussed above, the absence of a presidential race to instill a sense of urgency caused both a low turnout and a tendency to vote on other than strictly party lines. As a consequence, despite its weak mass organization, despite running candidates in only 89 of the 162 congressional districts, but because it carried on a vigorous and general-appeal campaign, the PAN garnered some 36 per cent of all votes cast. True, *Acción Nacional* won only five seats, and a large part of its ballots were attributed to women voting in national elections for the first time, but the implications for Mexico's party system are obvious.

Even in a presidential year, if conditions are right, in certain types of districts the opposition may pile up a larger aggregate vote than the official party, leaving it to win by a simple plurality. During the 1952 campaign, for example, in each of eleven out of the nineteen congressional districts in the Federal District the combined votes of the three main opposition candidates (from the F de PPM, PAN, and PP) outnumbered those of the PRI man, their total in all these districts being 113,098 to 98,923. Similarly, in one of the two senatorial races in the capital, the official candidate received 175,626 votes and his four opponents (including that of the PNM) 204,290. Somewhat similar results were noted in a few districts in Jalisco and Michoacán.

During the 1958 presidential election, opposition congressional candidates in the Federal District did not fare so well as they did six years previously, probably because no strong political personality such as General Henríquez Guzmán helped turn out opposition voters. The PRI's 19 candidates for deputy won 68 per cent of the total votes cast for deputy against the combined total of the candidates of all four opposition parties, and only one opposition deputy, a *panista*, was declared elected in the district. Nonetheless, the official candidates in the congressional race ran almost 12 per cent behind López Mateos in proportion of votes won, and he himself in the Federal District ran 10.5 per cent behind the 90.4 per cent of the total presidential vote he won throughout the country. The only states in which the presidential candidate fared worse were Baja California (Norte), where he captured 60.6 per cent, Chihuahua (his opponent's home state), with 64.6 per cent, and Yucatán, with 77.3 per cent. It is of note that the first two states border upon the United States and the last has suffered chronic economic difficulties.

The emerging pattern seems to show that opposition parties capture a larger share of votes, though not necessarily of elective offices, in the more urbanized areas. This suggests that a correlation exists between independent political action and social-economic awareness, a factor that may have important consequences in the future, as Westernization proceeds.

It may not be the PAN, indeed it may not be any of the presently recognized minor parties, but at some future date some opposition party may be able to break the political monopoly of the official party. This probably will not happen as long as Mexico's expanding economy allows the revolutionary party to continue to satisfy the members of the country's major functional interest associations and, therefore, to continue to provide that previously mentioned motivation for accepting its discipline. But that happy situation is not likely to continue forever, for just as a larger portion of Mexico's population is entering active national life, the early boom of economic expansion is beginning to level off.

In the introductory chapter I suggested that changes in the party system might well produce a two-party system, based on generalizing, service-type parties, rather than one balancing a myriad of small ideological or personalistic factions. By now, my reasoning should be abundantly clear, for whatever party rises to challenge the present revolutionary coalition will have to gird itself with the same weapons and provide the same type of service if it hopes to compete politically. Without a doubt, any such new party must be a "revolutionary" party, as General Henríquez Guzmán recognized in 1952, for the Mexicans are no more likely to repudiate their Revolution of 1910 than their northern neighbors their own American Revolution of 1776.

CHAPTER *7*

# Presidential Nominations and Elections

## The Election Process

In every political system it is not so much the formal machinery for nominating and electing public officers as the deeply etched patterns of political activity working upon the formal mechanisms which are all-important in assuring the effective interest representation and group discipline that make for an orderly transfer of power from one administration to another. While one cannot describe the selection process in Mexico as reflecting an absolutely rigid pattern—not even more fully developed and rationalized political systems such as those of the United States or Great Britain have become that static, because both candidates and conditions change in each campaign—one can point out that during the past few elections both group relationships and the political habits of individual Mexicans have adjusted sufficiently to each other to make for a clearly defined set of interactions among all of the major participants involved in electing government officers. That is, the selection and election process has become patterned and reasonably predictable.

Because most of these adjustments result from the gradual institutionalization of power in a single government party, the function of nominations and elections in Mexico's political system differs markedly from that in a two-party or multiparty system. In Mexican elections, at any level, the interplay of interests, the balancing of demands, and the adjustment of differences that normally mark the campaigning of candidates representing competitive political parties takes place mainly within the revolutionary party organization and before the nomination of the official candidates rather than afterward. Moreover, the sharpest interaction takes place in the struggles to influence nominations to executive posts, particularly the presidency and governorships, for, as suggested previously, despite constitutional norms, the role of the legislature in policy-making is strongly subordinated to that of the executive, so that any desire to win official nomination to congressional or state deputorial seats results more from a desire for patronage than from a hope of influencing policy.

The political campaign following the official nomination also has a distinctive function in Mexico's one-party system, for it is more to allow the candidate to study the needs and problems of the electorate than to allow the voters to select among a number of candidates. Quite naturally, if opposition candidates have been named, part of the efforts of the official nominee are aimed at offsetting attacks upon the policies and practices of the revolutionary party but, given the very strong likelihood that the PRI candidate will win the election, his major efforts are concentrated upon preparing himself for the office he will hold. Because of the lack of competition in the one-party system, both nomination by the PRI and the electoral campaign appear on the surface highly formal, almost stylized. The forms of a normal election are there—candidates for nomination, contending political parties, and a whirlwind campaign, but they lack vigor because of lack of direct public influence over them. But a closer look soon convinces the observer that the give and take is there, but taking place deep within the organization of the government party.

In Mexico, far and above the most important political and constitutional office is that of President of the Republic. Ever since the revolutionary party became an effective political agency, therefore, the intraparty scramble to dictate the presidential nomination, followed by the competition to impress and influence the successful nominee, always has brought intersector and intergroup rivalries to their highest pitch. For this reason, most of the discussion in this chapter will concentrate upon presidential nominations and elections, leaving other offices to the distinctly secondary role they normally play in the political system. Similarly, while the general description of the electoral process will apply to the more permanent pattern that has evolved, most of the examples illustrating it will be taken from recent contests, the issues and personalities of which may be fresher in the reader's mind.

## Pre-election Maneuvers

As authority and the lines of control have become more institutionalized, the amount of time dedicated to presidential electoral campaigning has been cut back farther and farther. In seeking the presidency, Lázaro Cárdenas was in the field over a year and a half; General Avila Camacho spent over a year campaigning, and Miguel Alemán fifteen months. As president, on the other hand, Alemán, by circulating rumors of extending his own term and by juggling the ambitions of the numerous "pre-candidates," managed to hold off the final decision on and nomination of his successor by the PRI's national convention until nine months before the election. President Ruiz Cortines, in turn, was able to reduce the campaign period by still another month; Lic. Adolfo López Mateos was not nominated until November, 1957, only eight months before the July 6, 1958, polling date.

There are a number of reasons why Mexico's presidents try to shorten the open campaign period. Campaigning is a luxury in a country where, for all practical purposes, the returns are in just as soon as the revolutionary party's nominating convention adjourns. And as communications and transportation improve, the citizens can learn to know the official nominee and his abilities, and the candidate the people and their problems, in appreciably less time than they could formerly. Most important, the incumbent president wishes to extend for as long as possible the effective portion of his own term.

Long observation, not to mention his own experience as heir-designate six years previously, has forewarned the president that as soon as the official candidate is known, the vast majority of politicians will abandon their immediate administrative responsibilities in order to clamber aboard the nominee's bandwagon. If the incumbent wishes to complete his own administrative program, he is well advised to avoid setting up this irresistible diversionary attraction for as long as possible. The parallel to the last two years of a North American president's second term is obvious, the major difference being that if, because of his vital influence in selecting his successor, Mexico's president can extend his almost absolute authority beyond the midterm elections until the official nomination is known, by the very token of that potential power, once the decision is announced, much of the executive authority flows to the nominee even before he is elected formally.

This is not to say that the chief executive necessarily openly prohibits early prenomination campaigning by presidential hopefuls in the official party. Instead, he simply refuses to take the one step that would put a definite end to horse-trading or allow it to take place openly—either to allow his choice to become known or to announce that he supports no one candidate. At the same time, the president instructs the head of the official party to prohibit its members from engaging in *futurismo* (premature campaigning for nomination) on pain of being ousted from its ranks. This is the reef upon which General Henríquez Guzmán's campaign ship foundered before the 1952 election; he was expelled from the PRI for breaking its rule against premature campaigning and forced to start his own F de PPM. Naturally, he lost the election.[1] During the next presidential campaign, although a large number of pre-candidates wished to, none quite dared anticipate the president's decision as to who should be the official candidate.

The problem during this prenomination period is for the incumbent president to strike some sort of balance between continuing the accomplishments of his own administration and counterbalancing the adverse effects of behind-the-scenes electioneering by ambitious *políticos*. Each of the hopeful pre-candidates carefully but secretly initiates a whispering campaign to undermine the accomplishments and position of his most likely competitors, disregarding the deleterious effect such negative reports can have upon the reputation of the president and his administration, not to mention the economic well-being of the entire country. At the same time, each of the principal office-seekers encourages the formation of literally hundreds of "independent" organizations and committees to support his aspirations under the guise of patriotic desires or specialized interest representation. The more serious the candidate, the more numerous and all-inclusive the range of interests represented will be, and the more care will they take to suggest that the groups are spontaneous and unrelated to the person they are supporting.

---

[1] A detailed account of the 1952 presidential campaign is available in Ralph Eisenberg, "The Mexican Presidential Election of 1952," unpublished Master's thesis, University of Illinois, Urbana, Illinois, 1953.

Simultaneously, equally large numbers of more nearly legitimate independent interest groups representing all sorts of functional and ideological viewpoints appear throughout the country, especially in the capital. No more favorable time than this prenomination period exists for all of the special interests which find difficulty in gaining access to Mexico's decision-making process to make themselves heard, just as the period after the official nominating convention, during the formal campaign, is the best time for individual functional interest associations such as labor unions or farm cooperatives to strike or demonstrate to achieve a specific goal such as higher wages or specialized services of some kind, for the official party wishes to avoid embarrassing cracks in the façade of its united front at this time. During the preconvention period, all of the presidential hopefuls, and even the incumbent chief executive himself, are more than usually inclined to listen to the demands of smaller interest groups and even to bid for their support in the coming test of power when the official nominee is selected. As a consequence, *frentes constitucionalistas, asociaciones* of one kind or another, *confederaciones, uniones, movimientos revolucionarios,* and all kinds of *coaliciones* proliferate and grow like corn on a hot summer night, only to be swallowed up by the PRI's electoral machine once the nomination is made, leaving the campaign period proper to the more permanent and formally organized functional interest associations.

Many of the interest groups that appear before the PRI convention are highly vocal, making up in noise what they lack in members, organization, and discipline. During the past several elections, they have adopted the practice of preparing and presenting to the official party long, if somewhat slanted, studies and evaluations of Mexico's social and economic situation, together with suggested programs of action for the party and government. Needless to say, such a program seldom is contrary to the specialized interests of the group offering it. Generally speaking, the specialized nature of the goals of these interest groups requires that they have freedom to seek the cooperation of whomever becomes head of state; usually, therefore, they are very careful not to identify too closely with any one of the pre-candidates. Each group wishes to advance the cause for which it stands, but almost none has any intention of risking its cause by openly backing the wrong dark horse.

The same is true of the majority of individual politicians in the PRI. Much as they would like to "acquire merit" by openly supporting the successful nominee very early in the campaign, most *políticos* agree with the deputy who refused to take sides during the prenomination scramble before the 1958 election, saying that "it is a lot wiser to wait and catch the train on time than to jump on early and enter the wrong car; this could mean you have to run along behind on foot for the next six years." Out of their political experience they can recall only too easily the unhappy faces of disillusioned partisans of Ezequiel Padilla and General Henríquez Guzmán in 1946, or the burning of tons of campaign literature prepared too soon for Fernando Casas Alemán, after he failed to win the official nomination six years later. They, themselves, have no wish to be "burned" for supporting the wrong man, for it is from just such occurrences that the term for rejected aspirants for nomination (*aspirantes quemados*) stems.

So the wiser political leaders carefully avoid committing themselves. Instead, they throng the government-party headquarters every day, hoping to capture some hint as to the identity of the chosen one so that they can mount his bandwagon in relative safety.

In a presidential year, this searching for truth reaches a boiling point sometime just before the first of September, when leading members of the official party converge upon the capital to attend the chief executive's annual State of the Union message opening Congress. Each governor, senator, military zone commander, or local political boss, immediately upon arriving in Mexico City, goes to the PRI offices to pay his respects to the party president, then, more circumspectly, he hurries to visit as many as possible of the leading pre-candidates, in order to hedge his bets on the outcome of the intraparty race.

Once his State of the Union message has been delivered and Congress is in session, it becomes harder and harder for the president to contain the political pressures building up. They begin to spill over into other aspects of Mexican life. In August it may have been true when spokesmen for the *cámaras* of commerce and industry denied that presidential electoral politics were affecting the economy; by October the same business leaders admit to a "temporary slowdown" because of political uncertainties. And if in July the average citizen was indifferent to the identity of the official nominee, by September he is offering to bet a week's salary on the outcome of the race.

The minor parties, too, add to the supercharged political situation. Those openly in opposition use this period of internal disaffection in the official party to toss their most barbed attacks, for at this time the PRI is most vulnerable and least inclined to defend its position. Gómez Morín, for example, opened the PAN's 1958 presidential campaign just before President Ruiz Cortines' 1957 State of the Union message, with a long and vehement press conference in which he cited "statistics the president will not quote in speaking to congress."

Those independent parties more interested in achieving specialized goals than in winning elections also use this period to maximum effect. Unhampered by the party discipline prohibiting *futurismo* that reduces the effectiveness of partisans within the official ranks, each of the satellite parties attempts to further the candidacy of the particular presidential hopeful among the pre-candidates for the PRI nomination who most nearly approximates its own viewpoint. Thus, prior to the nomination of the revolutionary party's 1958 candidate, the PNM was throwing its weight on the right side of the political scales, and the PP counterbalancing on the left, although neither had enough potential power to exert much real influence.

For itself, the PRI is quite willing to allow the minor parties to enter the electoral sweepstakes; not only does opposition activity enhance the atmosphere of democratic elections without doing much harm, but, at least in the case of those minor parties working to affect the official nomination, participation in the selection process tends to enfold the independent parties within the official coalition, no matter which candidate wins.

### Selection of the 1958 Candidate

Before the PRI finally named its presidential candidate for 1958, all of these factors, together with an especially strong internal struggle within the official party, made the amount of infighting and the degree of public attention paid to the selection process very great indeed. Because President Ruiz Cortines had managed to prolong the waiting period before the nominating convention, and because no opposition party centering in an ex-revolutionary candidate had formed to ease the internal party pressures, the official nomination loomed even more important than it had in earlier presidential contests.

Because, too, the country was reasonably prosperous and very well satisfied with the integrity of its chief executive, the Mexicans' well-developed political sense of humor turned the waiting period, with all its uncertainties, into an amusing guessing game. The as yet unannounced official candidate was christened *El Tapado* (the hidden or disguised one), and Mexico's best political cartoonist, Abel Quezada, created a series in the newspaper *Excelsior* featuring the political misadventures of *El Tapado* with a flour sack over his head to hide the face, accompanied by a menagerie of all types of political cohorts, grouped together as the *Tapadista* party. The joke won even the accolade of commercialization, with Quezada preparing a widely advertised series proclaiming that "*El Tapado fuma Elegantes.*" In actuality, when President Ruiz Cortines finally announced the official selection—after a long and difficult party struggle—it turned out that Lic. Adolfo López Mateos smoked an altogether different brand of cigarettes, Delicados.

Quite obviously, however, selection of the revolutionary party's candidate involves a great deal more than the brand of cigarettes he smokes. During the entire preconvention period, the president of Mexico is busily engaged in measuring the qualifications and political attitudes of all the pre-candidates against the disparate interests and currents of opinion represented by all of the groups and organizations springing into action at this time. As we shall see presently, in order to be *presidenciable*—that is, "available" for presidental nomination, in North American political jargon—the acceptable candidate must satisfy as many and dissatisfy as few as possible of the principal interests participating in the revolutionary coalition, no little accomplishment considering the wide range of viewpoints included.

During most preconvention periods, the problem of selecting a nominee who can balance these conflicting interests is a delicate but not necessarily impossibly difficult task. Although most of these interests are represented by real interest groups, united and motivated by consciously known goals which must be considered and to some extent satisfied if the revolutionary party is to retain the group's cooperation, the more widely supported interests usually are not so highly specialized that they cannot be accommodated within the broad scope of the PRI, while the majority of those interest groups which cannot be satisfied tend by their very specialization to be smaller and less important politically. Consequently, a candidate who is reasonably moderate and flexible enough to adjust his campaign to the most outstanding needs of the nation finds that most interest groups recognize the necessity of pragmatic compromise, so that there is little danger of their moving into open opposition. The possibility is reduced markedly, of course, by the absence of any politically effective alternative party into which to move.

At the start of the 1958 campaign, however, the very success of the revolutionary party in assimilating interests of all shades of political opinion during previous elections made for difficulty within the party. When the president sought to select the 1958 candidate, he found it necessary to attempt to satisfy the conflicting desires of newly active right- and left-wing factions which sought to dominate the selection process and, consequently, the PRI itself.

During the earlier revolutionary period, before political control crystallized in the official party, schisms in the governing faction usually resulted from frustration of the personal ambitions of successful military leaders; later, after the party of the Revolution became more firmly entrenched, splits occurred when the uncompromising leaders of one faction could not reconcile themselves to the nomination of a presidential candidate from outside of their own select group and started an opposition movement to the right—as in the case of General Almazán or Ezequiel Padilla—or to the left—say, those of Vicente Lombardo Toledano or General Henríquez Guzmán—depending upon the politics of the official candidate.

Today, with the structure of political power more nearly systematized in the revolutionary party, the proportion of party members likely to participate in such a schismatic withdrawal has dwindled to almost nothing, for most politically minded Mexicans have adjusted to the hard realities of party discipline and learned to remain in the party despite political disappointments, because only there can they hope to influence its policies effectively and thereby achieve their particular goals.

Over the years, however, as the revolutionary political organization has become more nearly all-inclusive, certain of the vastly different interest groups and associations subsumed within its three sectors have found it expedient to form themselves into right and left cliques in order to maximize the effect within the official organization of viewpoints which at one time might have existed as separate contending ideological parties. Given Mexico's tradition of

personalistic identification, it is hardly surprising that as a concomitant of their turning into live political-action groups during
Ruiz Cortines' administration, these cliques should cluster about
important political personages in whom their attitudes could be
personified, the faction to the left looking to ex-President Cárdenas
and that to the right toward ex-President Alemán.

Some evidence of the existence of these contending political factions within the government coalition had appeared during the process of selecting the official candidate in previous presidential elections, but until these new groups began to make positive and public
attempts to influence government policy, and particularly the presidential nomination, their activities were kept discreetly within the
party and limited primarily to negative influence, such as ex-President Cárdenas' veto of certain pre-candidates who leaned too far
to the right. Thus, these factions were no new phenomenon appearing suddenly and unexpectedly during the 1958 campaign; what
was new was the general identification of these extreme wings of
the revolutionary party with the two ex-presidents, as well as the
public acknowledgment of their existence through open discussion
in the newspapers and on the street. Both of these differences reflected the high degree of interaction that existed in both factions,
which enabled each to exert a great deal of pressure upon the
president in his attempt to find a suitable successor.

These extreme factions in the government party form effective
pressure coalitions because they represent the two traditional main
currents of revolutionary thought, one quite radical and the other
more conservative. In this sense, both Cárdenas and Alemán represent a complex of ideas and values identified in the minds of those
grouped around them as "the ideology of the Revolution," although
in truth there is little enough of real ideology involved in either
case. Cárdenas leans toward benefits for the small farmer and other
popular interests on a semisocialistic basis, as he always has, while
Alemán and his followers favor industrialization based upon private
ownership assisted by the government, somewhat as did the old
norteño group personified in Calles. The dichotomy is not quite so
clear-cut, of course, for emotional and sometimes even irrational
identification with one or the other leader results in both being
supported by functional interest groups representing all kinds of
activities from all over the republic. Moreover, the two wings of
the official party nearly equate in intraparty influence, for if the

interests rallying to Cárdenas' standard have a larger popular membership, those with Alemán are better organized, more politically aware, and in a position to spend greater amounts of money to further their ends.

Probably neither of these men suspected, on leaving the presidency, that before 1958 he would find himself at the head of a faction contending for supremacy in his own party. Each had good reason to believe that his particular interpretation of revolutionary dogma would be respected by his successors, because he left the party machinery in the hands of persons not too violently opposed to his own viewpoint. But such a belief failed to take into account the effects of changing circumstances and the almost unlimited political power placed in the hands of Mexico's president by the single-party system.

Even so, Cárdenas was able to withdraw to his own state of Michoacán for a relatively long time before he felt compelled to return to active defense of his own values, exercising in the meantime only a negative restraining influence over the conservative tendencies he saw expanding in the revolutionary party. When he stepped out of office in 1952, on the other hand, Alemán was soon disabused of the belief that in Adolfo Ruiz Cortines he had a tractable successor to continue his program. The very existence of two conflicting interpretations of the Revolution made it both necessary and possible for President Ruiz Cortines to exercise judgment independent of both and fully responsible to neither. He took a moderate stand in the center of the broad political spectrum embraced by the PRI.

The *alemanistas* found that their position of influence in the government deteriorated much more speedily than had that of the *cardenistas*, once they were out of office, because they forced the president's hand instead of accepting a gradual adjustment of policies to fit Ruiz Cortines' middle-of-the-road program. When the president sought to clean out the Augean stable of graft and corruption left by his predecessor, Alemán's former cronies organized to bring pressure upon the chief executive so as to protect their vested interests. This was a major tactical error, for political pressure of this sort always breeds counterpressures.

Not only did President Ruiz Cortines use the great prestige and power of his office to contain the attempts of the conservative faction but when some of the more liberal members of the PRI began to organize about the symbol of General Cárdenas, he used their movement, too, to counterbalance the *alemanistas,* providing the left with new entree into government councils. We have already seen evidence of the right-left struggle in the sectors of the revolutionary party during the administration of Ruiz Cortines; the dispute between the *alemanista*-influenced BUO and the CROC faction in the Labor sector is a case in point and so is the attempt to organize a new farm workers union. Utilizing such means, the president preserved a balance between the two conflicting factions, allowing neither to gain the upper hand during his term of office.

As a consequence, the main event in the contest for predominance between the two wings of the government party resolved itself into a struggle to control the nomination of the official presidential candidate for 1958. In this struggle the *cardenistas* managed at long last to enlist the General's active support, convincing him that if he failed to act, the right wing would be able to bring inexorable pressure upon the president to impose a candidate favoring their views. After over fifteen years abstention from public participation in active national politics and notwithstanding President Ruiz Cortines' attempts to hold down premature campaigning, General Cárdenas, as early as March, 1957, took the unprecedented step, for him, of making political fence-mending tours through several key states, even crossing the border into California to speak in Los Angeles, thus reinforcing his already vast political prestige and providing a standard around which the anti-*alemanistas* could rally.

The right wing too continued its political activities, until the intraparty pre-electoral contest reached its climax late in August, when the spokesman for the conservatives, Fernando Casas Alemán, openly admitted to newsmen that the *alemanistas* were a great deal more than "a group of friends who get together to talk over old times," as one of his more circumspect colleagues had suggested. On the contrary, he stated, this was a political action group that fully intended to engage in *futurismo* as soon as the president's State of the Union message was delivered in September. Meanwhile, both factions were preparing their own programs, in traditional style, to be presented to the PRI and its candidate, whoever he might be, in order to influence the campaign and the next administration.

The fact that despite the pressures brought by the two wings of the revolutionary party, with their unusually strong attempts at *futurismo*, President Ruiz Cortines was able to control the political situation and even to delay formal selection of an official candidate for a month longer than any former president, at the same time maintaining substantive neutrality between the contending factions, indicates graphically how greatly the political authority of the chief executive has developed with the institutionalization of Mexico's political system. Neither his own nature nor political design impelled Adolfo Ruiz Cortines, during his six years in office, to attempt to make himself the kind of strong president Miguel Alemán became, much less a popular *caudillo* in the Cárdenas pattern. Yet the very fact that he controlled the machinery of government and the day-by-day activities of the PRI gave him power enough to overbalance the political pressures brought by the interests surrounding the two stronger personalities.

One reason that President Ruiz Cortines was able to control the political situation is that, notwithstanding their ideological differences, both wings of the government party, and particularly their leaders, share a certain irreducible core of revolutionary values that encourages them to continue working in and through the PRI. For all their conflicts, both groups stem from a common revolutionary movement in which a nucleus of overlapping viewpoints was absorbed to provide a foundation for cooperation; this foundation in turn has been shored up by unifying effects of Western technology. Whether they know it or not, therefore, most of the members of the two wings of the PRI have evolved into "moderate extremists" who may fight long and hard for the nomination of one of their own for president but are neither willing nor able to leave the party if they prove unsuccessful, provided the official candidate seems to possess neutral characteristics rather than those of the opposite extreme faction.

In this sense, both Cárdenas and Alemán personify the men who surround them in a way that neither leader nor follower ever imagined. Having been presidents themselves, the two know only too well the necessity of compromise in trying to keep the revolutionary coalition intact; each, as chief executive and head of the government party, had faced the pragmatic problem of conceding to the demands of the other wing of the party in order to keep the working agreement between them operative. And each, in his turn, made the necessary adjustment in his thinking.

As president, Cárdenas set an example of political moderation by acceding to the suggestions of his more conservative colleagues that rather than a fire-eater such as General Múgica, his successor should be General Avila Camacho, an administrator who could consolidate the reforms of the past six years. Outside of office Cárdenas continued to show the way, refusing to support disgruntled liberal candidates who abandoned the official party and maintaining party solidarity by accepting instead more conservative nominees such as Alemán, retaining only the negative control of an informal veto of the most blatant right-wing pre-candidates such as he exercised in 1952 over Ramón Beteta and Fernando Casas Alemán. For its part, the rightist faction accepted Alemán in 1946 as a compromise between the more conservative Padilla and a possible candidate from farther to the left, and six years later President Alemán himself turned to Ruiz Cortines as a kind of balance between his two rightist favorites, mentioned above, and the more liberal General Henríquez Guzmán.

Another and perhaps even more cogent reason that the president was able to control the selection of his successor lies in the nature of the changes occurring in the structure of political power because of Westernization. If the social and economic effects of technology produced change at the extremes of the PRI, they have had even more profound effect upon its center, albeit indirectly. More and more of those "moderate extremists" mentioned earlier have ceased to identify with the periphery and now work with the party center so that the two traditional main currents of revolutionary thought are tending to converge at the center, providing a hard core of support for the political leader who can manipulate it. With the right and left wings of the party very nearly at an impasse, this core at the center wields the balance of power and, because of his position, the president controls the core. This does not mean that neither wing of the party has a voice in the nomination but that the negative influence of each precludes that the other's favored candidate can win, leaving the president to select from the more neutral contenders at the center. In this process, the wings of the PRI resemble Riesman's veto groups.

In other words, the government party provides a mechanism through which almost all shades of political opinion can find representation in the process of selecting the future president of Mexico, but as an inseparable corollary the candidate selected must tend more toward the center than toward either end of the political spectrum. This tendency to nominate the official candidate from among the center faction in the PRI has been in operation during the past several presidential elections, becoming more nearly institutionalized each time. The relatively neutral characteristics demonstrated by Avila Camacho and, to a somewhat lesser extent, by Alemán have been strongly reinforced in Ruiz Cortines and López Mateos until, by now, it is possible to describe a Mexican pre-candidate who is *presidenciable* with just about as much assurance as we do an "available" North American presidential candidate.

### Qualifications for President

Constitutional norms describing the qualifications and term of the President of the Republic in Mexico are more extensive and demanding than those of the North American law, but in neither country are they as limiting as the political requirements that an available candidate must meet. Legally, the Mexican president must be a male who is already thirty-five years old at the time of his election. He also must be a Mexican citizen by birth and the son of Mexican citizens by birth, a provision reflecting the high degree of nationalism endemic in the country and one which has worked against several otherwise qualified politicians. Although he was one of the founders and still is a principal director of the PAN, for example, Manuel Gómez Morín has never been its presidential candidate, because his parents were not both born in Mexico. Furthermore, the presidential candidate must have resided in the country during the entire year preceding the election, a provision that was aimed originally at possible military invasions by out-groups organizing in surrounding countries. It does not apply against individuals who have left Mexican territory on official missions. For that matter, it was not applied against Vicente Lombardo Toledano in 1952, when he registered as a presidential candidate after several trips to the Soviet Union during the previous year.

To be eligible for office, a presidential nominee must not have held office in the national cabinet, or have been governor of a state or territory, or have been on active military service for a term of six months before the day of his election. Despite the doubling of this "cooling-off" period, from three to six months, during the 1940's, most government party pre-candidates, successful or otherwise, are recruited from among the president's cabinet secretaries. Generals Cárdenas and Avila Camacho had been ministers of War and Navy before their nominations, while both Miguel Alemán and Adolfo Ruiz Cortines were Secretary of *Gobernación*, and President López Mateos Secretary of Labor and Welfare. This suggests that separation from office is not necessarily a major detriment to political success if the pre-candidate has been able to utilize his position to capture the official nomination. Finally, no minister or priest of any religious denomination ever may hold public office, including the presidency, in Mexico.

Once elected, the full term of Mexico's president is six years, but even if he has held office for a shorter period as interim, provisional, or substitute president, no individual once having been chief executive ever may be elected again. We have already seen the fatal consequence (for Obregón) of the one departure from this rule since promulgation of the 1917 constitution. Not even the augmented power of the president resulting from his control of the official party has served to change the precept of "No Re-election" that appears at the bottom of every official letter or document, for since Cárdenas set the mode by declining firmly to seek re-election in 1940, no president has attempted to extend his tenure of office beyond the time for which he was legally elected. The talk heard in 1951 of amending the constitution to enable Alemán to serve again, for instance, was nothing more than his way of holding off too much *futurismo*, which would have disrupted his administration.

Above and beyond the constitutional provisions, to be *presidenciable* a pre-candidate must possess, insofar as possible, a certain pattern of desirable political traits and must lack certain other traits, in accord with the political values and activities which have become systematized in and around the revolutionary party and the government. First, and so basic that it is an absolute requirement before any other combination of qualities is considered, the presidential hopeful must be acceptable to the incumbent chief executive. Acceptability presupposes that the president likes the individual both as a person and a politician, meaning that their political views are sufficiently similar for the man who wields the tremendous concentration of authority represented by the party and the state to place this power in the hands of his successor. Beyond this, on the basis of the political relationships which have evolved over the years among the principal interest groups and functional associations interacting to form Mexico's system of politics, as well as the major characteristics of those official party pre-candidates successful enough to move on to the presidency, we can forecast that the most available candidates will fit more or less neatly into the following pattern.

In very general terms, the *precandidato presidenciable* must have personal and even physical characteristics suitable to the office he seeks and the political environment in which he operates. He should be reasonably healthy, quite energetic, and at least not violently ugly. Although he may be considered as *muy hombre* (a he-man), the pre-candidate should avoid the reputation of being a *macho* (a woman-chaser); in fact, politically it is much more expedient to appear as a family man, with a wife who is interested in public affiairs but not so active that she will intervene in the concerns of those who already have carved out a position for themselves. Neither should she be a foreigner and certainly not a North American, as was Ramón Beteta's wife. The politician's religious views may range from practicing–Roman Catholicism to free-thinking, but should not in either case be so extreme as to brand him a *fanático* who will serve the Church blindly or a militant atheist who will attack the Church equally blindly. On the other hand, in nominally Catholic Mexico he must not be an active Protestant.

Taking for granted that all serious aspirants have revolutionary backgrounds of some sort, the most available pre-candidates will have struggled up from humble beginnings to the heights of material success as professional men and as professional politicians. They also will have had sufficient education to understand the national scene and to operate effectively within it; this may be self-education, but much more likely nowadays it is formal secondary- and even university-level training, probably in the law. Chances are, too, that most of these men will be of the middle class, if not in origin, certainly in outlook, for only a person with the relatively general and neutral approach of the middle class is apt to relate successfully with functional interest associations and social movements representing enough people at all levels of Mexican society to attract a personal political following of presidential magnitude.

When selected, the official nominee more than likely will come from a large and economically important state, probably one on or near the *mesa central*. Thus, Cárdenas came from Michoacán and Avila Camacho from Puebla, while both Alemán and Ruiz Cortines had been governor of Veracruz before moving onto the national political stage. President López Mateos, in turn, was born in the state of Mexico, one of the points in his favor regarding the nomination, for although one of the strongest contenders, Angel Carvajal, was Ruiz Cortines' very close friend and Secretary of *Gobernación,* he too came from Veracruz, and three presidents in a row from that state seemed impolitic.

Invariably, the successful pre-candidate has a broad foundation in practical politics and equally wide experience in administration. Alemán, Ruiz Cortines, and López Mateos each managed the presidential election campaign of his predecessor. Before taking office, every revolutionary president of recent years has been governor and/or senator from his home state, but never immediately before his nomination, reflecting the sad political state of both federalism and legislative influence. Instead, every official candidate has stepped into the nominee's role from a successful term as head of an executive department and member of the president's cabinet.

Increasingly, of late, the PRI's candidate reflects the broadening out and toning down of the revolutionary party's ideology. He must be relatively well known nationally and acceptable to all of the major groups included in the three party sectors, but at the same time he must not be too closely identified with any one of the strongest functional interest associations, for fear that he will favor it at the expense of other legitimate interests. For instance, Fidel Velázquez of the CTM and Raymundo Flores Fuentes of the CNC, neither of whom would have refused the 1958 nomination had it been thrust upon him, were not really available for nomination because of their positions in the bureaucracies of the labor and farmers organizations. Furthermore, the candidate may not have too strong an affiliation with the party's right wing or he will lose the approval of General Cárdenas, as did Casas Alemán and Beteta in 1952 and Uruchurtu and others in 1958. Similarly, views too strongly leftist in character will cost him *alemanista* support, also required for his selection.

As a corollary, the official nominee must traverse the narrow passage between the Scylla of economic nationalism and the Charybdis of lost potential foreign capital investment. As we shall see, López Mateos struck just the right note here, both in his pre-campaigning and after his nomination. The same was true of his public attitude toward the United States, a universally popular whipping boy in every Mexican election but an increasingly important factor in the country's economic development. He had never been closely enough connected to North American interests or activities to damn him in the eyes of the middle class, as was "Mister" Padilla before the 1946 campaign, yet neither had López Mateos demonstrated in his public or private political activities the potentially disrupting hostility showed by one of the other leading pre-candidates.

It is a moot question whether the availability of this man was more seriously weakened by President Ruiz Cortines' realization of the impediment such a nomination might provide to the growing economic interdependence of his country and its larger northern neighbor or by unfavorable public reaction to an extremely laudatory article about him that appeared in a widely read American digest magazine just at the height of the prenomination struggles. In one quarter he was suspect for being too unfriendly and in another for being too well liked by the *gringos*. In any event, this particular contender could never have won nomination because he was too closely identified with the right wing of the revolutionary party to win General Cárdenas' approval.

Under this heading of selecting candidates who reflect the gradual erosion of the extremes of revolutionary ideology so as to enable the PRI to represent a wider range of interests, we should note the evolution of a kind of rhythmic pattern that recurs in the characteristics of the successful men. Lacking a vice-president to balance the ticket as he does in the United States, the revolutionary party does so by alternating the presidential type it chooses from among the pre-candidates. A young and dynamic leader who effects great change—say a Cárdenas or Alemán—is followed in office by an administrator who can consolidate matters, a man like Avila Camacho or Ruiz Cortines. Perhaps this alternating of types is not part of any conscious plan; undoubtedly it is more nearly a reaction on the part of the incumbent president to pressures he has sensed building up during his administration as a direct result of failure to satisfy the desires of interest groups whose goals do not fall within the precincts of his own value system. Obviously, for example, a conservative president would not select a violently radical successor but evidence already has been offered—and much more exists which could be cited—to suggest that intraparty pressures do build up to force some adjustments, even in such cases. The gradual development of a liberal reaction to expanding *alemanismo* and its success in forestalling the nomination of a right-wing presidential candidate are a case in point.

Finally, by an amusing turn of the wheel of fortune, the growing tide of public disapproval aimed at the personalistic government of the old-style *caudillos,* when compared with the achievements of present-day civilian presidents, probably means that active military status makes a candidate less rather than more likely to win the official nomination, a direct reversal of the situation only a few years ago. Not one of the six leading hopefuls in the race for the 1958 candidacy wore a general's uniform. The old days of the flamboyant, personally attractive *político,* who could speak like an angel but was not very highly endowed with administrative skill long since have been replaced by the era of the managerial specialist who combines efficient service with his political oratory.

It hardly seems necessary to suggest that no single individual combines all of the qualifications, political as well as legal, to make an ideal presidential candidate. Still, on reviewing the life and career of each of the recent revolutionary nominees, it is little short of amazing to note just how closely they do hew to the ideal pattern. Perhaps this is not really quite so amazing as first appears, for in the final analysis it is the president of Mexico, sitting at his desk in *Los Pinos,* who selects the man who will succeed him. For all that he must take into consideration the possible vetoes of candidates by the spokesmen of the two wings of the PRI, as well as the wishes and demands of all the conflicting interest groups subsumed in the official party, the chief executive has had long experience in holding the most effective factors of political power in approximate equilibrium, so that he is not likely to be stampeded into naming an individual hastily, on the basis of irrational or emotional motivations rather than intelligence, experience, and suitability.

What is amazing is the high level of competence and political ability the official candidates have demonstrated in the presidency. Because of, rather than despite, the political factors he must consider, to date, the chief executive has found the one pre-candidate among the contenders who best suits the peculiar complex of conditions which he must dominate, making for a series of effective presidents, though, as in cases such as those of Avila Camacho and Ruiz Cortines, not necessarily "strong" leaders in the older, personalistic sense of the term. Control of the electoral process by a single effective political party and manipulation of that party, in turn, by the president, offers one real advantage. In selecting the next national leader, the incumbent must take into account all of the varied interests throughout the country but having done so he chooses a man to govern rather than simply to win an election, as so often occurs at North American nominating conventions, where the man is picked because of characteristics that mark him as a good candidate rather than as a good president.

Perhaps the best way to point up the extent to which the conventions for selecting Mexico's official candidates have adjusted to the changing demands upon the chief executive is to review briefly the careers of the PRI's two most recent presidential nominees. Like his predecessor, Adolfo Ruiz Cortines was a civilian of unimpeachable revolutionary background but, unlike Alemán, his reputation rested more upon success as an administrator and bureaucrat than upon the glamour of political campaigning. Ruiz Cortines was born December 30, 1890, in the state of Veracruz; his father died when the boy was only three months old, so his mother helped him to obtain an education until he went to work at the age of sixteen. His youth was the usual one of a lower middle-class Mexican until the outbreak of the Revolution, when he began his public career by supporting Madero.

Late in 1912, when he was twenty-two, Ruiz Cortines left Veracruz for Mexico City. He was there when Huerta ousted Madero from the presidency, so he joined Carranza's secret service, working against Huerta in the capital under Alfredo Robles Domínguez. When Carranza came to power, Robles was named governor of the Federal District and Ruiz Cortines stayed on as his aide. In 1914, when political circumstances forced evacuation of the capital, he returned to Veracruz, but shortly afterward entered the military service as second-captain, once again acting as aide to Robles, who was named governor of the state of Guerrero. Later, after acting as general paymaster for the Army of the East, he was promoted to major and served on the staff of General Jacinto B. Treviño, finally becoming his private secretary. When Treviño was named Secretary of Industry, Commerce and Labor in 1920, Ruiz Cortines continued to serve as his secretary. This early relationship with Treviño undoubtedly helps explain the success of the General's PARM in winning recognition as a national political party, for political loyalty is as strong a characteristic of successful politicians in Mexico as in any other country.

After Obregón became president, Ruiz Cortines returned to the army as an administrative officer, leaving it permanently in 1926 when he was named chief of the Directorate of Social Statistics in the Department of National Statistics because of his reputation for rectitude and administrative efficiency. In 1935 he was appointed *oficial mayor* or chief administrative officer of the Department of the Federal District but left the post two years later on being elected federal deputy from Tuxpán, Veracruz. While he was still a deputy, Miguel Alemán, then managing Avila Camacho's presidential campaign, named Ruiz Cortines treasurer of the group directing the campaign. Later, in 1940, he became for a short period secretary-general of *Gobernación* in the state of Veracruz, under a provisional administration headed by Fernando Casas Alemán, but with the inauguration of Avila Camacho in December of that year he became *oficial mayor* of the national *Secretaría de Gobernación*, serving under the younger and more dynamic Alemán.

Ruiz Cortines was elected governor of Veracruz in 1944, acquiring a reputation as an effective executive in that office, but he resigned his gubernatorial post in 1948 to join President Alemán's cabinet as Secretary of *Gobernación*. From this nationally important position he stepped into the presidency six years later as a compromise candidate. Despite having risen in political and government circles principally upon the coattails of more colorful politicians, his proven administrative ability, together with the authority concentrated in his hands as president, made Ruiz Cortines an able, independent, and very effective chief executive.

The career of Lic. Adolfo López Mateos parallels that of Ruiz Cortines in many ways but it also deviates sufficiently to show the Mexican law of political adjustment in operation. Like the man who selected him for the official nomination, López Mateos comes of middle-class revolutionary background and moved up through the political hierarchy in administrative and staff-type positions rather than primarily through electoral success. Unlike Ruiz Cortines, however, on his nomination President López Mateos was only forty-seven years old, one of the second generation of revolutionary leaders, and much more likely to provide vigorous leadership and new ideas for the revolutionary party than his mentor had been.

Adolfo López Mateos was born in a small town in the state of Mexico on May 26, 1910, making him a real son of the Revolution, as his supporters emphasized repeatedly during the campaign. He was the fifth child of a poor dentist. His father died soon after López Mateos' birth, whereupon the mother took the family to Mexico City. Already showing signs of his future brilliance and determination, the boy won a scholarship to the Colegio Francés, the notably Roman Catholic–influenced school where he completed his primary education; he then moved to Toluca, capital of the state of Mexico, to live with relatives of his mother while he earned his way through secondary school working in a library. After leaving secondary school, the future president taught literature and history at the Normal Institute in Toluca while working for a law degree at night school. In 1929, López Mateos found time to act as a delegate representing his state at the Aguascalientes anti-reelection meeting of the Socialist-Labor party, as well as to win the oratory championship of the state of Mexico.

After acting for a time as secretary to the governor of his state, Colonel Filberto Gómez, López Mateos was invited to become the private secretary of General Carlos Riva Palacio, who became head of the PNR in 1933. Later, as secretary-general of the PRM's regional committee for the Federal District, López Mateos attracted the attention of General Cárdenas for his activities in social reform. Then he worked for various national government agencies, in succession the Banco Nacional Obrero de Fomento, the National Printing Office, and the Treasury, spending eight years in the last agency, following which he was sent for three years as a troubleshooter to act as rector of the Institute in Toluca.

As a result of the same 1946 campaign during which President Alemán was elected, López Mateos rose to the post of senator from Mexico. He had already known Alemán, who acted as his mother's lawyer in securing her a pension as granddaughter of José Perfecto Mateos, a hero of the Juárez period. Now he also came into close contact with Ruiz Cortines, because as senator, Adolfo López Mateos represented his state in the political question it wished to raise with the Secretary of *Gobernación*. When *Don* Adolfo was selected as the official presidential candidate for the 1952 election, his younger namesake was called home from Switzerland, where he was heading Mexico's delegation to the UN Economic and Social Council; López Mateos was made secretary-general of the PRI and campaign manager for *ruizcortinismo*, moving from there to the post of Labor and Welfare secretary in December, 1952.

While Labor Minister, López Mateos worked long, hard, and efficiently, gaining the respect not only of labor and management alike, but of North American diplomats as well, the latter particularly for the intelligent manner in which he worked out the agreement that both protected and controlled the *braceros* who crossed the northern border to work in the United States. Furthermore, of over thirteen thousand labor disputes reported during his five years in *Trabajo*, only thirteen resulted in strikes, yet López Mateos managed to retain his reputation for being scrupulously fair to both employers and workers. Thus, the Secretary of Labor managed to please both the mass farm groups and organized labor, together with management, while he was in the cabinet.

It may well be that the single success which brought him into national prominence as a potential presidential pre-candidate was his masterful handling of the projected general strike called by the CTM for July, 1954, to support its demand for an immediate twenty-four per cent cost-of-living raise. Both the leadership of the revolutionary party and the general public were highly impressed by the way in which López Mateos averted the strike, satisfied Fidel Velázquez with smaller increases, and smoothed over the threatened crack in PRI unity.

### The Nomination of López Mateos

As the pre-campaign period drew near, other circumstances also worked in favor of the selection of the Labor Minister. For one thing, pressure was building up among the second generation revolutionary politicians for the selection of a younger man, one of their number. The old-line revolutionary leaders, who still ruled the official party, were in their sixties, or close to it; when he left office Ruiz Cortines was within a few weeks of being sixty-eight. Even they recognized that the time had come to look for a man with fresh attitudes, fully alert to rapidly changing conditions inside Mexico and capable of recognizing the country's growing concern with world affairs as it became more and more strongly linked to the world economy. Needless to suggest, not every "old soldier" was convinced that the younger generation as yet was prepared to assume control, and even among younger Mexicans a great many opposed vigorously any change in their country's traditional isolationism.

The emergence of the PARM, the Veterans of the Revolution, and the Association of Delegates to the 1916-17 constitutional convention all were indicative of a last flaring up of the original revolutionary flame before it burned out forever, just as the appearance of supernationalist movements marked a last-ditch stand of Mexican isolationism, for neither set of opinions was in step with the times, which called for young blood and new ideas to solve the challenging problems facing the republic. The vast majority of politically active and thinking Mexicans recognized and accepted this indisputable fact.

Clearly, if Adolfo López Mateos was a successful, well-known, and youthful cabinet minister, other members of President Ruiz Cortines' administration were equally successful and prominent, and well within the age limit to qualify as members of the rising generation. Moreover, by the very fact that they had been politically active for a longer period, some of the older presidential hopefuls in the cabinet had built political reputations and personal organizations which easily could compensate for the simple advantage of a few less years. But once again circumstance worked in favor of the Secretary of Labor. Because of the impasse between the right and left wings of the PRI, the major political leaders agreed with the president that the official candidate should be someone with few strong ties to any faction; this, in turn, meant a man who had not been very active or highly placed in the national executive branch prior to 1952. These two conditions effectively short-circuited the political ambitions of most of the other principal pre-candidates, young or old. After carefully measuring the qualifications of those who were left and evaluating their acceptability to ex-Presidents Cárdenas and Alemán, not to mention himself, President Ruiz Cortines finally narrowed the field to one man known to, trusted, and respected by all three leaders. After securing the reluctant but inevitable approval of his choice from the other leading pre-candidates, the president told López Mateos that he had been selected.

This whole process of elimination ostensibly went on behind closed doors, but given a free press and even freer political imagination, the Mexican man on the street managed to keep pretty well up to date on the general frame of reference within which the decision was being made. The only problem was to determine which pre-candidate best fitted the emerging pattern. In the old days the announcement of the chosen one was made more overtly; Avila Camacho did it for himself, for all practical purposes, by resigning from his post of Secretary of War and Marine, Alemán was launched by Lombardo Toledano, and Ruiz Cortines by Fidel Velázquez, both in the name of the CTM. But in the case of López Mateos, no clear-cut act occurred. Instead, the public had to narrow down the field much as the president was doing, but one step behind him. The process even earned the dignity of its own term in political jargon—*auscultación,* the plumbing or sounding process by which a physician tests a lung or other organ hidden inside the body.

Notwithstanding the discretion of the PRI hierarchy, the process of *auscultación* worked so well that by the time the revolutionary party's presidential nominating convention was called for the middle of November, most politically aware Mexicans had a strong suspicion about the candidate who would emerge from it. Their suspicions were confirmed before the meeting took place. Just as six years previously the president of the PRI himself predicted a week before the convention that Adolfo Ruiz Cortines would be nominated, so this time during the first week of November a combination of circumstances and trial-and-error tests, plus some quite accurate judgments and shrewd guesses, began to make the identity of *El Tapado* clear.

Unlike the two previous presidents, Angel Carvajal still was in *Gobernación* preparing the election machinery, so he probably was eliminated; Ernesto Uruchurtu had announced that he was not a candidate, and some of the election materials of Raymundo Flores Fuentes were seen being thrown out; various other pre-candidates had stopped electioneering. All of the evidence seemed to point to López Mateos; betting in his favor rose from even to five to one. Any lingering doubts were dispelled when the CNC leadership, eager to be the first on the bandwagon, broke the tradition allowing the CTM to announce the identity of the official candidate and stated unofficially on Monday, November 4, 1957, that the farm group would support Adolfo López Mateos.

Once his name had been mentioned publicly, the dam burst and the labor secretary was deluged with the usual mob of well-wishers, office-seekers, and special pleaders. The leaders of every conceivable interest association, do-gooder organization, professional group, or agency of government waited upon him, bought full-page newspaper advertisements extoling him, and otherwise sought to demonstrate that they had been *lopezmateistas* from the very start. One group of organizations from the state of Tabasco went so far as to antedate their advertisement to Sunday, November 3, in order to precede the rest, on paper at any rate. Assurances of support by delegations of senators, generals, labor union leaders, deputies, businessmen, farm politicians, and even women's clubs were reported daily, until López Mateos must have imagined that these were visitations upon, rather than visits to, him. And all of this before the nominating convention.

With the identity of its presidential nominee already assured, the PRI convention could scarcely hope to be more than an anticlimax to the nomination process, for only a few details remained to be ironed out. One of these details was to decide which organization should have the honor of nominating the candidate formally; the CTM still was outraged by the CNC's assumption of labor's prerogative by making the informal announcement. As it happened, the official party bureaucracy worked out a compromise formula that allowed all three sectors to nominate López Mateos simultaneously, in itself an indication that the CTM had indeed lost some of its former prestige during the administration of Ruiz Cortines.

## The Election Campaign

If the convention that nominated López Mateos as the PRI's 1958 presidential candidate seemed anticlimactic with regard to the nominating process, it was a great success as the first formal act of the campaign proper. Following what has become a fixed political tradition, López Mateos set the tone of the ensuing campaign in his acceptance speech made at the mammoth Olympic sports stadium in University City before a crowd of nearly 100,000 that spilled over into adjacent parking lots. Just as Alemán's acceptance presaged emphasis on industrialization and economic development and Ruiz Cortines' on consolidation and moral reform, López Mateos' speech forecast quite accurately the points he would stress in his campaigning. In sum, they added up to moderate liberalism, with the accent on both words in the term.

The new candidate presented a program calculated to satisfy both conservatives and liberals.[2] For the masses he promised to maintain agrarian reform vigorously, to support the right to strike and, in general, to protect the working class. To free enterprise he offered a continued climate of liberty to participate in industrial as

---

[2] See the Mexico City press for November 18, 1957, for the text of López Mateos' speech and program. It may be found also in *La Campaña Electoral de 1957-1958* (Mexico, D.F., 1958), which contains the programs and platforms of all the political movements active in this campaign, though the stress on left wing, *cardenista,* and Communist pronouncements is not an accurate indication of their relative role in the election or the number of votes they could muster.

well as agricultural development, stressing the need for collaboration between private interests and the state. Pointing out that with Mexico's three per cent annual increment of population, leveling-off of production really would be retrogression, he identified the government party's fundamental objective as industrialization, which "is creating a better standard of living. It is necessary, therefore, to maintain the system of preponderantly free enterprise and freedom of monetary exchange that has provided the economic structure which has enabled us to develop so satisfactorily." In recognition of the *cardenista* wing of the PRI, however, López Mateos declared that nationalization of the oil industry twenty years before was a conquest of the Revolution aimed at Mexico's economic independence, so "in nationalized petroleum, not one step backward."

With the star performance over, the political stage was left bare for the turn of the minor national parties, each of which held its own nominating convention. As had been forecast accurately in the press, three of the four independent parties—the PP, PNM, and PARM—voted to support the PRI's standard-bearer; only the PAN decided to name an opposition presidential candidate, picking a young and politically unknown textile manufacturer from the northern state of Chihuahua, Luis H. Alvarez. But neither the 38-year-old candidate nor the PAN itself generated much excitement. Contrast the packed Olympic stadium, jammed with shouting supporters of the PRI and festooned with colorful pictures and slogans, with the staid Mexico City ballroom, where three thousand tired PAN delegates, after listening to two long days of too-long speeches denouncing the PRI, tried to drum up enthusiasm for a young man they did not know, who was about to enter a contest the results of which they knew beforehand only too well.

In general, the 1958 presidential campaign was dull compared with previous ones. Six years earlier, for example, three legally recognized candidates, including Henríquez Guzmán, who had just left the revolutionary party, and at least one unrecognized man with a certain degree of organized support had run against Ruiz Cortines, and several of the opposition parties espoused political doctrines quite distinct from those of the PRI. This time, Alvarez offered the only legal opposition, and his party's platform was not much different from that of the government party, for the PAN had learned an eye-opening lesson in the 1955 congressional election campaign; it could attract a larger share of the votes by offering more and better revolutionary reforms than by opposing an accomplished and publicly accepted fact of long standing.[3] But "me-tooism" on a minor scale is hardly the tenet to produce a very lively contest; neither the general public nor those members of the opposition party who still opposed the Revolution responded very energetically to the exhortations of the earnest young PAN nominee. Nor did the campaign approach of the PRI's candidate serve to quicken the contest.

As we shall see in detail presently, López Mateos' strongest approach to campaigning was aimed at conciliation and adjustment of the differences among his organized supporters as well as among the people of Mexico as a whole. Furthermore, he rejected proposed alliances with the minor parties which were supporting him, effectively cutting the political ground out from under individuals such as Lombardo Toledano and General Treviño who, because of their more extreme viewpoints, might have added spice to the give-and-take between the *lopezmateistas* and *Acción Nacional*. In the same way, he sought to discourage the formation of large numbers of small and independent ideological and functional interest groups such as had clustered about Ruiz Cortines, adding a great deal of life to the 1952 contest but also compounding confusion and internal difficulties in the campaign coalition because they refused to submit themselves or their activities to party discipline.[4]

Lacking both basic ideological differences or strong personalities to motivate partisan disputes, it was difficult for either side to get the campaign off the ground in terms of its own members, and even more difficult to animate the general public sufficiently to accomplish a respectable showing in the formalities of free and democratic elections. For all that López Mateos was a popular candidate, the average voter was convinced, correctly, that the selection of Mexico's next president already had been made. Why, then, bother to register? The situation was complicated by the fact that although the Federal Election Law provides for permanent registration, constant changes in the norms of the law necessitated reregistration of the entire voting population, just as they had before the 1952 and 1955 elections.

As a consequence, by February 15, 1958, when the National

---

[3] The principal issues, or lack of them, in this election, were anticipated quite accurately in Rodrigo de Llano, *México y las Elecciones de 1958* (Mexico, D.F., 1957).

[4] See Eisenberg, *op. cit.*, pp. 58-59.

Voters List was to be closed, only some twenty-five per cent of the eligibles had been registered, despite a legal requirement of compulsory registration and voting. In hopes of obtaining a less embarrassing proportion of registrations, the period for enrolling was prorogued a month. During this period a high-pressure registration campaign took place, utilizing all mass media of communication to encourage lagging citizens to visit the registration booths, which remained open extra hours. Small merchants throughout the country, and particularly in the Federal District, offered a ten per cent discount on a long list of items to any person presenting proof of registration. Professional organizations, functional groups such as the Bankers' Association, and all of the interest associations affiliated with the PRI conducted their own campaigns to assist and encourage their members to obtain their voter's credentials. By March 15, the CROM was able to announce that every one of its members had registered, together with his family, but the same was not true of other Mexicans. On the second closing date total registrations of less than seven million still lagged behind even those for the 1955 congressional race and far below the estimated thirteen million that had been expected. So the period was prorogued a further two weeks, to March 31. By that date, registrations reached 10,443,465, somewhat more impressive but still hardly the sign of a hotly contested campaign.[5]

The only real political activity in and about the Federal District during the first few months after the November nominating conventions was taking place behind closed doors at PRI headquarters and in the offices of its three sector organizations, where hundreds of the leaders of the component interest associations were pressing to "sacrifice themselves for the country," as the Mexicans cynically call the rush to win nominations to legislative office that occurs every three years. In a presidential year the problem is always more complex, because in addition to 162 deputies, sixty senatorial candidates must be selected and, more important, all must be cleared with the official presidential candidate, to assure that he will have a cooperative and loyal Congress.

---

[5] Total registrations in recent national elections are as follows:

1952—4,925,900 registered (women did not yet vote), some 85 per cent of the eligibles;

1955—8,941,020 registered, some 67 per cent of the eligibles;

1958—10,443,465 registered, some 80 per cent of the eligibles, of which 4,649,983 (or 44 per cent of the total registered) were women.

The pre-candidates for these 222 congressional posts, together with an equal number of substitutes' positions on the ballot, are selected from persons suggested by three sources—the clique around the official presidential candidate, the three sectors of the revolutionary party, and the governors of Mexico's twenty-nine states. Not unexpectedly, this proliferation of sources results in approximately three times as many names as offices to be filled. In the winnowing process a great many basic policy decisions must be taken, the final results of which provide the earliest evidence based on acts rather than words of the political attitudes of the next president. While he is waiting, therefore, every *político* asks the same questions. What will be the share of posts allotted to each sector? Which factions within the sector will be given the largest part of its allotment? Which governors will be allowed a relatively free hand within their states, implying trust by the official nominee, and which will not? Most important, since the nominations come from three distinct sources, the final decisions also must be cleared through the same three sources, so that in 1958, as always, the governors' acceptance of the final decisions, the attitude of Flores Fuentes of the CNC, of Fidel Velázquez of the CTM, and of Caritino Maldonado of the CNOP, as well as the reaction of all concerned to Senator Alfredo del Mazo, López Mateos' secretary for political affairs, provided the answer to the most basic question of all—how effective a politician and leader is the revolutionary candidate when real policy matters are involved?

While nomination of the PRI's congressional candidates was not important of itself, given the lack of real legislative power in that agency of government, the play of competitive interests operating during the campaign did show up clearly here, just as the relatively easy acceptance of the allotment of posts by the interested parties indicated López Mateos' domination of the situation. When the list of official party candidates became known late in March, 1958, of the three party sectors, the Popular was allotted nearly half of the seats in the lower house (78 of 162) and a majority of those in the Senate (39 of 60), while the other two sectors divided the remaining deputies' posts approximately equally. The Farmers sector received no Senate places and Labor only the few remaining.

The proportional position of the three sectors remained, therefore, approximately the same as in the previous Congress, suggesting once again López Mateos' inclination against widespread alteration of existing conditions. In the same vein, although the congressional posts were assigned to the three sectors, it must be kept in mind that with the exception of labor, which usually allots its seats to various union leaders, many of the remaining places went to persons not really connected with the sector; again according to custom, in many states the governor appointed his own friends, relatives, mentors, or protégés, so that these officers too were substantially satisfied.

The government party's strategy during 1958 seemed to be to keep the active phases of the election campaign in the provinces and away from the larger cities for as long as possible, to avoid disruption of private business activities as well as of President Ruiz Cortines' administrative program. Even after López Mateos began his carefully planned series of campaign tours throughout the country early in December, 1957, the proportion of time spent in the cities as opposed to smaller towns and even villages, was much less than one might have expected. As late as the following April, the usual wall slogans, names cut into the sides of mountains, billboards, triumphal arches, and similar devices extoling the official presidential candidate were much more in evidence in rural areas than in the cities. Similar devices for Luis H. Alvarez were practically nonexistent in either environment.

By a coincidence, the two opposing parties began their formal campaigning on the same day, Saturday, December 7, but at opposite ends of the country. Alvarez spoke in his home state of Chihuahua and López Mateos at Chetumal, in Quintana Roo. For the official candidate this was but the first stop on a fifteen-day tour through seven states of southern Mexico, the prototype of the series of flying trips he made during his twenty-six week campaign, during which he visited some 480 towns throughout the country. These voyages by the PRI's nominee, blanketing the country, have assumed the status of a political institution in Mexico since General Cárdenas set the pattern during his campaign as official party candidate back in 1933-34. Over the years the techniques employed have been refined, but basically the trips perform the same function they always have, allowing the candidate to reach the people to reinforce the influence of the revolutionary party and at the same time enabling him to learn the needs and problems of all sections of the republic so as to prepare himself for his new responsibilities.

Both Adolfo Ruiz Cortines in his campaign and Adolfo López

Mateos during 1958 used the technique of holding social-economic conferences in the principal cities and sometimes even in market towns of the areas they visited on these trips, meeting with state and local government officials, party leaders, and the heads of whatever functional interest associations operated in the region. They also made a point of treating with individual businessmen, workers, farmers, and the like in order to get private as well as organizational opinions on possible government policies to improve conditions and alleviate problems where they existed. This device of conferences cultivated the sense of personal relationship between the future chief executive and the ordinary citizen, especially the opinion-makers of a community. Because it fitted so well into the personalistic tradition, the device was used extensively by both men.[6]

As future presidents, they found these meetings advantageous from another viewpoint, too, for both Ruiz Cortines and López Mateos demanded that the local government and party leaders prepare a good briefing of the social and economic situation in the district where each conference was held. This staff work allowed the candidate to make an intelligent analysis of the suggestions presented at the meetings but, equally valuable, it also allowed him to test the energies and abilities of persons in the field, to decide how much confidence to place in each when the campaign ended and the candidate became president. The one real weakness of the conference device is a defect endemic in all political life; the candidate found it nearly impossible to reach the real people, because wherever he went he was insulated from them by hoards of professional politicians seeking offices, pleading special causes, or simply building their local prestige by appearing close to the future chief of state. López Mateos, in fact, was forced to take positive action to limit the numbers of hangers-on who sought to accompany him on these trips so that he could speak to the people he had come to see.

Another campaigning device, used for the first time during the 1958 race, allowed the party to reach out into back-country districts where the official candidate simply could not penetrate, at the same time offering a sense of personal contact with him. Teams

---

[6] A recapitulation and discussion of the program of government worked out by Lic. López Mateos as a result of meetings with these *consejos de planeación económica y social* can be found in Juan Espinosa's *Presente y Futuro de México* (Mexico, D.F., 1958).

of young PRI stalwarts drove into the central squares of remote villages in trucks or jeeps plastered with campaign posters of López Mateos and loaded with portable generators to provide power for sound and film equipment. After offering a show to draw a crowd, the youthful *políticos* would demonstrate the operation of a tape-recorder and invite the citizens to record personal messages describing their needs and problems which, they promised, would be presented to the revolutionary candidate in person. Once the first natural timidity of the shy and unsophisticated Mexican had been overcome, the dam burst and hundreds of persons throughout the republic had the experience of speaking to their next president, though they had never seen him in person.

Clearly, the revolutionary candidate's campaigning consists of a great deal more than massive rallies, banners, parades, and speeches by and for him. In addition to the music, the dancing in regional costumes, the speeches in local Indian dialects, or the inevitable comparisons of the nominee to the local revolutionary hero, serious and productive work is accomplished. One can trace changes of emphasis in the candidates' thoughts as a result of new ideas learned during these campaign travels. Ruiz Cortines picked up the groundswell favoring national women's suffrage on one of his trips and promptly added a promise to sponsor the idea if elected. Similarly, in his earliest travels López Mateos sensed an attitude of dissatisfaction in rural areas because of the disproportionate advances of the city over the country. Consequently, without altering the basic tenets of his campaign, expressed in his acceptance speech when he promised moderate advances for all classes, the 1958 candidate shifted the stress of his later talks toward the idea of a more equitable share of the Revolution's benefits for the rural Mexican. Cleverly, he tied this concept of "balanced development" to the traditional regionalism of the country, suggesting that a dual industrialization must take place in the provinces. Just as commercial agriculture must be encouraged, by better channeling of public and private credit for *ejidos* and small privately owned farms, by expanding government-sponsored soil conservation programs, by building feeder roads, and otherwise providing services to farmers, he insisted, so primary processing of agricultural products and other forms of industry must be developed throughout all sections of the country rather than in the Federal District alone.

In his approach to this matter, López Mateos demonstrated quite clearly that he was indeed a candidate of the present, as his backers had claimed, because for all practical purposes he was adapting his campaign to contemporary circumstances, recognizing the need for and advocáting strongly the further Westernization of his country.

As a profitable by-product of his interest in the rural majority, in the midst of the campaign López Mateos won the positive approval of General Cárdenas. This can be considered an important indication of liberal support during his term, for the ex-president had contented himself with a cool neutrality or at best only formal support during the campaigns of Alemán and Ruiz Cortines.

In one sense, López Mateos observed faithfully the conventions of official party campaigning which have evolved over the years. He made the campaign tours to various regions of the country, he held the necessary conferences, he offered the expected speeches, and he did his best to satisfy all of the diverse factions which must be considered if the revolutionary coalition is to dominate the Mexican political scene. Furthermore, he faced and discussed the major issues which confront every candidate seeking the presidency. The general problems of advancing the economy, of social welfare, together with farm and land policy, the needs of organized labor and, more recently, the difficulties of inflation, are recurring items in every election. No quick and easy solutions exist, so each nominee in turn must offer his own formula for easing problems and improving conditions, even though he cannot resolve them completely.

Quite naturally, these standard matters took a large share of the campaign time, but Mexico's human and material resources had not multiplied with López Mateos' nomination, nor was he the type to seek immediate policy changes. Neither did the PAN have much to offer as an alternative program on these basic problems, having ingested the Revolution, as it were. Therefore, it was not so much the old issues as the new approaches to politics which were significant in this campaign.

In these, the 1958 presidential race indeed provided a departure from long-accepted norms. López Mateos' conception of balanced development for the entire country was no more than an application of a new and more widely accepted Western-style sense of political moderation and shared values, for which he simply stood as a symbol. His campaign reflected these new ideas as well as the old. Not the least of these was López Mateos' positive action to develop closer relationships between the government and the Roman Catholic church.

At first glance, one might be tempted to attribute the candidate's action to his early exposure to religious influence at the Colegio Francés but patently, whatever his own views, as spokesman for the Revolution he must have reflected a reasonably strong current within the PRI or he could not have acted so. Certainly the anticlerical faction within the Querétaro convention that included in the 1917 constitution provisions divorcing Church from State and particularly Church from politics could never have approved the sentiments the revolutionary candidate expressed in Tlaltenango, Zacatecas, during February, any more than old-style orthodox Roman Catholics could his statement in Huajuapan, Oaxaca, a month or so previously. In the Oaxacan stronghold of the PAN, a city known for strong, orthodox religious views, López Mateos repeated a stand he had made before, defending religious freedom for all creeds and exhorting all Mexicans to respect minority ideas and opinions. In Tlaltenango, on the other hand, the candidate appeared at a meeting to speak jointly with a Catholic priest for national unity in order to speed the progress of Mexico. The presidential candidate said that "the Revolution has won freedom of belief and thought for the people," to which Father Antonio Quintanar replied that although the Church is apolitical, as a Mexican he believed it was time to end internal national divisions, for "there is no fight among liberals and conservatives, only Mexicans anxious for social justice."[7]

The new rapprochement between the Roman church and the government party indicates a new interpretation of the reciprocal responsibilities of both. On the part of the Church it reflects the effects of a new Vatican policy for Latin countries, under which the Church seeks to identify itself with more liberal social and political doctrines than it has supported heretofore. Some of the recent events in Argentina, Colombia, Venezuela, Cuba, and even Spain, whereby the hierarchy opposed certain acts of authoritarian rulers, resulted from this new policy. Needless to say, neither in

---

[7] See the Mexican press of February 2, 1958, for reports of this incident. After the election, on his return from consecration ceremonies in Rome, the new Cardinal of Guadalajara went even further, saying, "The Mexican Catholic church is apolitical and will maintain an attitude apart from and outside all political parties. As to politics, we will keep far away from elections, exhorting the people simply to meet their civic duties." *Excelsior*, December 28, 1958.

Mexico nor elsewhere do all members of the Church, lay or clerical, identify with this new approach. Regardless of this, in Mexico the hierarchy has offered enough indication of changing attitudes, and the reforms engendered by the Revolution have become sufficiently institutionalized, to enable the government party to consider relaxing informally its long-established policy of tight controls over the Church.

One indication that adjustments in thinking have taken place on both sides is the aforementioned shift in the PAN's electioneering techniques during both the 1955 and the 1958 campaigns. From old-line, conservative, proclerical, and antirevolutionary doctrines have evolved a comprehensive reform program embracing all, or almost all, of the Revolution's accomplishments. A most striking illustration of the marked moderation shown by both parties' candidates during the 1958 presidential race was a cartoon published in the weekly magazine *Hoy* during carnival time, just before Lent. With the background of a costume ball, the two nominees are shown at the front, López Mateos wearing a priest's surplice and biretta and carrying a missal entitled PAN NUESTRO, and Alvarez in traditional revolutionary costume, wearing a wide-brimmed hat, guns, and bandoleers. Under the picture is quoted the well-known song, "Do you know me, do you know me, masked one?"[8] This reversal of party roles was typical of the whole campaign.

Another novel factor introduced into the 1958 election by López Mateos because of his perspective regarding Mexico's changing situation was a more positive approach to foreign affairs. Until he did so, most campaign references to the outside world were conditioned by the country's traditional isolationism and xenophobia, clear evidence that Mexico had not yet become sufficiently Westernized to feel any great interdependence with other nations. Instead of constructive observations upon the role of Mexico in world or even hemisphere affairs, most politicians seemed to prefer to expend their energies on negative attacks upon the Colossus of the North or upon England for refusing to accept Cárdenas' oil expropriation gracefully. At best, the leading candidates would exhort Mexico to accomplish some goal, be it paving the streets in a border town or solving the country's land problem, in order to preserve the nation's dignity in the world community.

These older attitudes of isolation, once so widely shared and so

---

[8] *Hoy*, February 22, 1958, p. 4.

near the surface, provide us with a striking example of how mass opinion can influence public policy despite the difficulty that non-functional interests have in gaining a voice in decision-making under the same semicorporative sector system of the official party. During the early months of the 1952 presidential campaign, a ground-swell of opposition to the military aid pacts being negotiated with the United States began to appear. Quick to ride this swell, the opposition parties united to attack the agreements and, rather than provide a ready-made major campaign issue, the government ceased negotiations until after the elections.[9]

Granted that this was a very "hot" public question, that it arose during an election in which a rather strong opposition group developed, and that the opposition parties provided already organized agencies through which to exploit these favorable circumstances, the fact remains that the interest group theory of political decision-making as propounded in Chapter I operated in Mexico in spite of the specialized conditions obtaining because of the existence of a single major party organized into functionally based sectors. For all that the conditions here were such as to bring the process to the surface, there can be little doubt that similar pressures just as broadly founded though less obvious to the outsider, operate regularly in the system to provide representation above and beyond the rather specialized forms offered by labor unions, farm groups, and the like.

As the Mexicans become more nearly united in their value system and, at the same time, more sophisticated, these broad, unorganized, but irresistible pressures tend to become more numerous and more influential than ever. Eventually, I suspect, they will cover so many aspects of Mexican life that the functionally based interest associations will find their areas of influence more and more restricted until, as in the United States and other more fully Westernized states, the campaign and its issues will become almost conventionalized, and the corporative organization of the single party will begin to disintegrate. In fact, such a situation may mark the opening of a period of a two-party system for Mexico, for once the deadly competition of incompatible ideologies is removed, a process that appears to be starting already, the way will be clear for political parties to compete for the support of functional interest groups on

---

[9] *Tiempo*, February 15, December 5, 1952; *New York Times*, April 1, 1952.

the basis of the service they can offer them rather than doctrinal differences. Such competition requires only two major parties.

To return to our consideration of foreign affairs in the 1958 campaign, it is to Mexico's credit that neither López Mateos nor Luis Alvarez treated international relations as a political football, but as a vital policy matter. Each of them made it clear that he regarded Mexico as having become a full-fledged member of the community of nations, both politically and economically, again pointing up how far Westernizing tendencies have spread even during the six years since the last presidential election. Both the PRI and the PAN candidate supported Mexico's present international economic policies encouraging foreign investment through free exchange but prohibiting monopolies, and both indicated political identification with the free world as opposed to the Soviet empire. Their only differences lay in detail and emphasis.

López Mateos even went so far as to invite North American newspaper correspondents to a special breakfast-news conference early in his campaign. Here he discussed Mexico's international position freely and openly. Alvarez later followed suit.

The fact that the 1958 presidential election campaign produced fewer real ideological clashes than previous contests does not mean that its seven- or eight-month span was entirely free of agitation. This would be contrary to the whole tradition of Mexican politics. Within the revolutionary coalition, between it and the PAN, and even among the minor parties allied to the PRI, the highly charged atmosphere of elections could not help but provide impetus for political activity and the kinds of related action that always accompany it.

As usually is the case, gubernatorial nomination struggles accompanying the presidential campaign produced interesting, if not always the most significant, clashes within the official party. In February, 1958, for example, the opponents to the nomination of Senator Norberto López Avelar as the PRI candidate for governor in the state of Morelos accused him of having been implicated in the assassination of Emiliano Zapata. Whether the accusation was true or not, it is typical of the sort of charges arising out of intra-party power struggles, as was the efficient manner in which the party hierarchy imposed López Avelar as its choice. Less typical, perhaps, was the strength of the refutation of the charges; one of Zapata's daughters spoke in favor of López Avelar at a CNOP meeting.

If, as so often is charged, the governors are no more than viceroys representing the President of the Republic, one might be tempted to dismiss such disputes as little more than the maneuvers of ambitious men. A few months before the Morelos incident, however, in speaking to the national council of the CTM about the change-over of governors in the state of Mexico, Fidel Velázquez proved just how vital to a given functional interest a governor's nomination can be. He pointed out that the departure of Governor Sánchez Colín from the state executive's chair would "completely change the political picture as regards labor," for his administration had protected captive unions and "repudiated the workers' right to strike." Although this may simply have been Fidel Velázquez's way of saying that Sánchez Colín sided with the anti-BUO faction in the Labor sector, it does suggest the kind of role governors can play in important power struggles inside the party.

Functional interests, too, took the usual advantage of this period of political activity to improve their own position. It is almost ironical that Adolfo López Mateos, who had averted so many strikes while Secretary of Labor, found his campaign plagued with a rash of strikes and threatened work stoppages, as the telegraphers, the telephone workers, electric company employees, and others sought wage increases just as the government hoped to avoid any demonstration of dissatisfaction to mar the election. The success of such tactics in prying increases out of employers (with government approval, or acquiescence, at any rate) served to multiply the number of unions resorting to them, for it is inherent in the nature of functional interest groups that they seek out and utilize every advantage; as in physics, pressure in politics seems to mount just where the barrier is weakest.

Several of these threatened strike movements were supported by the CTM and the BUO, offering clear indication that the specialized interests of particular groups or factions within a sector of the official party still may take precedence over the more general goals of the PRI. This is an interesting commentary upon the lack of complete party discipline, suggesting that despite its corporative structure and growing centralization of controls, the revolutionary coalition is not yet a monolithic organism in which particular interests are unable at least to attempt to protect or enhance their positions.

The same kinds of pressures, resulting from a desire to take advantage of the election period and attendant circumstances, also were brought upon the government from outside of the PRI. During the first months of 1958, for instance, agitators from Lombardo Toledano's UGOCM, led by Jacinto López, precipitated a series of invasions of privately owned farm properties by landless peasants in the states of Baja California, Sonora, Sinaloa, and Colima. In the largest of these invasions, some 6,000 *paracaidistas* (squatters or parachutists) took over nearly 20,000 hectares of irrigated truck farms in the valley of Culiacán, Colima, owned mostly by Greeks and other Europeans, or the descendants of non-Mexicans, just as the tomato crop was ripe for harvest. Only the exhortations of the state's governor, the counsel of the head of the CNC, and a firm promise of aid by Ruiz Cortines' Minister of Agriculture, backed by the presence of federal troops, convinced the squatters that they ought to decamp. A month later, they were allotted four thousand hectares of irrigable land elsewhere; as in the case of the strikers, this simply encouraged further attempts by other land-hungry *peones.*

Both of these cases, like that of the 1952 opposition to the U.S. military aid pacts mentioned earlier, demonstrate that for all of the difficulties of access to government, not to mention the sheer material limitations of resources under which government operates, it is possible for interests to bring pressure effectively in the Mexican political system in order to obtain specialized goals. All three cases indicate that the best time to do so is during the election period.

As the opposition party, *Acción Nacional* also provided a certain amount of life to the campaign, although, with all due respect to it for supplying the only legal candidate other than López Mateos, one can scarcely say that its activities set the political pot boiling. In theory, the PAN's campaign issues and campaign techniques were quite good, probably as effective as any that could have been devised, for, as mentioned earlier, the party had dropped its religious-conservative approach and begun attacking the PRI on policy. No great wisdom was required to discover the weak points in the revolutionary party's program and to hammer upon them. Overcentralization, inadequate consideration for agricultural areas in dispensing government aid and services, inflation undermining the standard of living of the urban workers, political corruption, and a thousand other complaints, real and imagined, soluble or not, irritate the Mexican citizen and, fairly or not, he is inclined to blame the party that has held power for all these years. Naturally, the PAN sought to capitalize on these real and fancied grievances, using pretty much the same techniques for reaching the populace as the official candidate. But for a multitude of reasons, in Alvarez' hands these techniques were not very successful.

*Acción Nacional's* political machinery was weak, restricted in scope, and badly organized. Worse still, the party itself was divided and not sure of its candidate. In addition to the basic division between the die-hard ideological conservatives and those who wanted the party to act within the extant political system, a large section of the membership felt cool toward Alvarez because they felt he did not have the prestige that a Luis Cabrera or a González Luna enjoyed, forgetting that it was difficult to get a candidate at all. Moreover, they had heard the stories of Alvarez' political dilettantism, how he very nearly had entered politics as a *priísta*, then had been in contact with the PNM, and, only when these two contacts failed, had he turned to the PAN to accept the hopeless nomination as candidate for governor of Chihuahua which later led to his selection as the party's presidential candidate; although they suspected some of these tales might have been planted by the official party, enough rubbed off to dampen their enthusiasm.

In actuality, this story probably was not inspired by the PRI; the campaign was hardly enough of a contest to require much in the way of underhanded political tactics. Both Alvarez and López Mateos easily could observe the Mexican convention by which leading political contenders leave the smear techniques to their underlings; better, smears could be omitted altogether. Certainly nothing quite so amusing occurred in 1958 as one event during the previous presidential election. General Múgica of the then non-recognized and now defunct left-wing *Partido Constitucionalista* suddenly alleged that candidate Ruiz Cortines' name had been found on a copy of the payroll of the United States military forces which invaded Veracruz in 1914, probably the most heinous crime a revolutionary Mexican could be accused of. The PRI sprang to the defense of its candidate speedily, but without much coordination. The *Comité Coordinador pro ARC de Córdoba* published a full-page newspaper advertisement headed "Múgica Lies" and explaining that the name on the payroll listed as A. Ruiz C. was not the candidate but one Adolfo Ruiz Cervantes. Almost simultaneously, in a second full-page advertisement another PRI group announced that the culprit really was a certain Adolfo Ruiz Cadenas, and a group of old revolutionaries appeared to swear that the official nominee had been away from Veracruz during the occupation. Finally, an official explanation, stating that the name had been added to the pay list in question in 1938 by persons who had been plotting against Ruiz Cortines during his congressional campaign, was accepted by the PRI-dominated state legislature which investigated and dismissed the charges. Furthermore, few if any voters believed the charges, for accusations and counteraccusations were flying thick and heavy, effectively negating each other to a great extent.[10]

Inevitably, in a situation where one party is for all practical purposes dominant, the opposition will find itself harassed to some extent; during the 1958 race, PAN meetings from time to time were interrupted by street repairs, or rival free carnivals were offered by the local official party organization on days when the PAN candidate was to speak. Alvarez once actually found himself in jail for a few minutes after a small riot that resulted when *panistas* tried to silence three loudspeakers which happened to be playing cha-cha-cha records during one of their meetings, but the central authorities disclaimed the action and disciplined the police chief involved. One serious clash between the two parties took place late in May, when at long last the presidential campaign began to warm up in the capital; there, partisans of the official candidate broke up a large rally for the PAN nominee. Another took place near the end of the campaign, during June, when a PAN party worker was killed in Chihuahua. But the number of clashes and deaths was well below that of any previous recent election.

In truth, little enough need existed for official party attempts to weaken or disrupt Alvarez' campaign; the combination of circumstances working against the PAN and its candidate required no impetus from the PRI. Some of the negative factors we already know—a divided party, lack of depth in the party organization, a large amount of "me-tooism" in its platform, a spirit of defeat, and a virtually unknown candidate. Add to these disadvantages a large amount of bad luck and bad campaigning. The bad luck came in the form of heavy rains, motor trouble, and even snow, which im-

---

[10] See Eisenberg, *op. cit.*, pp. 109-11.

peded Alvarez' efforts to reach his scheduled meetings. And all too often when he did arrive on time, his and his aides' lack of political experience led them to do the worst possible job of campaigning. On one occasion, for instance, a PAN speaker suggested facetiously that since Congress really had little authority it might just as well not exist; the newspapers carried the story under the heading: PAN Would Do Away with Congress. Another time, in introducing Alvarez, one of his followers spoke of the sense of democratic responsibility associated with North American elections; this was reported as: *Acción Nacional* Asks that Mexico Imitate U. S. in Politics. Such stories, carried in not unfriendly newspapers, did nothing to allay and much to firm up already existing suspicions in the minds of the masses about the true motives and goals of the PAN.

If political ineptitude damaged Alvarez' campaign, his political ignorance harmed it even more grievously; every speech the PAN nominee made betrayed not only his inexperience in practical government but, worse still, his inability to formulate a positive administrative program because he simply had too little knowledge of his subject. By February these facts were so obvious that a devastating full-page newspaper advertisement was prepared by a pro-López Mateos group, the *Universitarios y Profesionistas de México*, listing side by side the programs and public statements of the two candidates; even discounting the bias in the ad's selection process, Alvarez came off very badly, as newspaper editorial comment demonstrated.[11]

Under these circumstances, it is hardly surprising that although Alvarez attempted to adapt the PRI's successful campaign technique of trips associated with social-economic conferences to his own uses, it did not begin to suit his needs. Without an effective political organization to turn out the citizenry, without the support of many functional associations, without much in the way of a positive program, and without the drawing power of a well-known name, the PAN candidate consistently attracted small and dispirited crowds which not even his most enthusiastic newspaper supporters could convert into the hoards of shouting people who attended the meetings for Adolfo López Mateos. One inevitable consequence of the kind of campaign it waged was the suspicion, held both by

---

[11] See the Mexico City press for February 10-12, 1958.

disgruntled members of the party and by outsiders, that the PAN
had sold out to the government party, an allegation hotly denied
by Alvarez and Gómez Morín. Nonetheless, as the campaign progressed—or perhaps it would be more nearly accurate to say, failed
to progress—many former supporters of *Acción Nacional* lost faith
and withdrew, usually silently but sometimes publicly and with
strong words. One of the members of the local committee in Tuxtla
Gutiérrez, Chiapas, for example, not only resigned from the committee but from the party itself, citing the marked lack of enthusiasm shown for the PAN's presidential candidate during his tour of
the state, as well as Alvarez' "ignorance of the problems affecting
Chiapas."

Notwithstanding the poor campaign waged by the PAN, it contributed more politically interesting action to the 1958 presidential
race than any of the other minor national parties or unrecognized
political groups, perhaps more than all the rest combined. We have
already seen that during the 1952 campaign not even the absolute
common goal of wanting to defeat the official party's candidate had
been strong enough to unite the opposition parties into a single
and united cooperating group; despite expanding Westernizing influence, they had not yet become that pragmatic. Much the same
was true of the 1958 presidential election, though the possibility of a
united opposition was neither so important nor so likely because of
the complex of conditions under which the so-called independent political movements made their decisions whether to ally themselves
with the PRI or to remain in opposition.

Not even those minor parties which nominated López Mateos
as their candidate participated very much in his campaign. For
one thing, the PRI candidate early in the campaign specifically rejected any alliance with other parties, whether or not they had
nominated him. For another, the other parties found it expedient
to avoid campaigning which might expose publicly their numerical
and organizational weakness.

Other than the PAN, the only organized groups which provided
any real political activity to balance the revolutionary party's campaigning were not legally recognized as national parties. The *Unión
Nacional Sinarquista* waged a negative battle against the PRI,
ordering its supporters to cast blank ballots marked "R. E." for
*reforma electoral,* in an attempt to force reforms in the election laws
that would assure what the *sinarquistas* call free and uncontrolled

elections. At the opposite extreme of the political spectrum, the Communist party decided, after a great deal of indecision, to nominate a candidate although the party was not listed on the ballot. To the surprise of everyone, the nominee was a 74-year-old lawyer who called himself a Catholic with Socialist ideas. Miguel Mendoza López long had been associated with ultraleft politics, having been in 1952 a member of General Múgica's *Partido Constitucionalista* which supported Henríquez Guzmán, but he never had belonged to the Communist party. In actuality, his nomination was a farce, for if he himself was sincere, quite obviously his Communist sponsors were not; they used him as a cat's-paw in their attempts to retain some measure of political influence.

The only real result of the nomination of Mendoza López by the Communists was to further divide Lombardo Toledano from the Mexican Communist party, if not from international communism. As in 1952, when he refused to give up his own candidacy, in 1958 he refused to jeopardize whatever standing the PP had by supporting a nuisance candidate. The resulting public recriminations between Lombardo Toledano and the Communist party leadership, and between the right and left wings of the Popular party, finally dragged in interested outsiders such as the leftist painter David Alfaro Siqueiros, who attacked both sides for dividing the "progressive" forces of the nation, and the PAN, which saw the whole thing as a plot against it as the only real opposition party. Speaking through Segundo Ramos, a well-known Ecuadorian Communist, the Kremlin itself censored Lombardo Toledano, but in terms mild enough to allow further use of his services when convenient.

Despite all of this ancillary political activity, the real political drama long since had taken place at PRI headquarters and *Los Pinos,* with the selection of the official presidential candidate and his congressional and gubernatorial running mates. The results of the polling held on July 6, 1958, prove this. According to the official canvass made by the Chamber of Deputies early in September, López Mateos won 6,769,754 of the total 7,485,403 individual votes cast for president. Although this 90.4 per cent of the total vote was much higher than the 74.3 per cent Ruiz Cortines had garnered six years previously, the latter had faced stronger opposition; moreover, only a disappointing 71.4 per cent of the already reduced total of registered voters turned out to vote at all in 1958. Nonetheless, the election was a smashing victory over Alvarez and the

PAN, for he gained only 705,303 votes throughout the country. A final 10,346 votes went to "non-registered" candidates, including Mendoza López of the Communist party and Leonardo García Pérez, who was supported by a small write-in movement labeled the National Democratic Alliance, but in the capital a third of the write-in votes went to Ernesto Uruchurtu.

The PRI's congressional election victory was equally complete and continued the pattern of the previous term. Not one Senate seat went to an opposition candidate. Similarly, in the Chamber of Deputies the opposition parties won nine seats, as they had three years before. In spite of the PAN and PP refusals to participate in the vote counting and certifying functions of the Federal Election Commission and the Chamber, both parties were declared to have defeated PRI candidates, the PAN in six districts and the PP in one. As we saw earlier, both of these parties prohibited the successful candidates from accepting the seats assigned but four of the six *panistas* and the single member of the Popular party insisted upon entering the Chamber.

The final results in the Chamber of Deputies were as follows:

PRI— 153 members
PAN— 6 members, of whom only four accepted. Those who refused represented the third district in the Federal District and the first district of Zacatecas (Zacatecas City); those who accepted represented the first district of Yucatán (Mérida), the second district of Baja California Norte (Tijuana), the second district of Chiapas (San Cristobal de las Casas), and the fifth of Puebla (Acatlán).
PP— 1 member, representing the second district of Guerrero (Iguala).
PARM— 1 member, representing the first district of Morelos (Cuernavaca).
PNM— 1 member, representing the third district of Puebla (Cholula). He also had been nominated by the PARM.

It is difficult to discover any general pattern in the election of opposition members to the lower house, though it might be pointed out that, with the exception of the two PAN deputies from Chiapas and Puebla, each of the successful candidates represents reasonably large towns or cities where political awareness is greater and chances for the formation of effective opposition party organization better.

CHAPTER *8*

# The Presidency

## The Changing Role of the Presidency

No clearer example exists to show how profoundly Mexico's political decision-making process has been affected by Westernization
than the way in which the president's political function has changed
to keep pace with the country's evolving political system. Even
today it would be hard to overstate the amount of political power
the president wields, but one could easily misunderstand the source
and nature of that great power, for although the president remains
far and away the strongest single political leader in the republic,
the basis of his strength has shifted radically from what it was only
a few years ago.

All major policy decisions still are made by the president but,
speaking figuratively, he no longer reaches them at PRI headquarters; instead, he makes them at *Los Pinos*, the official residence of
Mexico's chief executive. That is to say, the center of the locus of
power gradually has been moving away from the extra-official
mechanisms of the revolutionary party toward more formal, constitutional government, though the process is as yet by no means
complete. Emphasis in the president's political role has shifted
correspondingly, from primarily that of a personalistic party leader
toward director of an increasingly powerful government bureaucracy
that arbitrates among the reasonably well-adjusted functional interest associations which submit themselves to the discipline of the

emerging governmental system. Both the change in the political system and the shift of the president's role in that system parallel closely the institutionalization of political agencies and activities described in previous chapters of this study as part of the process of Westernization.

Some such systematization and formalization of political activities was bound to occur in Mexico sooner or later, because no political movement, not even an all-powerful, easily joined semiofficial party such as the revolutionary coalition, could hope to substitute indefinitely for the established government in servicing the political needs of over thirty million Mexicans rapidly entering national life. Multiplication of functional interests and of specialized groups to represent those interests has made the fabric of Mexican society more complex, requiring stronger threads to bind that fabric together. These binding threads are really nothing but more complicated techniques for dealing effectively with intricate political relationships, techniques which cannot be administered successfully by the haphazard agency of a constantly changing party hierarchy subject to the all too often irrational will of a charismatic leader. Modern Western society requires more rigidly structured political agencies to provide continuous and predictable controls which allow the citizens to live a patterned and orderly life; almost by definition, these must be constitutional agencies.

None of this is intended to deprecate the importance of the role played by the revolutionary party, first in providing informal machinery to meet the challenge of changing political circumstances and later in providing a core of power to allow the formal governmental agencies to assume their necessary political responsibilities. During the 1930's, the need for additional political control-mechanisms was met largely by the revolutionary party and its three sector organizations, which supplied not only a kind of extra-constitutional means of access to the decision-making process but also auxiliary machinery for adjusting conflicts among the competing interests making demands upon government. Later, starting in the forties, when the interests which had to be considered grew so numerous and so varied that they could not be subsumed within its three sectors, the revolutionary party provided a solid foundation upon which to build constitutional stability, because by then the internal relationships among the functional interest associations participating in the sector organizations had become so formalized, so nearly frozen into place by long-established habits of cooperation and discipline, that government agencies could step in to exercise controls successfully over both the old and the new interest groups.

Significantly, in terms of the subject matter of this chapter, the key to integration and synchronization of the political activities of both the formal and the informal mechanisms of government has remained in the hands of one political officer who is, simultaneously, president of Mexico and head of the revolutionary party. The very act of strengthening the part taken by formal government agencies in the decision-making process, with a corollary sublimation (though not necessarily elimination) of the extra-constitutional interest associations acting to influence public policy through the official party, implies a basic change in the nature of the function of the officer who manipulates the two sets of mechanisms. But it does not imply that the president is weaker now than before the institutionalization of the political system; on the contrary, now that the system is more nearly rationalized, as long as the chief executive keeps within the bounds of political propriety, as delineated by custom, he can bring to bear upon any recalcitrant individual or interest group all of the concentrated and organized strength of both party and government.

Mexico seems to have solved the main problem of charismatic government—how to transfer power from one leader to another—in the only way possible, by doing away with the emotional tie between leader and follower through the institutionalization of the presidency. That is, by replacing charismatic government altogether with a less personal, mechanistic, and semiconstitutional system. Some of the average Mexican's tendency toward personalistic identification with a specific president carries over, of course, but the man toward whom that personal loyalty is directed now is more a product of the system than its progenitor. The fact that each six years a new person can take office to perform the presidential function demonstrates that in a very real sense the position has become more an institution than an individual. The further fact that each new president in turn has been successful in performing his twofold role as chief of government and head of the PRI, despite a constant and almost frantic accretion in the number and type of interests to be balanced, suggests, too, that in Mexico's developing political system it is not the president alone but the entire office of the presidency, supplying essential staff assistance to assure his effectiveness in all aspects of political activity, that makes the political system work.

In the earlier years of the Revolution, we know, neither party mechanisms nor formal governmental agencies were sufficiently influential in the political system to supply a president with this auxiliary strength, so that if he did not possess personally the great energy and individual ability required to capture loyal support and to assure the authority of the constitutional agencies, he could not fulfill his legal and political responsibilities. Then some *caudillo* might appear to oust him or to act as the power behind the throne; Huerta played the first role when he ended Madero's tragic administration and Calles the second while dominating Portes Gil, Ortiz Rubio, and Rodríguez from behind the scenes.

Today, with the development of stabilizing political institutions and proliferation of specialized interests, the incumbent in the presidential office must have very different qualities than did his dynamic and hard-driving charismatic forebear, because he must provide equilibrium among all of the diverse interests which have to be accommodated inside of the political system. In the last chapter we saw that a pre-candidate's availability for the official nomination is enhanced by neutral or semineutral characteristics such as those possessed by Alemán, Ruiz Cortines, and López Mateos before their selection. Because of the president's serious attempt to pick a man who is, at least, somewhat acceptable to a majority of the principal interest groups or, at best, the enthusiastic choice of all, at the end of a presidential term the interaction among the multifold interests operating in and around the sectors of the PRI does not result in prolonged refusal to accept the nominee by most functional association leaders.

A comparison of the type of politician who held the presidency early in the Revolution with more recent nominees of the government party is enlightening in this respect. Of the twelve men who have been president of Mexico since 1920, five have been generals, two leaders of armed forces without a corresponding military rank, and only five civilians, but three of those five civilians held the presidential office most recently. It is no coincidence that the transition in 1940 from charismatic-type presidents to leaders who could balance representation of conflicting interests corresponds exactly to the maturing of institutionalization of Mexico's political system. The change-over was facilitated, however, because General

Avila Camacho, who was elected president that year, enjoyed a certain aura of authority as a military man but was much more an administrator than an old-style *caudillo*.

Significantly, when President Alemán delivered the sash of office to President-elect Ruiz Cortines in December, 1952, the outgoing executive was the first civilian since Juárez in the 1860's to complete a full presidential term; not even Madero had managed to accomplish that. Yet Alemán as well as Ruiz Cortines and López Mateos used the constitutional agencies of government to hold contending interests in check and to provide stable and even fruitful government such as their more militaristic predecessors only dreamed of attaining.

In sum, the presidential function does not now make the same demands upon personalistic leadership to evoke singular and immediate emotional response by followers in the heat of battle that it once did. Instead, the surge of response to a dominant personality whose public aims are few and not very specific cannot displace the more prosaic response to the manifold operations of government. The individual in the presidency can count upon a sure positive reaction to the operation of his office, which has become a necessary part of multitudes of lives and activities throughout the country. In the Mexican political system, where the real task of politics is not camouflaged by the struggle to capture public office because this now is assured by the official party's nomination, the role of the president in the most constructive work of politics, adjusting differences among complex and continuing interests, is obvious to most politically minded citizens. Consequently, a good deal of popular support exists for the machinery—government and party agencies— by which these adjustments are made, as well as for the president who controls both sets of machinery.

## The Strong Presidency

Because of the factors working to institutionalize the vital role of the presidency in Mexico's political system, the individual entering the office of president assumes a great deal of authority automatically, so that while a strong-willed political personality may become president, a less forceful man may find winning the official nomination a great deal easier but still can take office with reasonable hope of success. In fact, as it now operates, the system appears to make even a relatively unassuming presidential nominee such as Avila

Camacho or Ruiz Cortines independent of a more dynamic predecessor and, quite early in the game, the dominant political personality in the country.

This mode of thought accepting the president's political authority is deeply ingrained in the Mexican political mentality. Note how even an anthropologist, in describing the pre-Columbian ceremony of the new year, refers to the power of the new chief of state:

> Even after the Fifth Sun had been created no one knew from which direction it would rise, but finally it came up in the East. The animals which had faced the wrong way immediately were sacrificed in its honor. . . . The Indians conceived of historical occurrences in closed cycles, independent of each other, and the cycle of one sun had nothing to do with another, other than order of appearance. It was as though with each sun the world would come to an end. (In reality, this way of looking at things still exists, for each President of the Republic is a species of New Sun. Today, too, the politicians who do not know how to forecast where he will spring from are sacrificed, just as were the animals which guessed wrong.)[1]

The high degree of independence of action an incumbent president can safely take upon himself because of the power inherent in his twofold party-constitutional position was first demonstrated in the struggle for supremacy between Calles and Cárdenas, which the latter won. But it was not until later, and partly because of Cárdenas' example on leaving the presidency, that an incoming president seemed automatically to assume authority to make him independent of his immediate predecessor. General Cárdenas withdrew from national political life, as we have seen, and so did Avila Camacho, each permitting his successor to dominate the machinery of political and constitutional control. They also brought moral pressure to bear, forcing Alemán to do the same for Ruiz Cortines, though by this time the combined institutionalization of party and constitutional control mechanisms probably had begun to provide the new chief executive with sufficient authority of his own to sanctify a kind of unwritten "law of the presidential succession" under which he could achieve freedom of action to the extent necessary.

A politically important corollary of this law of presidential succession is, I suspect, an understanding that the ex-presidents of

[1] Wigberto Jiménez Moreno, *Historia Antigua de México,* Publicaciones de la Sociedad de Alumnos de la Escuela Nacional de Antropología e Historia, No. 1 (Mexico, D.F., 1953).

revolutionary Mexico are sacrosanct in their persons, so that no matter what differences may exist among the revolutionary leaders, they avoid public washing of their linen. This stems from the need to preserve the façade of legitimacy surrounding the presidency, which serves to unite the several factors operating in the political-constitutional system and, therefore, to provide political stability for the country.

As the first semi-independent civilian president since Madero, Alemán was expected to face a certain degree of difficulty during his term, but by the very fact that he was president he exercised sufficient influence to meet a serious challenge very early in his administration, before he could have had time to build a personal political organization within the executive branch loyal only to him. Within a few months of Alemán's inauguration, a serious strike broke out in the important Atzcapotzalco refinery of the government petroleum monopoly, reputedly instigated by Communist leadership in the petroleum workers union. Alemán used troops to put down the strike, ousted the union leaders, and emerged a strong president, despite the defection of certain left-wing elements in the PRI. It was soon after this, for instance, that Lombardo Toledano broke away to form his *Partido Popular*.

The Alemán administration was noted for its grandiose economic activities, for the building of new industrial sites, for the construction of huge irrigation and hydroelectric dams, for the expansion of school facilities at all levels, including the entirely new National University campus just outside Mexico City. It also became noted later by word of mouth and in the Mexico City newspapers for the corruption accompanying all of these projects, and for the very profitable economic strangleholds reputedly held by such men as Jorge Pasquel, with his oil distribution monopoly in the capital, Aaron Sáenz, who betrayed the agricultural masses' interests to dominate the sugar industry, or Antonio Díaz Lombardo, who made a fortune in transport and by milking the Social Security Department.

Given the revelations emerging afterward, it is hardly possible that the newspapers, the opposition politicians, and at least some members of the general public who praised Alemán and his administration so fulsomely did not know of these evils, but the position of the Mexican president is such that they hardly dared hint at irregularities while Alemán was in office. Newspapers and newsmen were subsidized for printing friendly reports, but in several cases bloody retribution followed unfavorable stories. Nor did members of the opposition care to jeopardize the legal recognition of their own parties or to bring personal reprisals upon themselves by becoming too specific in their charges.

Alemán and his administration offer a striking example of a major weakness inherent in the type of strong presidency that has evolved in Mexico during its period of transition to full Western-style constitutional government. Because presidential power still is based in part upon control of a single party, and formal mechanisms of government are subject to the PRI's influence, it is very difficult to hold a given chief executive politically responsible for his acts. As a consequence, it was not until Alemán was out of office and Ruiz Cortines sworn in as his successor, because Cárdenas and Avila Camacho vetoed Alemán's preferred pre-candidates, that the full magnitude of corruption became public knowledge.

That it became public knowledge at all is indisputable proof that in spite of his relatively inconspicuous background, Ruiz Cortines, too, speedily assumed the president's mantle of broad authority when he took office in December, 1952. Although he had very carefully appointed an experienced cabinet representative of most interests in the revolutionary movement,[2] it soon became clear that he intended to bow to none of them. The proportion of *alemanistas* in his cabinet or among those appointed to higher policy-making posts was much lower than had been anticipated and many of the leading figures in the former administration were encouraged to leave the country on temporary or semipermanent diplomatic assignments; others were retired to their home states or to private life in the capital. Alemán himself left for an extended European visit in March. Meanwhile, President Ruiz Cortines was cleaning up, ending unlawful or unfair monopolies, firing grafting politicians or venal public employees, and even suspending payment of claims on the government until their validity could be reviewed. To assure the loyal support of most public servants, he increased bureaucratic salaries ten per cent, but at the same time insisted upon drastic tightening-up of the *Ley de Responsibilidades* that required publi-

---

[2] The collective political experience of Ruiz Cortines' cabinet included four governorships, two cabinet posts, nine other high executive posts, two military leaders for Defense and Marine Affairs, two high PRI party bureaucrats, and one ex-senator. The heads of the executive departments included men identified with *cardenismo*, *avilacamachismo*, and *alemanismo*.

cation of financial statements from all upper-echelon public officers, appointed or elected. Finally, he enforced the land laws against some of the highest figures in the old regime, who had acquired huge estates illegally while in office, and divided their holdings among the landless country people.

The clearest single manifestation of Ruiz Cortines' power during the first reform-packed years of his administration was the successful avoidance of the threatened general strike of July, 1954, mentioned in the previous chapter as a triumph for Labor Minister López Mateos. This indicated that the presidential power was sufficiently established to contain the pressures brought by so well-organized an interest group as the CTM, whose leaders still tended toward *alemanismo*, giving a certain amount of credence to an earlier denial that the Alemán clique was seeking to organize against the president. As Enrique Parra Hernández, a leading *alemanista*, said, "that would be impossible because the power of a President of Mexico has no limit but the limit of time, his six years in office. If there were any *alemanismo*, President Ruiz Cortines would have only to snap his fingers to crush it. Such is the power of Mexican presidents." [3]

If *alemanismo* did not become a potent force in President Ruiz Cortines' administration, it was not for lack of trying as much as for lack of strength, as Parra Hernández suggested. Using his own political-constitutional presidential authority, bolstered by support from the *cardenista* wing of the PRI, Ruiz Cortines maintained his position of control against the pressures from the right. Lest we overvalue the president's dependence upon the left wing of his party in this contest, however, let me point out that Ruiz Cortines possessed enough independence of action to use the left successfully in containing the *alemanistas* without committing himself irrevocably to it. Even though his dealings with the left wing were complicated by rather basic ideological differences stemming from the president's support of a centrist position against the more radical views of the left, these differences were kept at an abstract level rather than descending into a personal struggle between Ruiz Cortines and the strongest *caudillo* in Mexico, General Cárdenas.

Two separate events during 1954 marked the conflict between right and left. The first was Cárdenas' message of support and sym-

---

[3] Quoted in the *New York Times*, July 23, 1953.

pathy for Colonel Arbenz Guzmán's leftist Guatemalan government in its dispute with Castillo Armas and the United Fruit Company, sent May 29, and released to the press by the Guatemalan embassy on June 17. Public response to this message was stronger than expected; some of it was favorable, for Cárdenas represents a strong current of left-liberal opinion, but a surprisingly strong negative reaction also resulted, sparked to great extent by the rightists who were contending with the *cardenistas* for dominant influence in the revolutionary party. The issue might have continued to simmer unresolved just beneath the surface of public consciousness if another clash of opinions had not precipitated an open right-left conflict a month later.

This clash resulted from a series of events surrounding the death of painter Frida Kahlo, wife of Diego Rivera. As a meritorious national artist, her body lay in state at the Palace of Fine Arts, where many prominent persons, including General Cárdenas and his son Cuahutémoc, stood as part of the guard of honor. The difficulty arose because during the rites the coffin was covered with a Communist party flag. Mexican rightists and nationalists united to object so strongly that Dr. Andres Iduarte was dismissed as Director of the National Institute of Fine Arts for not having prohibited the use of the red flag. The *alemanistas* took advantage of the Kahlo incident to make a concerted double attack on General Cárdenas, for his left tendencies and for what they hinted were dishonest activities in a relatively minor, semihonorary post he held as executive director of the Tepalcatepic hydroelectric and irrigation project in his native state of Michoacán. Turning the tables on his accusers, Cárdenas deliberately forced the issue by resigning his post, making the president select publicly between him and the right wing. Ruiz Cortines chose Cárdenas, declining the resignation because the general had "been carrying out his duties satisfactorily." [4] Cárdenas returned to his position, where he remained until March of 1958,

---

[4] During this period President Ruiz Cortines was alternately attacked or praised by both sides, depending upon his latest act. On August 31, 1954, I picked up this throwaway, crudely lettered with crayon on cheap paper; its poorly spelled message is typical of the kind one found—"Down with the power of this old man, Ruiz Cortines. Death to the filth. All thinking Mexicans ought to unite in demanding the resignation of the grafting gringo-lover, Ruiz Cortines, who should leave the presidency for honest men."

ABAJO DEL PODER DE ESE VIEJO RUIZ CORTINES MUERA LA RONA TODOS UNIDOS LOS MEXICANOS CONSIENTES DEVEMOS PEDIR LA RENUNCIA DEL INJERTO AGRINGADO RUIZ CORTINES QUE DEJE LA PRECIDENSIA PARA LOS HOMBRES HONRADOS

when he resigned because the project was substantially completed, being careful before he did so to offer public approval for López Mateos as the PRI's presidential nominee, so as to preclude his action being used against the candidate.

The use to which Cárdenas put his consolidated political position, vetoing the leading *alemanista* pre-candidates for the 1958 presidential nomination, has already been discussed. But we should note that this was all he did, for President Ruiz Cortines was sufficiently independent of either the right or the left wing to make his own selection. Certainly Adolfo López Mateos had characteristics that fell between rather than at either end of the political spectrum encompassed by the revolutionary party.

The first few months of President López Mateos' administration showed somewhat the same pattern as had those of his two predecessors. That is, early in his term the new chief executive was forced to demonstrate that the institutionalized authority of the presidency is sufficient to permit him to control serious challenges to his position, even before he had time to consolidate his government. The labor disorders, student disturbances, and invasions of occupied farm lands by landless peasants which had begun during the election period carried over after López Mateos was inaugurated, culminating in the Holy Week railroad strike of March, 1959, just four months after the new president took office. As we have seen, like Alemán and Ruiz Cortines before him, López Mateos acted promptly and effectively to prove that he had control of the situation. On the basis of his experience in Mexico's political system, the new president knew full well that if he was to fulfill his essential role in organizing and balancing the activities of all major factors of political power in the country, the man heading the executive must be a strong president in his own right. Only thus can he satisfy the president's primary responsibility to the political system at this stage of Mexico's political development—providing the necessary authority for the political agencies which operate a stable and workable national government.

This he must do even at the expense, sometimes, of constitutional niceties, a point to be noted, for although the trend is toward more formal government, the high degree of respect for constitutional formalism, prescribing that outward forms be observed, may betray the incautious observer into believing that the political system very nearly has come to coincide with the structure of government described in the constitution. This simply is not so. As a few case studies will quickly prove, when left to their own devices the adjustment of various formal agencies of government to the norms of the constitution leaves much to be desired. That is to say, departure from the constitutional concepts of division and separation of powers is not so much an indication of a power-hungry president as it is evidence of the continuing failure of the basic law to meet the country's present-day political needs.

Mere listing of powers and responsibilities of governmental units in a constitution does not necessarily carry with it an inherent and automatic ability to exercise the assigned mandate; notwithstanding nominal federalism and presidential government, neither the national legislature nor the judiciary, much less any state government, has proved itself sufficiently capable to capture enough political authority to fulfill its governmental functions independently. In the present political system the other agencies of government do not perform the function of, and therefore cannot be considered as, independent, coequal, or sovereign units in relation to the national executive, particularly with regard to major policy questions.

Although a complete swing to strict constitutionalism has not yet been achieved, the complex social and economic relationships of modern society do demand orderly government, the mechanisms of which can provide access to policy-making for all the major interests participating in national life, together with reasonable assurance that public policy will be more or less predictable and equitable for all elements in the society. In order to provide such government, Mexico's presidents have allowed—even forced—certain of the government agencies to perform their legal duties efficiently in relation to the day-to-day needs of the average citizen, but have been unable to allow them to assume their formal roles as independent or coequal units in the constitutional system because, for all its recent mushrooming, the broadly based national political value system has not yet become deeply enough institutionalized to assure loyal and coordinate cooperation without some firm directing hand. For this reason, as Westernization proceeds in Mexico, an auxiliary policy-deciding mechanism under the direct control of the chief executive has evolved in the presidency.

Because of its extra-constitutional status, this decision-making apparatus adjusts quite easily to the ever-expanding needs of the country for effective political controls; over the years it has come to include all of the principal factors interested in national policy— the president, his staff aides of various sorts, the heads of the executive departments, functional interest representatives from organizations both in and out of the revolutionary party, as well as professional government and nongovernmental bureaucracies, all interacting together. As it now operates, the presidency combines admirably the traditional pattern of strong executive influence with an adequate administrative system that services the political needs of a modern nation-state, both of which are required during the present period of transition toward a working constitutional system.

Significantly, in Mexico, as elsewhere, legalization of function tends to follow the established political practice. Soon after assuming office, for example, President López Mateos sent to Congress for approval his proposal to restructure portions of the executive departmental system. Among other changes, he set up a *Secretaría de la Presidencia* which assumed legally many of the functions the presidency already assumed informally. The new Secretariat of the Presidency under Lic. Donato Miranda Fonseca has planning, coordination, and review controls over both general policy and budgetary activities of all national government agencies, including independent bodies and state-national units. At the same time, López Mateos established a new Secretariat of National Patrimony that not only registers and controls all national property but acts as a control over the operations of many of the formally independent agencies. In accord with these two steps to formalize the high concentration of authority in the presidency, the same law dropped several secretariats, added several more, and shuffled the functions of others, to clarify the lines of control and to rationalize the operations of the executive branch. All of this was nothing more than legal recognition of the auxiliary governing mechanism that has grown up in and about the office of the president over the years in response to the needs of the country.

Authority for the chief executive to construct such an auxiliary governing mechanism stems chiefly from three sources—broad constitutional grants of power, political influence growing out of control of the official party, and the deep-rooted tradition of a strong executive. Though they appear separately on a list, obviously the three intermingle almost completely in actual practice, building one upon the other to form the internally consistent and complementary pattern of political habits that centers power in the executive and provides the hard core of Mexico's postrevolutionary political system.

Mexico's constitutions always have allotted an exceptionally large proportion of governmental authority to the executive at the expense of the other constitutional branches, much more than do the laws of the Western states from which the Mexican documents were adapted. In this respect the Constitution of 1917 is no exception. Again, the greatest bulk of organized political power, as well as the majority of functional interest associations, continues to lie inside of the PRI's ranks, and it is the president who controls the activities of the official party. Finally, Mexico's political realists long have recognized the need for a strong executive, free to employ other than strictly legalistic means in assuring the hegemony of the central government throughout the republic. By combining the broad powers derived from law and politics with the general patent of authority granted by tradition, the presidency has become the focal point for all really effective political activity in Mexico.

It would matter very little if during his administration President López Mateos wished to abandon this concentration of power in the presidency so as to bring the Mexican political system into closer approximation of the formal constitutional system. Undoubtedly, if he were to try, he would have no more success than did President Eisenhower during the first years of his administration, when he sought to treat with the United States Congress as the absolute coequal that the North American constitution envisions rather than to provide the national leadership that pragmatic experience dictates to be an essential factor in the success of the United States political system. In Mexico the need for strong political leadership to motivate the one effective aggregating agency is infinitely greater than in the United States, so great that it molds the public personality and actions of the man who personifies government, no matter what his private inclinations may be.

For all his high position, in his role as chief of the political system the president no more can exercise completely free and rational choice, or act independently of the values that motivate the political system, than the newest member of the *ayuntamiento* in the smallest *municipio* in Mexico. The political requirements of his office very nearly force the president to fall into the pattern of the dominant executive. For that matter, being a Mexican, motivated by the same values and a product of the same history as all other Mexicans, not to mention having risen politically to the apex of the political hierarchy within this same political atmosphere, it is doubtful whether López Mateos or any other president would wish to change the political system very much, even if he were able to do so.[5]

All this does not mean to suggest that the private feelings and attitudes of each incumbent have no effect whatsoever upon the tenor of his administration; the concentration of power in his hands is such that almost without willing it the president has a tremendous political impact. What it does suggest is that despite his vast personal influence, the function of the presidency that the chief executive heads has become so much more all-inclusive and so institutionalized that a discussion of its activities no longer describes the acts or personality of one man, no matter how dominant his character; instead, it describes the entire political environment in which the president operates.

### The Grid of Power

Until such time as all of the formal constitutional machinery becomes more operative in the political system, the presidency will continue to function as a control unit over the interlocking grid of power factors which work on politics, exerting pressure upon functional interest associations, political organizations, and the other agencies of government to force conformity with the needs of a stable political system. In reality, it has no choice but to do so if the country is to enjoy government adequate to the requirements of its proliferating national society and expanding economy.

The president, working through the presidency, can exercise this control function successfully for two very good reasons. The first, we know, is that by now the greatest proportion of politically minded Mexicans accept the legitimacy of the revolutionary government and the political mechanisms through which it works. The second reason is that the political control mechanisms used by the presidency can bring almost irresistible pressure to bear on any recalcitrant individual, group, or political unit. The executive has

---

[5] See Stephen S. Goodspeed, "The Role of the Chief Executive in Mexico: Politics, Powers and Administration," unpublished Ph.D. thesis, University of California, Berkeley, California, 1947, for a more complete description of the evolving role of the president. For a general description of President López Mateos' political outlook and for substantiation of his disinclination to reverse the pattern of Mexican politics, see Josep Barrales V., *El Pensamiento Político de Adolfo López Mateos* (Mexico, D.F., 1959).

so many different resources in its arsenal of power that the president always is prepared to mount an "offense in depth" against his opponents, utilizing whichever of his sources of strength—legal, political, or popular-traditional—he deems most expedient, or all of them if he so desires.

In effect, the structure of political power consists of a hierarchy of interrelated groups and associations, the loyalties and relations of whose leaders culminate in the president, who in turn uses the mechanisms of the presidency to play one individual and interest against another in his attempt to assure political stability. No local, state, or national political figure or functional interest representative can hope to exercise his influence over the unit he represents for any appreciable length of time if he is in open conflict with the rest of the interests in the coalition and especially with the executive coordinating their activities. If he happens to hold public office, the politician's independence of action is even more restricted because he must depend upon the presidency in trying to meet the dual responsibilities endemic in the polyfunctional role assigned him in the Mexican political system. Without the support and assistance of the national executive, which assures a certain amount of adjustment (if not active cooperation) among all of the factors active in a given situation, the individual official never could succeed in satisfying his two separate and at times antagonistic publics—the functional interest organization that named him for office and the more general constituency that the office serves.

As in most hierarchical systems, the president is at the apex of the pyramid and influence and control still seem to flow from the top down to the lower echelons of government and functional association. But here there are horizontal as well as vertical lines of control working at every level and upon every unit of government; each local government, already dominated by the president's "viceroy" in the state—the governor—and the PRI organization he heads, also is splintered by the shared loyalties of its members, to the *municipio* they serve and to the sectors in which they act politically and economically. And, as we have just seen, the individual members themselves are torn by their dual responsibilities to functional association and legal agency.

At the state level, too, the political system allows the president a wide choice of pressure tactics to assure a reasonably docile and cooperative administration. If, as the president's representative, the governor generally is the dominant figure in state politics, he too must deal with cooperating sectors in the PRI whose component members are in close and constant contact with their national interest association at the capital. The national leaders of these functional organizations, in turn, are dependent for their success, even for their positions in the organization, upon the good will of the president; he can, therefore, use them and their groups whenever necessary to bring pressure upon uncooperative state officials. Failing in this informal suasion, the president can turn to the alternate route of direct action. Given his control over Congress, the chief executive can always use one of several constitutional grants of authority to the national government in order to remove an offending state officer of any kind; in fact, given his control over the interest organizations which nominate state officials, from time to time the president finds it more convenient politically to instigate the necessary formal action through other officers of the state government itself. In either event, the *Secretaría de Gobernación* can approve the action and national troops enforce it if necessary. Normally, however, none of these recourses is required, for the governor cooperates to the hilt with the national executive; if he does not, the political system so concentrates authority in the presidency that the dissenter usually can be persuaded either to change his mind or to leave the office to a more tractable successor.

The fact that functional interest associations in the PRI's sectors are used by the presidency to hold difficult government officials in line does not mean that in seeking their own specialized goals the interest group leaders can act as independent agents contrary to the wishes of legally seated officials, unless the chief executive so wills it for purposes of his own. Remember the inability of the CTM to force Governor Sánchez Colín to change his labor policy in the state of Mexico. As in the case of persons holding formal government office, the heads of functional interest associations are bound to the political system by a common stake in the activities of the revolutionary coalition, but they depend even more completely upon the good will of the president than do other politicians because of the sharp competition for government favors with other sectors in the official party and, for that matter, with other functional interests in their own sector. The same dependence upon presidential good will is even more marked in the case of persons representing those interests which must operate within the political decision-making system but from outside of the revolutionary fold.

The president's power to make or break functional interest leaders is vast. For labor and agrarian leaders, and even for the representatives of the growing business and manufacturing interests outside the PRI, his power to recognize strikes, to grant or refuse road or irrigation projects, to remit state and *municipio* debts to the national government, to apply or relax taxes or trade regulations, and all the other discretionary decisions he can render make the president master of their destinies. The executive's control over substantive policy matters and dispensation of job patronage at the national level and his influence over the governors who exercise the same power in the states, together with his strong influence over the making and enforcement of professional standards, leaves even the Popular sector leaders dependent upon the cooperation and friendship of the president. If he delegates some of his powers to the governor of a state, to a sector bureaucracy, or to one of his cabinet ministers, it is done through the extra-legal mechanism of the presidency more than the formal processes of the law (though these too may be changed for appearances' sake); he can, therefore, always withdraw the powers he has granted and bestow them upon competing interest leaders.

All of this talk of interest representation should not, however, blind us to the fact that in his governing activities the president deals with men and not simply with abstract concepts. For all that the interest representatives must produce some gains for the forces they speak for, they are still individuals and Mexicans, with all of the personality quirks and human motivations this implies, including a marked tendency to serve their own immediate interests at least as much as they do their broader responsibility to their respective groups or associations. Because of this, the chief executive often can control these disparate allies of his by manipulating, with consummate tact backed by steel power, the jealousies and cross-purposes of the political and functional leaders he leads and serves.

## Case Studies of Presidential Control

Perhaps it would be worth while at this point to offer several short case studies of the relationship between the executive and some of the other formal units of government, in order to point up the manner in which the president uses his authority to make the façade of constitutionalism work in spite of the difficulties already alluded to. It is hardly necessary to suggest that each of them deserves more detailed treatment than I can attempt here, but I shall endeavor to compensate for the limitations imposed by space by supplying citations to other sources whenever possible.

The constitutional unit that demonstrates most clearly just how widely yawns the gulf between legal form and actual political practice is the Congress of the Union because, as every informed Mexican knows, its principal function—policy- or law-making—has been assumed by the presidency almost *in toto*. Apart from their subordination to the executive on major policy issues, members of the national judiciary and state government officers maintain some freedom of action within the sphere of their official duties because the local units of government and the mechanisms for resolving legal controversies between private persons must be able to exercise a certain amount of authority or the whole fabric of modern society would break down. As long as their acts or decisions do not run too strongly counter to the broad policy lines laid out by the executive, therefore, judges and state officials may carry on their duties with reasonable independence and self-respect. Not so the congressmen, for the legislative function resides in the two chambers only in the most sterile, legalistic sense, depriving the senators and deputies of even this small pretense of independence with which to salve their bruised egos.

Actually, the situation is not quite so black as I have painted it, for most of the members of the revolutionary party who sit in Congress accept the political convention that calls for primacy in policy-making to be exercised by the presidency, while many Mexicans who have a vital interest in public policy but are not professional politicians recognize that, as now constituted, the Congress does not and could not perform a successful aggregating function. Those who complain that, since Cárdenas, the official party has stolen the power and constitutional role of the legislative branch too easily forget the fruitless debates and endless internecine warfare which used to mark congressional sessions when the undisciplined and irreconcilable personalistic power-blocs made constructive lawmaking impossible. Could Cárdenas or anyone else steal what did not exist?

The president's domination of the national legislature is almost absolute, as it is based on all three prime sources of executive authority and extends not only to legislative but to other allied functions of the two chambers. We already know that the balance of power tips far in favor of the president in regard to constitutionally allocated powers. In addition, under Mexico's traditional system of code or civil law the executive always has enjoyed a wide prerogative in administrative rule-making, with little or no effective congressional review of the use to which he puts this privilege. Furthermore, although the 1917 constitution emphatically forbade granting the executive "extraordinary powers" to legislate, except in the most stringent emergencies, the emergencies seemed to come so thick and fast during the twenties and thirties that the president always seemed to have a high degree of legislative authority. Finally, in 1938, at President Cárdenas' request, the constitution was amended again, to strengthen the prohibition. Nonetheless, during the emergency period of World War II the chief executive reassumed the power, and a few years ago, during the Alemán administration, the constitution was again amended to allow the president greater freedom of action in certain customs and excise tax matters.

In point of fact, now that the official party is so well organized, the executive has little need to go outside of Congress to assume legal approval of his acts. By constitutional fiat the president has much broader powers of initiating bills than most presidential systems assign; at the same time his legislative initiatives and the cabinet ministers who are granted the floor of Congress to support them both enjoy special privileges not granted to private bills and their sponsors.[6] But then, privately initiated bills are virtually unknown, for even if introduced they seldom can compete with administration measures being shepherded through the legislative mill by the *control político* of the PRI, which regularly returns divisions of 140 to 3 in the Chamber of Deputies or unanimous votes in the Senate.

With such perfect discipline, the president never need worry about having his veto overridden; indeed, since only two vetoes, and both on minor, technical questions, have been cast since the Revolution, it is not a very lively worry anyway. The chief executive has little need to veto bills written by his own ministers and passed without alteration by Congress.

---

[6] See the discussion of such advantages in most Latin American legislatures in my chapter on "Legislatures and Legislation" in Harold E. Davis (ed.), *Government and Politics in Latin America* (New York, 1958).

The legislative record of the Forty-first Congress offers a fair representation of the role of the executive in policy-making. During its 3-year term, some 138 bills passed both houses; of these, 72 concerned new or amended statutes, 31 related to foreign medals and decorations, 7 permitted Mexicans to work for foreign governments, and 28 authorized special pensions. Not all of these acts emanated from the presidency; seven were initiated in the Congress itself, mainly from the Chamber's *Comisión de Estudios Legislativos*. Three of the president's initiatives still were pending in one or the other house when the session adjourned for the last time.

In a separate study of Mexican budget-making, I learned that even in this most basic of public policy questions, the national legislature regularly makes no attempt to meet its primary responsibility of exercising fiscal controls. By law and by custom, initiative lies with the executive and once the budgets of government income and expenditures have been sent to Congress, usually during the last two weeks of the session, almost no discussion of their terms is offered and no attempt is made to discover the criteria upon which allotments were assigned, much less change made in their content.[7] Little wonder, then, that on one occasion a lonely opposition deputy from the PAN wistfully remarked that it was no coincidence that the budgets had been sent down to Congress on the Day of the Holy Innocents.

To suggest the legislators' subservience in other congressional functions, let me cite just one example from several I have discussed elsewhere.[8] Just after he had been inaugurated, President Avila Camacho sent a number of nominations for the Supreme Court of Justice to the Senate for ratification. To the immense surprise of the capital, the Senate, meeting in closed session, refused to ratify three of the president's choices, terming them "reactionaries." One senator remarked that these were men of age and "naturally not in accord with new theories or modern thought." President Avila Camacho does not seem to have been in accord with new theories either, or at least that branch of modern thought permitting the Senate its constitutional function of free ratification, for he soon changed the decision. After a committee of senators waited upon the president to inform him of the action, they hurried back to

---

[7] Robert E. Scott, "Budget Making in Mexico," *Inter-American Economic Affairs*, IX, no. 2 (Autumn, 1955), 3-20.

[8] "Some Aspects of Mexican Federalism, 1917-1948," pp. 59-60.

set things right. The next day the Senate ratified the entire list, and the Senate president stated that the earlier press reports on the secret session had been in error. The Senate had never refused to ratify; it had merely kept action pending while more information was gathered on the three men. The president's contribution to the affair was, of course, to provide the opportunity to gather full information on the three between Friday night and Saturday morning.[9]

In short, as it now operates, the legislative branch of the national government is not really fulfilling its constitutional duties and it is not likely to in the foreseeable future. On the whole, it serves as little more than a convenient training ground for ambitious young politicians who wish to spend a few years in the national capital, as a kind of convenient patronage for certain political and functional interest association leaders, or as a quiet tapering-off appointment for older politicians who no longer are as efficient as they once were but are not quite ready to retire, or, perhaps more nearly correctly, to remove their names from the public payroll. One former Supreme Court justice who won a Senate seat was conspicuous for having missed almost every meeting of his chamber, but very prompt in picking up his salary.

By a strange quirk of fate, the low quality of members of Congress and the even lower standard of debate by the overwhelming PRI majorities in the two houses, coupled with an apparent willingness to allow free speech to the few opposition members, has made the Congress a worth-while sounding board for public opinion. Of itself, this might not be of great value in a legislature that has no real power to make policy, but the presidency, which can make policy, is flexible enough to use such indications when they are available. A case in point was the reaction to certain mechanical weaknesses in a former federal election law. After the 1952 election, deputies from both the PAN and the PP objected to a provision under which senators already declared elected by the Federal Election Commission had sat in judgment on a disputed Senate seat for the Federal District. The opposition deputies pointed out that outside of the capital, declarations of election to the Senate were made by another agency, the state legislature, rather than by the Senate itself. Accordingly, when the election law was changed, a

---

[9] *Excelsior*, December 28-29, 1940.

provision was added referring such cases to the Chamber of Deputies in lieu of a local legislature.[10]

The uncompromising weakness of the legislative branch is one of the unsolved problems of Mexican postrevolutionary political development, for it is a weak link in the constitutional mechanics of responsible and limited government. That it has not become a more pressing problem results only from the fact that Congress has no vital role in the real decision-making process. So long as the president continues to provide fairly easy access to the political process, there probably will be no really violent struggle by interests outside of the PRI to win seats in Congress or to give it the true legislative function the constitution describes. If, however, the presidency should not be able to follow its balancing routine, or if the locus of power should begin to shift toward the legislature, we can anticipate a much stronger demand for a larger share of seats in both chambers. Meanwhile, governmental responsibility is assured only by the will of the president and his associates, though that will constantly is being more strongly supported and even forced into reflecting the needs and desires of the general citizenry by a growing social sophistication and political awareness. rise of M.C.

Lest the reader be overwhelmed by a sense of futility in the search for observance of constitutional forms, let us turn away from the legislature, the principal function of which cannot begin to be operative until conditions change enough to allow Congress at least a share in the decision-making process, to the judicial branch, where far more of the regularities of the courts' constitutional functions are observed, including even those regarding their relations with the executive agencies of government. In doing so, I have no intention of presenting an exhaustive discussion of the mechanical operation of Mexico's judicial system, which has been done elsewhere.[11] Instead, I wish simply to suggest that the presidency has been able and willing to restrict its own unlimited freedom of action by accepting legal restraints in order to meet the demands of modern society for orderly government.

---

[10] Eisenberg, op. cit., pp. 118-19.

[11] See, for instance, Chapter V of my "Some Aspects of Mexican Federalism, 1917-1948"; Tucker, The Mexican Government Today, Chapter 8; Helen L. Clagett's chapter on "Law and the Courts" in Harold E. Davis, Government and Politics in Latin America. For a general source of references, see John T. Vance and Helen L. Clagett, A Guide to the Law and Legal Literature of Mexico (Washington, D.C., 1945).

The primary function of any court system is to interpret and enforce law, particularly constitutional law. In Mexico, disputes at law between private citizens are disposed of quite adequately and equitably by the courts, especially the national courts, where the bulk of judicial business falls because of the wide jurisdiction assigned the central government by the constitution and by political practice. Enforcement of constitutional provisions against laws enacted by the legislature or unconstitutional acts carried out by the executive could be another question altogether, for the tradition of civil law under which the courts operate acts as a barrier to the development of judge-made law by outright declarations of unconstitutionality. Until very recently it was argued that to assume this prerogative would be to invade the jurisdiction of the other branches of government.[12] As a consequence, while theoretically extant, the power of judicial interpretation and initiative is limited strictly to decisions on specific application or enforcement of the law in a given case, rather than upon the constitutionality of the law itself. If the legislature takes cognizance of the courts' findings it will, it is hoped, amend or repeal the offending law; similarly, the executive may cease to act under the law until it is changed. Meanwhile, each individual must apply separately to a national court for protection.

The Mexican recourse from actions based on unconstitutional laws or acts is to ask a national court for a writ of *amparo*, a kind of cease-and-desist order to the authority involved. The writ applies in cases arising out of acts by government offices at all levels involving infringement of constitutionally guaranteed rights, out of national-level laws or acts invading state sovereignty, or out of state-level laws or acts invading national jurisdiction. Although *amparo* also includes certain personal procedural rights under the "due process" clause of Mexico's constitution, it is inoperative in political matters, as defined by the courts themselves. Moreover, it must be requested by a specific aggrieved person in a national court (state courts are clearly prohibited from issuing such writs), and if issued applies only in the case at hand, the law involved or the act committed not being enjoined in general terms. Hence, any other person similarly affected also must seek *amparo*.

[12] *Jurisprudencia Definida de la Suprema Corte,* pt. 1, pp. 187-88. In February, 1958, however, the court did declare a law unconstitutional, though it was not one closely related to the president's major policies. See *El Universal,* February 19-27, 1958.

In order to provide a guide to the lower-level national courts in issuing writs of *amparo*, however, it has been necessary to develop a kind of precedent for acceptable procedure. When five consecutive decisions on the same point of law are rendered by the full bench of the Supreme Court or by one of its four subject-matter *salas*, without an intervening contrary decision, a fixed application of the law (*jurisprudencia definida*) is established. The court may, of course, reverse itself but naturally it is slow to do so; therefore, a reasonable degree of consistency is achieved.

It is of particular note in terms of the subject matter of this chapter that *amparo* is applicable against acts of government authorities and government authorities only. For all of its limitations, the writ must be sufficiently effective against acts of government, including the executive, to encourage resort to it, for the number of writs of *amparo* requested over the years as Mexican society has become more complicated has multiplied fantastically. The upper-level courts in the judicial system, which get mainly the appeals against contrary decisions in the District Courts, have been so swamped, for example, that they have had to multiply and specialize in order to handle the flood of cases.

The Supreme Court of Justice, which according to the 1917 constitution was to have consisted of an eleven-man, single bench, was divided in 1928 into three special subject-matter *salas* (civil, criminal, and administrative), with a fourth, labor *sala* added in 1934. These four specialized sections, consisting of five justices each, together with the full court (*corte pleno*) for general constitutional matters, spent almost their entire time on appeals in *amparo*. Nonetheless, by 1950 the Supreme Court was falling so far behind that although it handled 33,957 pieces of judicial business, it still had a backlog of 27,026 pieces, almost all concerning writs of *amparo*. The civil *sala* alone was behind 11,791 cases.[13] Because the lag had been growing yearly drastic steps were taken to ease the problem.

In 1951, amendments to the Organic Law of the Judicial Branch temporarily added a fifth *sala* to the Supreme Court to assist the court in cleaning up the backlog of cases. At the same time five collegial Circuit Courts were set up solely and specifically to hear requests for *amparo* as a further means of easing the burden on

---

[13] *Informe Rendido . . . a la Suprema Corte de Justicia . . . 1951,* "Informe de la Presidencia," pp. 15 ff.

the Supreme Court. After four years the authority of the High Court's auxiliary *sala* to sit on *amparo* cases was removed, leaving it simply as a source of temporary replacement for judges, but the previous year, in 1954, a second collegial Circuit Court was set up in Mexico City, making a total of six throughout the country. For all of this extra help with *amparo* cases, the jam of unfinished cases continued to rise each year, until in 1955 rather extensive changes had to be made in the procedures under which the writ is issued, in hopes of reducing the number awaiting solution. The Supreme Court itself established tighter rules for obtaining the writ, prohibiting it in certain types of criminal cases, and requiring re-petitioning at stated intervals in civil cases.

The 1951 changes in the Law of the Judicial Branch also did much to professionalize the Mexican judiciary. The Supreme Court, appointed for life by the president with ratification of the Senate, not only has administrative jurisdiction over inferior courts, but appoints judges to the lower courts. If reappointed after a four-year term, these judges acquire permanent tenure. Furthermore, the tendency now is to name District Court judges from the J. P. courts, the so-called Public Ministry (prosecuting attorneys), and es-pecially from among the clerks of the courts, and to appoint Circuit Court judges from the District Courts. Within the past few years, visitations by Supreme Court justices to District and Circuit Courts and much more careful scrutiny of inferior court activities have resulted in a notable improvement in judicial administration. In short, the courts seem both to provide an essential control function over the acts of the political branches of government and, at the same time, to be improving their personnel and techniques for act-ing effectively as the needs of the country for such service expand.

Undoubtedly the reason that the executive has been able to allow this growing judicial control over its activities is that in reality the court does not interfere in the basic policy questions decided by the executive. Even if the law of *amparo* did not specifically exclude all political matters from its jurisdiction, there is a great deal of evidence that the judges at all levels of courts would hesitate long before they attempted to act against a major policy decision of the president. No matter how strongly the constitution institutes the concept of balanced powers, the Mexican generally agrees with a justice of the Supreme Court of Justice (who later became its president) when he wrote that in his opinion "It is not true that the judicial power exists as an independent agency, with the characteristics of a real branch [of government], as jurists seem to believe because of article 94 of the constitution. . . ."[14] This attitude stems not simply from the ease with which the executive can bring pressure upon judges, though I have cited a number of examples of threats of impeachment and the like in another study,[15] but from the general acceptance of political leadership by the president that is part of the political system.

Let us turn to a quick consideration of another nonjuridical power of the Supreme Court, this one more discretionary than is *amparo*, to demonstrate how the court cooperates with the presidency in political matters. This judicial power is found in constitutional article 97, paragraph 3, which in addition to other items empowers the court, on request of the national executive or Congress, or of a state governor, or on its own authority, to "investigate a violation of any individual right or abuse of the public vote, or any other offense punishable by federal law." According to the terms of the article in question, investigation is mandatory upon the court if one of the other constitutional officers or agencies so requests, but not so if some private or nongovernmental group asks that the Supreme Court act on its own initiative, which usually occurs in connection with elections. In such matters, the numerous investigatory facilities of the political branches of government, including those of *Gobernación*, are apt to be suspect because the administration is involved in reviewing its own acts, a dismal prospect for those seeking impartial corsideration of their cases. So they turn to the court as the least political of the three branches of the national government, but *amparo* being inoperative in political cases, the complainants base their request on the court's discretionary authority under article 97.

In practice, the High Court never has attempted spontaneously to investigate a political dispute resulting from an election, and its record of acting on request points up clearly that political factors influence its decisions. A review of the cases in which the court did act demonstrates that requests from a national authority, and especially the executive, are likely to produce an investigation but that almost from the first years of the present constitutional era, starting in 1917, the court has preferred not to accede to petitions

---

[14] Salvador Urbina, "Nuestro Sistema Constitucional," *El Universal*, August 5, 1936.

[15] "Some Aspects of Mexican Federalism, 1917-1948," *passim*.

from state officials to review elections at that or the municipal level, on the grounds that such action would invade state sovereignty. This despite the clear mandate to do so in the constitution. Petitions from opposition political parties, which seem to come as a matter of course after every election now that the revolutionary party has become all-powerful, are even more apt to receive short shrift.[16]

As a general judicial precept, the court has evolved a rule refusing private and party petitions unless they are "in the national interest," which seems to mean that the investigation might ease a political situation embarrassing to the PRI. A striking example of the different uses to which the court puts its discretionary power in this respect occurred during 1946. The strained political situation that obtained in Mexico as a result of imposed municipal officers in the 1945 elections has been mentioned before; two of the most loudly protested impositions took place in León, Guanajuato, and in Monterrey, Nuevo León. Up to a point the two elections both followed the common Mexican pattern whereby the dominant party announced victory for its candidates and proceeded to attempt to install them in office over the protests of the opposition. The point of difference was that in León a riot occurred, shots were fired by the opposition demonstrators and the military, and some fifty people died.

Both the *Partido de Acción Nacional* in León and the *Partido Liberal Nuevo Leones* petitioned the Supreme Court of Justice for investigation of the two elections, under its discretionary power. In the first case, the court sent two justices, not to study the contested election which, it was claimed, had been settled by the state authorities through appointment of a *Junta de Administración Local Municipal*, but to study the later events, which were suspected of depriving citizens of their civil rights, including their lives in the case of fifty persons. After the investigators presented their report, the court decided that sufficient evidence existed to imply violations of individual rights and of the vote, as well as other national statutes, so copies were sent to the president, to the governor of Guanajuato, and to the PAN. But with the exception of ousting Governor Hidalgo as a sop to public indignation, no further action came of the report, which had served its purpose in easing the ten-

---

[16] A review of the history of Supreme Court actions and refusals to act was made in a decision rendered on August 9, 1949, denying a PAN petition for a study of the July, 1949, national deputies' elections. It was reported fully in the PAN publication *La Nación* for August 15, 1949, pp. 2-3.

sion of the situation. In the case of Monterrey, the court was not moved by public scandal, so it refused to investigate, basing its decision on the lack of any statute implementing its authority under article 97, in spite of the investigation being conducted in León at precisely the same time.[17]

The problem of Supreme Court action under the terms of this constitutional provision has been a source of frequent and prolific, if fruitless, discussion both by the justices and by outside commentators.[18] Several suggested amendments to the constitution have been offered, but this semipolitical power of the Supreme Court of Justice has never been strengthened by adoption of a statutory elaboration of the provision, nor has the provision been deleted from the constitution. This is probably because at present there is no real need to change the legal relationship of the court with the other political branches of the government, because a satisfactory adjustment of all three branches to each other and to the political system as it now operates already exists. The average citizen is well aware of this; knowing that the real and ultimate source of policy decisions, and the determination of their constitutionality as well, resides with the person in whom real political authority resides, the chief executive of the country, he looks to the courts for technical interpretation of the law or for protection against arbitrary applications by capricious individuals, and to the presidency when he wishes to influence basic policy.

As one last illustration of how other agencies of government subordinate themselves to the presidency in the real political system, let us consider the role of the states. We already have seen how the government party controls nomination and election of state as well as national officers. Perhaps during the twenties and thirties much of the political control exercised so ruthlessly over state governments by the *Secretaría de Gobernación* was a necessary concomitant to the virtual anarchy existing in the country at the time. By manipulating the formal constitutional powers granted the central government for protection from domestic violence under article

---

[17] This and other cases dealing with article 97 are detailed in my "Some Aspects of Mexican Federalism, 1917-1948," pp. 280-96.

[18] See the *Informe Rendido . . . a la Suprema Corte . . . 1944*, pp. 142-43; *ibid.* (1946), pp. 21-23; *ibid.* (1947), pp. 11-13. Also see Rafael Chávez Chávez, *La Intervención de la Corte en Materia Política* (Mexico, D.F., 1946), and Ricardo Domínguez Rodríguez, *El Artículo 97 Constitucional y el Voto Público* (Mexico, D.F., 1946).

89, section 4, and by using the threat of military reprisal, the executive determined the legality of state elections, chose between competing state governors and legislatures, and forced state administrations to accept its interpretation of state and national constitutions and statutes, all in order to assure state administrations which could work with the central government. Later, as the organization of the official party became more refined, the president's control over Congress allowed him to resort with confidence to article 76, sections 5 and 6, whereby the Senate may declare that all constitutional powers of a state have disappeared and appoint a provisional state administration. My study of Mexican federalism, cited just above, includes many but by no means all of the available examples of these early struggles for control of the state governments.

Today, as the political system becomes more all-inclusive, new and more subtle controls are available to the presidency, so that the older resort to force, masked by a façade of constitutional authority, almost never need occur. Whatever disputes do take place are apt to happen within the official party, where the president can bring his whole arsenal of political weapons to bear upon the clique with which he disagrees. This does not mean that political struggles do not occur at the state level, but that the causes and means of resolving them now differ sharply from those of a few years ago, in response to the new conditions under which they take place.

Declarations of disappearance of state powers by the Senate at the president's instigation under article 76, for example, virtually have disappeared over the years, and those which are made today have quite a different purpose than they once did. During the forty years since some semblance of national government was restored to Mexico after the chaos of the first period of the Revolution, some forty-seven declarations have been adopted by the Senate, or by its permanent committee when the upper chamber is not in session, as follows:[19]

$$
\begin{array}{l}
1918\text{-}27 - 24 \\
1928\text{-}37 - 16 \\
1938\text{-}47 - \ 5 \\
1948\text{-}57 - \ 2
\end{array}
$$

[19] See my "Some Aspects of Mexican Federalism, 1917-1948," Chapter III, and especially pp. 124 ff.

Many of the earlier declarations were what might be called justified in terms of the constitutional ends of article 76, for they represented removals of state officers in rebellion against the central authorities. Thus, in 1920, twelve state governments were ousted before the Carranza Senate itself was dissolved. In 1924 three vacated state governments were involved in the de la Huerta uprising, while two removed in 1927 had taken part in anti-reelectionist disturbances, followed in 1929 by two ousted for participating in the abortive revolt of that year. During this same period not a few other state administrations were removed for refusing to accept the domination of the central authorities in less dramatic ways.

Since 1930 and the organization of the revolutionary party to provide more complete machinery of central control, the need to resort to this drastic method of enforcing the will of the executive largely has been obviated, so that the power associated with article 76 now is used only sparingly, and less for direct rebuke of local political officers than for enforcing intraparty discipline or to provide a solution for otherwise embarrassing political dilemmas. This is not to say that it is never used for control purposes; President Cárdenas used it to oust five pro-Calles governors when he publicly demonstrated his political independence from the ex-president late in 1935.[20] But despite the fact that we see at the beginning of each presidential term a kind of shakedown among the governors' posts to assure that the state administrations are loyal to the new chief executive, the president has other means of asserting his ascendancy than the rather public washing of dirty linen that earlier revolutionary leaders employed.

An excellent case study in the methods of presidential control over recalcitrant state governments, and the diverse motives for national intervention in state-level affairs, can be presented simply by reviewing the activities of President Ruiz Cortines in this area of political control during his term. He was faced with an unusually challenging situation because of two related facts. First, his predecessor, Miguel Alemán, had been unusually active in imposing state administrations close to his own viewpoint, because of an abnormally strong interest in patronage and graft, so that President Ruiz Cortines met with unusually strong opposition to his relatively mild attempts to control the state governments, particularly in regard to

---

[20] *Ibid.*, pp. 131-32.

his clean-up campaign. Second, the situation was complicated by the behind-the-scenes intraparty struggle between the *cardenistas* and the *alemanistas* for influence at all levels of government including the states, which kept state politics seething.

Nonetheless, President Ruiz Cortines managed to contain the political situation with a minimum of public friction and at the same time was able to control the worst peculations of the state administrations carried over from the Alemán regime. Utilizing the tremendous prestige of the presidency, together with the very wide latitude in discretional policy-making placed in his hands by domination of the presidency, the chief executive kept the state governments in line until gradually the terms of their elective officials came to an end and new, more loyal officers could replace them. Even so mild-mannered a politician as Adolfo Ruiz Cortines could use the broad legal powers of the central government, aided no little by the fact that the national government spends some 80 per cent of all government monies in Mexico, to accomplish this end.

In the twenty-nine states, only six state governors or entire administrations had to be removed before the end of their fixed terms, and this was for a variety of reasons ranging from political disloyalty to the president to fantastic political corruption which could be ended in no other way. And, significantly, of these only one case was resolved by declaration of disappearance of state powers by the Senate, acting for the central government under the terms of article 76. The other five were accomplished either by action of other agencies of the state government, such as the legislature, or by "voluntary" resignation of the officer or officers concerned; in every case, however, the closest possible liaison existed between the state-level persons involved and the central authorities, through *Gobernación* and/or through the bureaucracy of the PRI.

The only direct constitutional action against a state by the national government during President Ruiz Cortines' term took place in May, 1954, when the Senate vacated all three branches of the government in Guerrero on well-substantiated charges of widespread corruption. In the other five situations the governor was encouraged to request a leave from the state legislature, which promptly granted it and appointed a substitute more suitable to Mexico City.

The first case of enforced leave, and by far the most serious, actually began as early as March, 1952, before Ruiz Cortines took office, when *henriquista* leaders organized a public protest in Oaxaca against an extremely unpopular tax law. In the resulting riots and general strike, which lasted for a week, several people were killed; despite the attempt of Governor Manuel Mayoral Heredia to save his own position by firing the state's secretary of *Gobierno*, treasurer, *procurador* of justice, and his own private secretary, because they "had failed to merit the confidence of the people," public pressure during this presidential campaign period became so intense that the central government forced the governor to request a leave of absence. Later, in April, 1953, after Ruiz Cortines was president, Mayoral Heredia was persuaded to resign, and the new president designated his successor.

A somewhat similar set of circumstances took place in Tabasco during March, 1955, when the people of the state rioted against Governor Manuel Bartlett Bautista because of maladministration and corruption. Again, the central government convinced the governor that he should request leave from the state legislature. Although the state lawmakers legally were then free to appoint a new governor, the pattern of presidential domination persisted and the decision seems to have been made in the national capital for ". . . President Ruiz Cortines had decided to name General *don* Miguel Orrico de los Llanos interim governor of Tabasco."[21] Another Alemán protégé, who was imposed from the national capital, Governor Tomás Marentes of Yucatán, also resigned, in June of 1953, when he was unable to solve the long-festering problems of the southeastern peninsula. After many complaints to the new president from students and from the henequen-producers union, Ruiz Cortines sent a representative of *Gobernación* to investigate, and almost immediately the governor requested and was granted leave of absence. His successor, Professor Victor Mena Palomo, also named by the state legislature on recommendation of the central authorities, had a difficult time with the local lawmakers and the *yucatecos* in general, for he too was unable to solve the problems of the state, but, having at least the neutral support of the president, he managed to survive.

The last two cases during the Ruiz Cortines administration were relatively minor. In March of 1953, Governor Pérez Arce of Sinaloa developed "symptoms" and requested leave, which the state legis-

[21] *Tiempo*, March 28, 1955, p. 5.

lature promptly and gratefully granted. This was no case of dishonesty but of magnificent ineptitude. Pérez Arce simply had turned out to be a clown who produced grandiloquent monthly reports which he insisted on publishing in the newspapers, writing about the president as "a courtier of Versailles might have about Louis XIV, and making Mexicans laugh almost as much as Cantinflas."[22] Even the newspapers in his own state began to make fun of him, calling him "Pérez *Abuelo*" (Grandpa Pérez) every time they had to write about his difficulties with state politicians. The state legislature had complained about his poor work to the secretary of *Gobernación,* but before the central government could decide on action, Pérez Arce took the hint and withdrew.

Finally, in August, 1955, Governor Oscar Soto Maynez of the state of Chihuahua took leave after minor riots and a popular campaign against him, including his being shot in the shoulder, convinced both the governor and the president that a new state executive should be appointed. Governor Soto Maynez did not even have the distinction of being grandly corrupt, but five years of such minor graft as his five-dollar levy on all streetwalkers in the border city of Juárez, about which they wrote protesting letters to the newspapers, mounted up to an intolerable situation against which the citizens finally reacted so strongly that the central government had to force Soto Maynez out of office.[23]

The reader may well be curious to learn not only how individuals so corrupt or so inept manage to capture high posts in Mexico but also how they manage to hold them in the face of their obvious inadequacies. The answer lies, of course, in the nature of the political system, which places so much authority in the hands of the president. As I have stated repeatedly, given Mexico's present political development this can be a good thing if the president is honest and capable. If he is not, the power can be misused, as these cases of governors who took office under President Alemán clearly show. Ruiz Cortines' predecessor was so interested in placing his cronies in positions of influence that their moral or mental inadequacies were a secondary consideration, so that it was only after Alemán left office that the worst of them could be ousted.

One final case showing how the president can influence state

---

[22] *Hoy,* March 7, 1953, pp. 6-7.

[23] *Ibid.,* February 12, 1955, p. 23; *Excelsior,* August 10, 1955.

politics to protect a protégé should prove my point. In March, 1951, while the governor was in Mexico City, the state legislature of Colima, meeting at the Hotel Casino in the state capital, voted to oust Governor Jesús Gonzáles Lugo for illegal and corrupt acts. Gonzáles Lugo immediately visited Alemán's secretary of *Gobernación*, Adolfo Ruiz Cortines, who sent the *oficial mayor* of *Gobernación* to investigate. The latter returned and reported that the legislature had not observed proper state and national constitutional procedures in removing the governor. Furthermore, just a few months earlier the president of the PRI's central committee had spoken in Colima attacking Gonzáles Lugo's enemies. As a consequence of the official and unofficial interest expressed in the national capital in support of the governor, the local congress announced that it had changed its attitude "in light of the interests of Colima, on the express wish of the president of the republic. . . ." [24] On March 29 the local legislature revoked its former action, greeted the governor in friendly terms, after which they all walked over to a local restaurant for a celebration banquet. A few months later, when elections to the state legislature were held, both President Alemán and Governor Gonzáles Lugo saw to it that more tractable men were selected. So much for the influence of the chief executive over state governments.

Under presidents less aggressive than Alemán, the amount of presidential intervention in state affairs is appreciably less than the case of Colima might seem to indicate. As long as the governor keeps within the general terms of presidential policy, and if he does not stir up political unrest by refusing to take into account the principal functional interests which have a legitimate concern with state administration, or incite popular dissatisfaction by inefficient or corrupt practices, the chief executive is apt to allow the state official a relatively free hand. In turn, the state administration is likely to act in close and loyal collaboration with the national government, from which all blessings, political and legal, as well as economic, flow.

### Policy-making in the Presidency

If there is any one term by which application of the vast authority described in these case studies as reposing in the president can

---

[24] *Tiempo*, March 30, 1951, pp. 10-11.

be defined, it is "government by consultation." Utilizing all of the formal and informal, legal and extra-legal agencies of the presidency, the chief executive heads a mechanism that hears and considers the competing needs and desires of all the major functional interests concerned in any given policy decision.

Because he stands as a symbol of authority in whom the Revolution is made manifest, most actions of the political process are taken in the president's name, but with the broadening of the base of politically aware citizens, the chief executive must rely more and more upon the organization that has evolved in the presidency. No longer is he in face-to-face contact with all of his followers or even all of the leaders of the major power factors in the political system. Instead, consultation and decision-making have been systematized, so that discussion takes place at lower levels, between interest representatives and the bureaucracies both of the government and of functional interest associations. Only then does a policy question move up through the ministers heading the executive departments or through the sector leaders of the PRI to the presidential level where high policy is decided. This policy, in turn, is applied and administered by the intermediate members the presidency, who relate with the lower echelons of the PRI's sectors or to other functional interest associations not included in the party's organizational structure.

The policy problems which reach the president are formulated in various ways. Some of them have their origins in the press, others are presented by functional interest associations, perhaps through the PRI's sector organizations, or perhaps from outside, and a very few arise in the speeches or publications of opposition party members. With the formalization of government activities, however, the largest proportion come directly from the executive departments, which have the day-to-day task of facing and trying to solve the multitude of problems plaguing the country. Congress, on the other hand, hardly enters the picture at all, for reasons we already know.

The agencies which participate in formulating and resolving policy matters are a confusing mixture of official and semi-official government units, political bodies representing both geographic and functional interests, commercial and manufacturing interest associations not identified officially with any political party, and a myriad of other specialized interest groups which are consulted when their particular interests are concerned. Because aggregation of all these interests is not achieved in the legislature no single consultative agency other than the president and his staff aides exists to provide integrated policy. The chief executive is, therefore, the key to the whole process of decision-making.

With few legal rules for reaching major policy decisions, the personality of each president is apt to influence the process even more than it does in a highly formalized political system, but the basic conditions under which each Mexican executive must operate do not shift markedly, and the interaction among the various power factors now follows well-worn channels, so we can suggest certain characteristics of the political process which will remain constant no matter who is president.

The absence of an effective legislature or some single substitute legal body for decision-making, together with the disparate nature of the interest associations and government agencies involved, makes for a tendency to assign consideration of individual matters to specialized committees rather than reviewing them in some one collective group. Not even the heads of the executive departments meet regularly as a cabinet with the president. Instead, the chief executive holds frequent sessions with each minister individually. That is, the president will assign work or responsibilities to his ministers but he limits the scope of decision-making more than his North American counterpart does. The degree of control exercised depends, of course, upon the individual president.

When the nature of a policy question requires broader consideration, the chief executive is likely to set up a committee consisting of representatives of the *secretarías* concerned and spokesmen for whatever nongovernmental interests are involved, together with members of his personal staff to coordinate the activities of the whole group. Working together, they prepare a policy recommendation that the president either can accept and implement or reject, as he sees fit.

In attempting to clarify a problem, the presidential organization is much less likely to engage in public debate than are North American or British statesmen, and certainly the decision will be reached and appropriate legislative proposals prepared in the executive agencies before the matter is referred to Congress for rubber-stamp approval. In fact, the tendency is to seek some workable solution through administrative action, perhaps by technical consultants and the bureaucracy, rather than to turn the question over to the legislature at all.

The executive must be careful also not to carry a major problem directly to the people without a long and careful educational campaign through planted newspaper stories, speeches of prominent government officials and revolutionary party leaders, and discussion in the member associations of the PRI's three sectors. During his first two years in office President Ruiz Cortines attempted to use a shock-treatment technique to force his countrymen to face up to the nation's most pressing problems, but public reaction was so negative that he soon abandoned the plan. Even if they themselves are suffering from certain of the Revolution's failings, the Mexicans seem to prefer to be told that all is going well.

Among the government officials assisting the president in the performance of his duties, the best known are the line officers heading the eighteen executive departments,[25] the attorney-general of the republic, the attorney-general of the Federal District, and the president's private secretary. Although the existence of executive departments is determined by law, both their number and organization are quite elastic, to suit the desires of each president. For example, article 2 of the Law of Secretaries of State empowers the chief executive to name at will two additional ministers, with or without portfolio. At one time, there was supposed to be a difference between *Secretarías* and *Departamentos*, the heads of the former being considered policy-making officers and the latter simply technical experts, but the distinction now has disappeared, probably because neither really acts independently in policy matters. Both may countersign executive decrees, orders, and regulations, as re-

---

[25] According to the *Ley de Secretarías y Departamentos de Estado* passed by the Chamber of Deputies on December 16 and by the Senate on December 19, 1958, there are fifteen *secretarías*: Government, Foreign Affairs, Treasury, National Defense, Marine Affairs, Industry and Commerce, Agriculture and Animal Industry, Water Resources, Public Education, Health and Aid, Labor and Welfare, National Patrimony, Communications and Transport, Public Works, Presidency; there are also three *departamentos*: Tourism, Agrarian and Colonization Affairs, and Federal District. A description of the legal duties of each can be found in the *Directorio del Gobierno Federal*, which is published periodically. Despite recent changes in executive organization, the most complete available discussion of the organization and activities of the executive dependencies is Wendell K. G. Schaeffer, "National Administration in Mexico: Its Development and Present Status," unpublished Ph.D. dissertation, University of California, Berkeley, California, 1949, especially Chapter IV, "The Organization of Mexican Administration."

quired by article 92 of the constitution, but this means little because they are appointed by the president without even Senate confirmation and serve during his pleasure only. Furthermore, although the constitution requires that department heads submit an annual report to Congress, this now is mere formality, as each secretary speaks in the name of the president who, in turn, dominates the legislative branch. Repeated attempts by opposition deputies to interpellate cabinet ministers, particularly the Treasury secretary, which are quite permissible under the rules, have failed, for questioning the minister's policies would be to imply an attack upon his chief, the president.

Because of the primarily administrative nature of their work for the president, the strongest characteristic required of the heads of line departments is technical competence, followed by political adaptability, but as in the case of the United States cabinet, a serious effort is made to include spokesmen for all political viewpoints representing major power blocs operating inside the official coalition. In appointing his cabinet, President López Mateos did not follow the example of his predecessor in this matter, however, for instead of naming men from both wings of the PRI to achieve balance, he did so by appointing primarily technicians. He also followed another pattern extant in Mexico as well as the United States, by naming one cabinet member to act as his representative in political matters. Alfredo del Mazo, who had been his political secretary during the campaign, was named Secretary of Water Resources.

In addition to the executive departments, Mexico's government is characterized by a great many independent or semi-independent agencies which carry on varied activities ranging from management of government corporations and nationalized industries or services to providing for agricultural credit or other specialized functional operations. Even for a country where constitutional doctrine and political practice presuppose a high degree of state intervention in social and economic affairs, the number and scope of these agencies is little short of amazing. Their total is too great to list here, but they can be found listed in the *Federal Government Directory,* cited just above.

From an administrative viewpoint, the problem of coordinating the activities of an army of independent agencies long has plagued Mexico's presidents, who are responsible for providing an integrated and positive program. As the society and economy have become more complex, so has the number and diversity of these agencies and the difficulty of controlling them. As part of his December, 1958, reorganization of the executive dependencies, President López Mateos incorporated many of the smaller independent agencies into the newly created *Secretaría del Patrimonio Nacional,* in order to clarify the lines of control. Nonetheless, many of the largest and most important independent entities still operate outside of the executive secretariats.

In his desire to consolidate policy, the president, who appoints the administrative boards and the executive officers of the remaining independent agencies, supervises their activities closely, especially in the case of units whose function could have a direct effect upon the success of his own administrative or economic program. The policies followed by the management of *Petróleos Mexicanos* (the government oil monopoly), the National Railways, *Nacional Financiera* (the small business credit agency), CEIMSA (the agency that supplies low-cost articles of prime consumption to provide a hedge against price-gouging and inflationary tendencies), and the workers' and farmers' credit banks, for instance, constantly are being measured against the broader policies of the national government to assure their mutual integration.

Strict presidential controls do not mean, however, that appointments to these semi-independent agencies are reserved only for official party members, to the exclusion of individuals or interests outside the governing clique. On the contrary, these agencies provide one of several links between the policy-deciding mechanism in the presidency and those functional interest associations not subsumed in the revolutionary party. As early as Avila Camacho's administration, for example, the president appointed Guillermo Guajardo Davis and Eustaquio Escandón to the administrative council of the National Railways as representatives, respectively, of the nongovernmental National Federation of Industrial Chambers and Federation of National Chambers of Commerce, which will be discussed presently. Both of these representatives of private business interests also happened to be members of *Acción Nacional.*

This tendency to include a voice for functional interests outside of the revolutionary party's three sectors has grown, if anything, during the three administrations following Avila Camacho's term. The Mexican Bankers' Association, a wholly private business organization, now elects representatives to various governmental fiscal agencies such as the National Securities Commission and the National Banking Commission and it is consulted regularly by official credit agencies and banks concerning national economic and fiscal policy. The same is true of the Mexican Employers' Federation, which was given legal status by the Federal Labor Code of 1931. Similarly, although they do not necessarily participate *ex officio* in national government dependencies, private and voluntary functional interest associations such as the Mexican Association of Insurance Institutions or the Association of Tourist Agents collaborate closely with government officials in the appropriate *secretarías* and commissions.

In fact, by far the largest proportion of organizations associated with nonagricultural economic activity, be it manufacturing, processing, or commercial, are related to the decision-making process not voluntarily but because they are legally required to. According to laws enacted in 1936, 1941, and 1950, every industry or business capitalized at over 500 pesos must belong to one of the fifty-odd functionally specialized chambers grouped together in the National Federation of Industrial Chambers (*Confederación de Cámaras Industriales de los Estados Unidos Mexicanos*, or CONCAMIN) or 250 geographically based chambers organized nationally as the Federation of National Chambers of Commerce (*Confederación de Cámaras Nacionales de Comercio*, or CONCANACO), depending upon the nature of the function performed.[26]

This required participation in one or the other of the two national federations is directed to the rationalization and stabilization of relations in the industrial and commercial fields, in the hope that the regulation of unhampered competition and the solution of outstanding problems will encourage the expansion not only of business but also of the sense of responsibility of businessmen in general. Despite the independent nature of the component members of the two federations, both law and political practice give them a semi-official status. In addition to mandatory membership, the *Secretaría* of Economy decides which functional chambers of CONCAMIN shall be set up, and settles disputes over the proper chamber to which a given manufacturing or producing unit should adhere, if any question exists. The law also determines arbitrarily

[26] See Gábino Fraga, *op. cit.*, sections 235 and 236 for a legalistic discussion of the functions of these *cámaras*.

that the Chambers of Commerce in CONCANACO be divided into two classes, according to the amount for which the firm concerned is capitalized. Furthermore, observers from the Secretariat of Economy attend all national meetings of both CONCAMIN and CONCANACO.

The organizational structure of the two federations is basically similar. Each is divided into its component functional or geographic chambers, which are represented at the national level by a general assembly held annually or on special call by the directing council or the *Secretaría de Economía*. National federation policy is adopted by the 50-to-75-member directing council representing a profile of the member chambers, and implemented by the smaller executive committee, under an elected president; in both federations, council and committee are assisted by a paid professional staff that does much to formulate the policies and to plan the activities of the organization.

The role of CONCAMIN and CONCANACO in the political process cannot be overstated, for although business and commercial interests are not provided with access to government councils through the PRI's sectors they can and do make their voices heard through these organizations. The presidency has found it very convenient to consult both the national federations and their individual chambers concerning proposed changes in administrative regulations and new legislation on matters affecting their particular interests.

Not all of the members of the industrial and commercial federations are entirely satisfied with the nature of their representation in these groups. As they point out, the tendency is for the larger, better organized, and more efficiently staffed firms to dominate the activities of the individual chambers, and for the richer or larger chambers to dominate the policy of the national federations. There seems to be a parallel here to the preparation of industry codes under the NRA before it was declared unconstitutional in 1935 and today to the activities of the NAM or the National Chamber of Commerce in the United States.

This is possible in Mexico not only because the larger firms or chambers have greater initiative, but because the mechanics of federation organization give them an additional advantage. In CONCAMIN, votes in the national assembly are proportioned according to the amount of dues paid by each chamber, enabling richer or larger industries to dominate the executive positions and to direct the federation's bureaucracy; the same is true of dues paid to individual chambers by specific member firms at the chamber level, with similar results. In CONCANACO the federation itself has two classes of National Chamber of Commerce. The first, composed of businessmen whose stores, hotels, or other activities are capitalized at over 5,000 pesos, dominates the federation. The second class, consisting of small merchants whose capital investment lies between 500 and 5,000 pesos, are called *comerciantes en pequeña* and have their separate *cámaras*. Despite the multitudes of small businesses which legally are required to affiliate with the National Chambers of Small Business, less than one-tenth of the chambers in the Federation are of the small-merchant type. We have already seen that in February, 1958, a group representing 40,000 *comerciantes en pequeña* spoke at a meeting for PRI candidate Adolfo López Mateos, requesting that they not be forced to join the Chamber of Commerce of the City of Mexico because it did nothing to protect their rights although it collected dues from them.[27]

It is because of these organizational inadequacies that many business and industrial activities have developed completely separate and independent trade associations to resolve their common problems and to coordinate their viewpoints so as to present a united front in dealing with the government, in order to bypass the federations whose executives and bureaucracies may be dominated by representatives of interests hostile to their own. The president and his staff are aware of this problem and the presidency consistently has shown itself prepared to take into consideration the views of such independent associations along with those of the semi-official federations.

An informative description of how the consultation process operates in Mexico's automobile assembly industry appeared lately in *Fortune*.[28] It shows how the association of auto producers and the

---

[27] After preparing this section on CONCAMIN and CONCANACO, I saw Frank R. Brandenburg's excellent study on these organizations, published as "Organized Business in Mexico," in *Inter-American Economic Affairs*, XII, no. 3 (Winter, 1958), 26-52. The reader is urged to consult this article for a more complete discussion of the role of business and industry in Mexico's politics.

[28] Daniel Seligman, "The Maddening, Promising Mexican Market," *Fortune*, LIII (January, 1956), 103 ff.

association of auto dealers, meeting together, seek to set up an optimum production figure for the assembly industry. The producers favor a free market and increasing the total number of vehicles assembled, while the dealers want a quota system in which a more or less limited number of vehicles are apportioned among the existing sellers, assuring the sale of each dealer's quota with a minimum of effort. Usually, when the compromise figure agreed upon is sent to *Economía* as a recommendation, the *Secretaría* lowers the total number of units before sending its own recommendation to the president for final approval. The automobile assembly industry leaders then try to get the chief executive's ear to argue their case, but when he finally picks a figure it is apt to be nearer that of his Secretary of Economy than the one desired by the industry, though they have been known to improve their case by direct appeal to officials in what is now the secretariat of the presidency.

Much the same process takes place in deciding the quota of units to be produced by each assembly plant and the subquotas of various styles of car and truck each may assemble. A great deal of lobbying goes on both in *Economía* and in the presidential secretaría, for each company wants to acquire a larger share of the fixed number of units to be produced, and to turn out proportionately more passenger cars than trucks, for the profit margin is higher on these models. In this case, as in that of the number of automotive units to be produced, consideration of the interests of the industry concerned are weighed against the executive's conception of the public interest, and the most satisfactory solution for all concerned is adopted.

Because of this willingness to allow economic interests not affiliated with the PRI access to the political process, there has been relatively little pressure from industry or business for a sector of its own. The few sporadic suggestions to this end have been made mainly by politically ambitious individuals rather than by the real representatives of these parts of Mexican society and economic life. For the reasons listed in the introductory chapter of this study, as long as they can accomplish their goals outside the revolutionary party, Mexico's economic interest associations have no desire and less need to subject themselves to the possible hazards of party discipline. *Excelsior's* political cartoonist, Abel Quezada, expressed this point of view very effectively when one of his political characters announced during the 1958 presidential campaign that he was going to leave his imaginary Charro party and join CONCANACO, because its members seemed to get more concessions from the government than did active and deserving party members.[29]

Nor does the presidency confine itself to consulting economic interest associations. One is struck in observing the operation of Mexico's political process by the variety and number of specialized interest groups which manage to gain access to the decision-making process when matters of concern to them are being considered. This is not surprising in the case of politically neutral organizations of highly trained professional persons such as the bar, the medical association, or the engineers' professional groups, but when a previously antirevolutionary institution such as the Roman Catholic church is consulted in cases of proposed policy which might concern its interests, one becomes forcibly aware of the degree to which the aggregating function is carried out by the presidency.

The machinery through which the chief executive fulfills this important function has already been alluded to. To coordinate the activities of the eighteen line departments and the army of independent and semi-official agencies, a large and highly trained group of staff aides gradually evolved into the agency known as the Presidential Office, which in turn became the *Secretaría de la Presidencia* late in 1958. The work of this unit extends far beyond the supervision of the daily activities of the line departments into long-range staff planning.[30]

Under President Ruiz Cortines there existed a tendency to organize this important activity of the executive into representative, consultative committees. For example, in 1953, he set up a Committee on Investments (*Comisión de Inversiones*) to investigate needs and to plan for expenditures for public works. The committee was charged with making studies to coordinate the economic, fiscal, and social goals of public policy, and to present to the executive an integrated policy for public expenditures. Finally, it was responsible for keeping this integrated policy up to date as changes occur in the country's society and economy. To complete its mission, the *Comisión de Inversiones* was staffed with a Director, Sub-

---

[29] *Excelsior,* September 27, 1957.

[30] The beginnings of adequate staffing of the Mexican presidency are described in Schaeffer, *op. cit.,* Chapter VII, "Planning." Unfortunately no study carrying the description beyond 1949 exists, and space precludes doing so here.

Director, Juridical Assessor, a Chief of Economic Analysis, who heads a group of technically trained research aides, and adequate administrative personnel. Under López Mateos, most of this responsibility was transferred to the new *Secretaría de la Presidencia*.

To date, the work of the committee and the new secretariat has not produced any panacea to cure all of Mexico's social and economic ills, because the political considerations which must be considered in every political system are operative here too. Strictly logical and rational planning must give way before the demands of organized and vocal pressure groups with vested interests, just as they must in other countries. As the chief personality in Mexican politics, in this respect, the president is no more a political man with absolutely free determination to accept or ignore the existence of interests working in the political system than was Adam Smith's economic man anything but a convenient fiction to personify absolute rational and independent economic choice in a world where such choice is humanly impossible. Nonetheless, the existence of such an agency has done much to provide a context within which broad policy decisions concerning public works expenditures can be taken.

Another collective consultative agency, set up by President Ruiz Cortines in 1954, has as its function the study of production problems and the preparation of recommendations to help balance agricultural development with industrial development. The Council for Development and Coordination of National Production (*Consejo de Fomento y Coordinación de la Producción Nacional*) differs from the Committee on Investments in that it is not primarily a staff agency for study of planning problems but a mechanism for bringing together representatives of the two major economic interests in the country, agriculture and industry, to discuss common problems and to formulate recommendations upon them. As such, it is not really a part of the policy-making machinery of the presidency, but rather an auxiliary to it.

The twenty-eight members of the *Consejo*, who are appointed by the president, consist of a President, a secretary-general, ten agricultural counselors, eleven industrial counselors, and five more persons named jointly by the two groups of functional representatives, together with an administrative staff. The functional members represent major functional interest associations for the most part; for example, Fidel Velázquez of the CTM is an industrial delegate, along with representatives from the two federations of industrial and commercial *cámaras*, and Rodolfo Elías Calles, son of the former president, represents the farm interests not covered by the CNC's delegates.

The Production Council reports directly to the president, from whom it has authority to request data, information, and technical assistance of all sorts from any executive department, agency, or dependency. Among the matters being studied are the following:

(a) In agricultural policy: (1) participation of private investment in irrigation projects; (2) public and private credit for agriculture and the livestock industry; (3) technical and social aid against erosion; (4) improved methods of cultivation; (5) agricultural insurance; (6) guaranteed farm prices; (7) distribution and marketing of farm products; (8) related subjects of interest to agrarian and livestock activities.

(b) In industrial policy: (1) increased exports; (2) tariff policy; (3) import policy; (4) encouraging of basic industry; (5) increased production; (6) channeling of greater private resources to industry; (7) policy on foreign investments; (8) related subjects of national interest to industry.

The example set by the presidency has been carried down to lower executive levels too. There exists, for example, a consultative council for the Federal District, consisting of representatives of labor, business, and professional organizations. The CTM, the Unions of Professional Men and Women, the government bureaucrats union (FSTSE), the *Cámara de Comercio*, the Small Businessmen's Association, the Landlords Association, and the Tenants' Organization all aid in advising the presidentially appointed governor of the district in which the national capital lies. Undoubtedly they provide as effective representation for the interests they represent as would an elective city council, given the tendency toward executive domination in the country.

In the final analysis, for all of these technical and staff aides assisting him, it is the President of the Republic who must perform the classic work of politics, making the final decision on high policy questions. He cannot delegate much of the real authority to his subordinates, even if he wishes to, for the political system makes him the figurehead of government to whom, theoretically, the last appeal in every major policy question must be addressed if the contending parties are to feel satisfied that final determination of the matter has been achieved. Too great a delegation of this kind of authority would be as foreign to his nature as to that of the people he serves and governs.

It probably is fair to say that the strong current of executive leadership emanating from this concentration of authority and from the one-party system that makes its possible has led Mexico away from presidential government in the North American sense toward a form of government more nearly analogous to the parliamentary system of Great Britain. The present political system forces all of the factors of political power either to discipline themselves in accord with the policies and programs of the presidency or to be prepared to pay the consequences.

Because no other politically effective unit such as the House of Commons exists, to which the presidency would render automatic responsibility and in which political disputes can be settled on the basis of a formal vote, an unsuccessful revolt against the decisions of the chief executive can mean temporary or permanent excommunication from the decision-making mechanism for the individual interest spokesman, though not for the interest itself for any length of time. Without a doubt only a unified front including a very large proportion of the major power factors could hope to succeed in dethroning the president, and this success would be accompanied by so many disastrous side effects upon economic as well as political stability that the interests which require a strong central government as a check against centrifugal forces would refuse to join such a front, preferring to limit their own aspirations to assure success for the broader system. They prefer to do this particularly because in deciding policy the presidency does take their views and interests into account to some extent.

The one real fault of this particular version of an executive-centered governmental system is the lack of any institutionalized agency, again like the House of Commons, through which individuals can gain access to the decision-making process as do organized groups and associations. Only if he belongs to some association can the average citizen hope to make his voice heard in public affairs, and then it reaches the policy-makers filtered through several layers of organizational hierarchy. The common practice of purchasing full-page advertisements in Mexico City's principal newspapers in order to smash through these barriers to reach the president is one answer to this problem of communication, but it hardly offers a practical solution to the masses of citizens who are hard-pressed to pay for a single copy of the newspaper, much less buy a full-page ad in it. These Mexicans must rely upon the president's awareness of the need to retain popular support for his government and party and his personal sense of political responsibility for protection of both the individual's rights and the general public interest in the battles of Titans carried on by the leaders of the strongest interest associations.

Actually, time may solve this problem of weak representation for individuals in the real political system, for the seeds of political awareness which were planted earlier during the Revolution already are beginning to sprout. Spreading knowledge and deepening sophistication are producing a citizenry that begins not only to demand a louder voice and a stronger hand in public matters but to hold its immediate functional representatives more accountable for the trust lodged in them. The low-level performance of government tolerated during the nineteenth century, when the rewards of political activity were shared only among the small politically minded part of the population rather than trickling down to the masses in whose name they governed, no longer is adequate today. In fact, because in Mexico the practice is to tie development activities, business concessions, and most social and economic advances to government, and particularly to the administration in power, the presidency already feels and responds to pressures from those citizens who do not share in the disproportionate benefits captured by the more effective functional interest associations for their members, despite the relatively higher-level performance of present-day government.

For all its mechanical inadequacy in regard to individuals, the governmental system centering in the presidency is infinitely more efficient in satisfying the needs of the citizen than were earlier political arrangements, in spite of the multiplication of social and economic problems inherent in Westernization. From the viewpoint of service, the real weakness of government by a single strong man, be that government based on naked force or on the emotional ties of charisma, is the same one that undermines government by a small ruling faction, whatever its basis or theoretic justification. Such governments operate outside of the political and/or constitutional norms that offer the bulk of citizens a sense of continuity and administrative efficiency, two acknowledged requirements of modern economies and societies.

As Mexico's present political system has evolved into an institutionalized governing mechanism, the disruptive and debilitating government processes that once worked against the average citizen have reversed themselves. A cadre of career officials has been developed to apply policy decisions through effective administrative techniques based upon written records, legal and administrative precedent, and other less erratic but more permanent methods of conducting public affairs. Although the operation of this governing mechanism does not adhere perfectly to the terms of the written constitution, it works to provide a predictable and constructive pattern to which the individual can adjust, and that is the important fact.

The revolutionary governments have not shown themselves adverse to making adjustments in the political system to satisfy, insofar as possible, the demands of citizens as they become politically potent. For the first time in Mexican history the opportunity to utilize the services of government is open to all citizens who are sufficiently aware of the possibility, though, to be absolutely honest, one must recognize that those Mexicans politically astute enough to channel their activities through the collective power of interest associations have fared far better than those individuals who insist upon acting alone.

The evolution of the presidency as a means of including organized power factors in the political process without regard to their association, or lack of it, with the revolutionary party, is the best evidence of political flexibility to meet the rapidly changing environment. Whether the aggregating function will continue to operate through the extra-constitutional agency of the presidency as the number and variety of factors in the political system increase, or shift to the legislative branch as the constitution envisions, or perhaps pass to some altogether new mechanism, is impossible to forecast. For the time being, however, the aggregating function will remain where it is, because the authority of the presidency is deeply ingrained and is now as effective as conditions will permit.

CHAPTER *9*

# Democracy in Mexico

## Government and the Individual

This book has attempted to describe the development of systematic, Western-style government in Mexico, even though the transition is not yet complete. There is no real need to repeat here what was said in general terms in Chapter 1 and more specifically throughout the rest of the study, but one important question does remain to be considered. How well does Mexico's evolving political system serve the individual, whether he participates in one or more of the interest groups which share in the decision-making process or whether he remains outside of the active machinery of policy determining?

This is a significant question in determining the success or failure of the transition toward a Western system of government in any country. As Roy Macridis says,

> The test of any system is the opportunities it provides to the individual to live peacefully with his fellowmen, that is, internal security and the development of institutions for the adjustment of individual and group conflict. A political system should provide men with opportunities for employment and economic security as well as for political participation. This means that the system should provide for education and freedom in the widest possible sense of the word —freedom of thought and expression, religious freedom, and freedom of association and political action. Above all, men must be treated by the government on a footing of equality. This means

that they should not be differentiated on any basis other than ability and achievement; it also means that no handicaps should be placed for any reason whatsoever upon the potentiality of a man's development.[1]

The fair-minded reader will admit readily that Mexico already has traveled quite a distance along the road to this ideal, but even the most friendly observer, one who identifies emotionally with the hopes, desires, and struggles of the Mexican people, must concede that Mexico's political system has not yet arrived at this stage of perfection. From the viewpoint of a study concerned primarily with the long-range pattern of political development and the gradual evolution of working political institutions for the satisfactory adjustment of individual and group conflicts, however, the vital point is not simply the degree of achievement at this particular moment. Instead, it is found in a question posed earlier in the book—whether the kind of responsible and effective government normally associated with the democratic aspirations of Western man reasonably can be expected to evolve in time. On the basis of what has taken place since 1910, and especially since 1930, I believe that such a political system can be expected to develop in Mexico.

Democratic government, in the Western sense of the term, is a great deal more than a political idea, or even ideal; as Macridis suggests, it involves the social situation and the economic conditions under which the individual exists, in addition to his political freedom. As such, a democratic political system reflects a whole way of life, in which the normal, daily human activities of the citizens are as important as the operations of formal government agencies. Democracy as a political system cannot long coexist with social or economic inequity and, conversely, a fluid society and viable economy are apt to produce conditions favorable to democratic government, for all human activities and values must be reasonably consistent with each other if stability is to exist in a given society. This does not mean, however, that every country in which social change or economic development is taking place may be classed automatically as a future democracy, for in addition to material conditions, the concept requires the acceptance of a particular set of values by a broad cross-section of the society. Consider the reversals suffered recently by the hopeful democratically inspired governments of the emerging Asian states because of the lack of

---

[1] *The Study of Comparative Government* (New York, 1955), p. 62.

any commonly shared understanding of what democracy entails. Or consider the alien form, by Western standards, that "people's democracy" takes in the Soviet Union, where the traditional value system supports authoritarianism and orthodoxy at the expense of responsible, representative government and individual freedom in social and economic matters as well as in political activity.

Growing as it does out of the social activities of large numbers of persons, democracy eludes formal or mechanistic definitions; it can be discussed best by means of a working definition that takes into account the action of people and the fluidity of the concept itself. One way to test Mexico's ongoing system of politics for evidence of democratic tendencies is to search for a democratic syndrome; that is, a significantly strong pattern of observable signs and symptoms which characterize democracy, occurring together in sufficient proportions to render any existing nondemocratic characteristics less and less operative, until a diagnosis of effective democracy is possible. Every political system contains some of the elements of democracy, just as it does some nondemocratic factors, so the important fact is not the existence of either but the respective roles they play in the political process; this offers an indication of a trend toward democratic government, if one exists.

As a minimum, Mexico's democratic syndrome must include a degree of limited, responsible, and popular government within a formalized, though not necessarily written, constitutional system. To operate successfully, such government presupposes relatively widespread public agreement on basic social and political values, so that the limits of governmental action prescribed by the political system are acceptable to and enforced by a large enough part of the citizenry to assure orderly administration. This, in turn, requires that the largest possible portion of the people be politically aware and well enough educated to demand effective action in matters of their concern. Corollary to this active popular role in government, and an absolute requirement for democracy, is the need both under the law and in the popular mind for recognition of the essential equality of all human beings and at least some acceptance of the fundamental dignity of the individual in relation to other individuals.

In testing for Mexico's democratic syndrome, we must consider carefully the political process in which these general factors operate, being equally careful to measure their role in that process in the currency of the country. That is, we must recognize that we are studying social institutions and political habit patterns which have meaning in Mexico rather than in some other country with different values, ideologies, and political culture. Taking this into account, we must seek to determine whether the political process operates in an environment of broadly enough shared values and understandings of the role and function of government for the minority to accept the decision of the majority and for the government in power to offer a high degree of toleration to the opposition. If most politically active persons, no matter which party or faction they belong to, are loyal to the general concepts of the political and constitutional system, chances are that the usual mechanisms of democratic government will operate effectively. Freedom of speech, press, and assembly will exist to assure that fair and free elections may occur.

Mere outward evidence of democratic-type factors in the formal constitutional system does not always indicate that working democracy is an operational reality in a country's politics. We must look behind the façade to determine just how deeply rooted such factors are in the general pattern of political action. Most modern constitutions, including that of Mexico, establish the external forms of responsible and representative government, but only as these forms are implemented by institutionalized patterns of action do they take on real meaning. In fact, as in the case of Mexico, the most meaningful democratic institutions sometimes operate almost completely outside of the formal constitutional agencies.

Because of the essentially interactive nature of the social, economic, and political forces which go to make up a democratic syndrome, any attempt to legislate democracy as a political end in itself appears foredoomed to failure. The several factors involved must evolve together so as to provide a balanced pattern which can act as a check upon extremes of every sort. Too little respect for the individual, for example, can lead to despotism in a social system, too much to anarchy. Attempts at obtaining social and political cohesiveness through enforced conformity can lead to dictatorship, just as refusal of large factions to conform to a generally accepted value system can lead ultimately to civil war. In this sense, stable democracy must result from an evolutionary process rather than from the off-the-cuff decisions of a revolutionary clique. The amount of inertia inherent in such an evolutionary process is strikingly evident in the history of the slow formation of Mexico's present political system, which is not yet completely stabilized.

Fortunately, the very interdependence of the forces which make up democracy means that once they have become institutionalized in a political system, they tend to support and build one upon the other. After all, a pattern of action becomes institutionalized because it is in harmony with the system in which it operates. If it clashes, either the action pattern proves unworkable and disappears, or the system adjusts to absorb it. Given the existence of, and the growing interaction among, forces which make for democracy, the speed with which a democratic syndrome becomes reality depends a great deal upon the intensity of influence each and all of the democratizing factors can bring upon the governmental process as compared with those forces which hinder limited, responsible, and popular government.

No precise formula can determine just when the democratic syndrome becomes operative in a given country's political system and makes itself manifest to the world. More than likely, once the minima of social and economic conditions have been achieved and had time to work upon the country's politics, the breakthrough comes when the majority of thinking and politically aware citizens begin to conceive of themselves as living in a democratic state and to conduct themselves accordingly. Once this happens, the individual citizen finds himself in a situation in which he reasonably can anticipate that his legitimate day-to-day needs and desires—social, economic, and political—are limited only by the wealth of the country and his own ability to satisfy them. Despite a carry-over of some antidemocratic practices, most of the major patterns of life in the democratic system will complement each other, for the very concept of system implies continuity as well as adjustment among the activities of persons.

## Democracy in Mexico

As suggested above, the Mexicans have not yet accomplished a complete syndrome of democracy, even in terms of their own culture and value system. Just before the 1958 election, one Mexican observer wrote that ". . . we have democracy 364 days a year and lack it only on one—election day."[2] This statement overstates the

---

[2] Rodrigo García Treviño, "Defensa de Nuestros Defectos Políticos," *Excelsior*, March 11, 1958.

case, both for democracy during the year and against it on election day, for within our definition of the term a political system cannot be democratic most of the year, only to reverse itself on election day. But this does not mean that the pattern of symptoms which could combine to produce a democratic syndrome in Mexico is not well advanced. On the contrary, in spite of the negative forces which continue to impede the evolution of a complete working democracy for Mexico at this time the development of conditions favoring the concept is advancing rapidly.

Examples of the factors hindering democratic government have appeared throughout this book. We know, for example, that Mexico's political system still does not rest upon a sufficiently broad base of nationally oriented, economically secure, and politically aware citizens either to assure representation of every legitimate interest in the deciding of public policy or to produce in certain of those who govern a fully developed sense of political responsibility to every individual, regardless of status or position. We know, too, that strategically located functional interest associations such as the government bureaucrats union or certain other labor groups enjoy unusually advantageous positions in the political process, and that these and other associations often are manipulated by their leaders for personal benefit, even at the expense of the rank-and-file members. We know that neither the internal nominating procedures of the official party nor the elections themselves are entirely free of pernicious influences intruding themselves for the personal benefit of certain politicians. We know, finally, that in the political process the individual unaffiliated with some formally organized interest association, be it inside or out of the PRI, finds it very difficult to make his voice heard, and that this condition probably will endure so long as the broad mass of Mexicans lack any strong sense of political initiative because of inadequate education, economic insecurity, or an incomplete feeling of participation in the nation.

On the social and economic level, as opposed to the political, even those citizens who have adjusted successfully to the conditions inherent in Western life do not have deeply ingrained in their consciousness and in all of their habit patterns that solid core of shared values and respect for the other individual per se that seems so important an ingredient in the formation of a democratic syndrome. Only too clearly, the benefits of industrialization, of easy communication, of Westernization in the material sense, have not spread out evenly throughout the country. Until quite recently, the urban areas have taken the lion's share, and even this portion flowed principally into the pockets of a relatively small middle and upper class. The very reform clauses of the Constitution of 1917, of which the Mexicans are so proud, have been subverted to this end at times, for they contain lists of material rights for certain groups of individuals. Although the economy of the country has not been able to satisfy all of these stated rights, the constitutional promises not only tempted but seemingly encouraged those individuals or interest groups which were stronger or better organized to bring pressure upon government, demanding their "legal rights," perhaps at the expense of the less competitive, who sometimes were pushed below the subsistence level, or even at the expense of the development of the country as a whole. In spite of all of the advanced social legislation contained in the constitution, this sudden-death kind of "collective Social Darwinism" too often has been the practice in Mexico.

Without for a moment ignoring the negative factors mentioned here and elaborated throughout this study, it appears to me that opposing, positive factors favoring responsible, representative, and limited government are in the ascendancy in Mexico today. In time they should grow in strength, each complementing the other, until at last they join together to provide the country with an operating democratic syndrome based upon its own culture and values.

In fact, the evolutionary process already is well advanced, for side by side with the negative factors noted in the earlier chapters of this book is evidence of a great deal of positive accomplishment in the struggle to establish working democracy in Mexico. As the operations of the political decision-making process become more institutionalized, an effective constitutional system has evolved, even though it does not always follow identically the letter of the law laid down in 1917. Despite obvious weaknesses in this governing system, it does seem to take into account all of the principal and most active interest groups and associations when the highest public officers are being selected and when major policy questions are decided. Moreover, the political system is flexible enough to permit access of new groups and associations representing developing interests which grow out of changes in the social and economic environment.

More important still, from the point of view of the individual, changes in the Mexican environment are both speeding up and proliferating at an almost geometric rate, as Westernization reaches out with roads and radios and schools to embrace all of the Mexicans in a single national life. Not only are the vast majority of Mexicans being exposed to new ideas and the possibility of material change, but the value system within which they operate is being affected by these new concepts. More important in this context is the way in which, as Westernization turns more and more Mexicans into nationally aware and politically conscious citizens, the medium through which it occurs—the Revolution of 1910—has become identified with the values of democratic government.

To date, the propaganda line of the revolutionary governments, that Mexicans live in a democratic environment, has not been fully implemented because, as suggested in Chapter IV, the dilemma of the Revolution was that it had to set about providing suitable social and economic conditions before the political goals of democratic government could be achieved. Now that new and more suitable conditions do exist, the minds of many Mexicans are ready to absorb new understandings of the role of the individual in society and of his responsibilities to his fellow man. The seeds of these ideas have been planted in minds already open to change, so that they can take root and bear fruit in the form of socialized action later. In the Mexican world of violently conflicting values, the most consistent and dynamic force of the past half-century has been the Revolution, which does equate with an urge toward democracy, no matter how differently each Mexican may understand the meaning of that word. The social myth can have profound influence over the political activities of men; for Mexico, the myth of democracy, believed by and acted upon by enough citizens, could provide the final tie to bind together the increasingly strong democratic influences into an operative democratic syndrome.

No one who knows Mexico would argue that the country already has attained a working democratic system, or that it is the most democratic country in Latin America today, though one might well argue that in the fifty years since the outbreak of the Revolution more has been done there to solve the real problems hindering development of such a system than in any of the other republics of the area. Political scientists who specialize in Latin American politics tend to rate Mexico rather high in democratic traits, particularly in comparison with the other "Indian" countries of Latin America which face similar social and cultural problems. A continuing study of Latin American democracy has been conducted by Russell H. Fitzgibbon among a group of Latin America area specialists. On the basis of such criteria as freedom of speech, press, and assembly, freedom of party organization and elections, independence of legislative and judicial activities, responsibility of the government to the citizens, and the like, Mexico stood seventh out of the twenty republics in 1945 and 1950, and in 1955 rose to fourth place; during the last mentioned year, no other country with an appreciable Indian population stood higher than tenth.[3]

My more sporting colleagues tell me that fourth takes no prize in a horse race, and considering the nature of the competition in the Latin American democratic sweepstakes, fourth place may well be considered a somewhat dubious honor. But considering too the number and nature of the handicaps Mexico has had in its bid for democracy, I should say that the country is moving up fast. Some recent events in Mexico's political life suggest that this is so.

## Democracy Under President López Mateos

During the interregnum period between the nomination of Adolfo López Mateos and his formal inauguration on December 1, 1958, and even during the first period of his administration, scattered but impressive evidence appeared to suggest that some of the democratic concepts which have taken root in Mexican soil are beginning to sprout. Despite the somewhat disappointing turnout of voters, due to the absence of qualified opposition, the presidential campaign itself indicated that a higher proportion of thinking Mexicans have begun to concern themselves about politics, not with the old goal of immediate and personal aggrandizement but with the understanding that honest, effective, and responsible government is a worthy goal in itself, one that could pay them valuable dividends in the long run, no matter what their means of livelihood or role in life may be.

New political attitudes were not limited to essentially passive intellectualizing, however, for hitherto quiescent interest groups throughout the country took advantage of the relaxed election and presidential transfer period to press home demands for particular

---

[3] See Professor Fitzgibbon's article, "Measurement of Latin American Political Phenomena; A Statistical Experiment," *American Political Science Review,* XLV (June, 1951), 517-23, and his "A Statistical Evaluation of Latin-American Democracy," *The Western Political Quarterly,* IX (September, 1956), 607-19.

interests which the leaders of the interest associations nominally representing them had failed to win. Some of these movements already have been mentioned. The attempts of leftist, anti-BUO leaders to capture control of the labor unions representing railroaders, oil workers, electrical workers, and primary-school teachers in the Federal District, among others, using real and fancied grievances as a lever, and the consequent efforts of the established CTM and other BUO leadership to protect their positions by initiating their own threat of a general strike to win wage increases for their followers are a case in point. So are the attempts, again led by leftists, of large numbers of landless *peones* to obtain their own farms by invading already cultivated lands held by others, particularly in the northwestern states of Sinaloa, Sonora, and Baja California. In the context of this study, it matters less that these movements were led by leftists than that these leaders were able to find persons among formally apolitical and passive portions of the citizenry who were willing to take action on their own behalf, indicating a growing popular initiative that had lain dormant since the violent days of the Revolution of 1910.

This same growth of popular initiative manifested itself in broader political terms at the state and local level of government during this same period. In at least two states, San Luis Potosí and Zacatecas, late 1958 and early 1959 saw a general cross-section of the citizens uniting in attempts to oust long-entrenched state political bosses. In both cases the struggle centered in attempts of the state *cacique* to impose his hand-picked candidates in *municipio* elections and, unlike previous disturbances at this level, such as that at León in 1945, the popular reaction was widespread and cut across party lines. Social development had at long last reached a level at which the general citizenry no longer was willing to tolerate the type of strong-man government that has continued to control some of the local units long past the evolution of more responsible authority at the national level. In the case of San Luis Potosí, at least, the governor was forced out in favor of a more popular person.

President López Mateos himself demonstrated, both in his reaction to the above incidents and in his general administrative program, that he recognizes and encourages the expansion of popular participation in government affairs and the activities of the revolutionary party. Among his first official acts in the presidential office was a general amnesty freeing student leaders who had been involved in incidents at the Polytechnical Institute and the National University, together with anti-BUO labor leaders who had precipitated the series of strikes which marked the transfer of presidential power, and radical farm leaders who had led the landless *paracaidistas* in their invasion of farm lands. As his predecessor had done in controlling the extreme wings of the revolutionary party before 1959, however, so President López Mateos made it very clear that his acts of conciliation in no way indicated abrogation of presidential power. To demonstrate that in a democratic system rights carry with them a corollary responsibility, the new chief executive did not hesitate to resort to force in the face of irresponsible or illegal acts upon the part of popular leaders, if the occasion demanded force.

Early in January, 1959, when farm lands in Ciudad Obregón again were invaded by landless peasants, President López Mateos promptly authorized the use of troops to remove the *paracaidistas* and to order the instigators held for criminal trial. And a few weeks later, troops again were used to halt the wave of disturbances involving students and leftist labor elements protesting the proposed raise in bus fares. Finally, as we have seen, the president took very harsh measures indeed in retaliation for the continued recalcitrance of the railroad workers union, breaking the 1959 Easter strike, replacing Demetrio Vallejo and his fellow union officers with a more moderate committee, and subjecting them to arrest for criminal activities.

Most Mexicans approved the apparent harshness of the president's reaction, for two reasons. First, López Mateos had to demonstrate that he would not allow public policy to be dictated by force, particularly considering the unsettled conditions marking his accession to office. Second, the chief executive already had demonstrated good faith with the restive groups. Not only had he freed their leaders, but agencies of the national government were attempting to resolve the problems which motivated their action. The students were to be consulted both in academic matters ranging from tuition and housing to educational policy questions and in more peripheral subjects such as increased bus fares. Labor leaders, both dissidents and BUO, had won concessions to improve their personal status; the former knew that wage increases they had won for workers had been confirmed and the rebellious leaders themselves were seated in the union posts they captured in the process; the latter were allowed to use the threat of a general strike to pry increases out of employers for their own followers, thus protecting their own established positions in the labor hierarchy. Even Jacinto López, who had been freed by the president's amnesty, wired his UGOCM followers in January, 1959, to stop inciting land invasions, because he was in the process of discussing establishment of new agricultural colonies to absorb landless peasants with the *Departamento Agrario y Colonización.*

If President López Mateos' reaction to the pressures brought upon his administration by specific emerging interests indicates a readiness to allow them access to and participation in the decision-making process, his general program went far beyond reacting to pressures brought upon him. It encouraged the kinds of governmental and private activity which would speed up and expand preparation of Mexico's masses for popular participation in public affairs and politics. During his first year in office, expenditures for education made up the largest single budget item, and his Education Minister, Sr. Jaime Torres Bodet, inaugurated a crash program for a drastic increase in numbers of schools and teachers and, very important, for a strong improvement in their quality. Carrying out his campaign promise, President López Mateos sought to use government spending policies to encourage the geographic diversification of industry away from Mexico City and into the hinterland. He also tried to make more money available for government development projects in the nonurban areas of the country—first by attempting to operate the government petroleum monopoly on a more businesslike basis, cutting back labor featherbedding, and raising the retail price of petroleum products out of the subsidy class to allow a small profit for reinvestment by the government; next by removing the government's small business loan agency, *Nacional Financiera,* from control over some of the more successful businesses it had financed, through sale of its stock holdings to the public; and finally by easing the drain on the national treasury that poor management and inefficient labor on the nationalized railways had forced.

All of these activities suggest that President López Mateos not only sought to extend as many as possible of the benefits of the Revolution to the broad mass of population but that he was both prepared and strong enough to do so in the face of the opposition of long-entrenched labor and business groups which had enjoyed a favored position in their economic and political roles. He strengthened the popular feeling that his administration would attempt to serve the interests of every Mexican who was sufficiently aware and politically active enough to participate in politics by insisting that General Alfonso Corona del Rosal, who was appointed new president of the central committee of the PRI, institute a reorganization of the party's internal operations on much more democratic lines, including the slight liberalizing of *municipio* nominating procedures mentioned above. López Mateos even went so far as to encourage the two chambers of Congress to assume a slightly stronger role in discussing policy before them for passage. In fact, certain fairly important provisions of the president's bill reorganizing portions of the executive departments were amended in the Chamber of Deputies and these amendments were upheld by the Senate, so that they became part of the law.

Quite clearly, the rapidly growing number of examples of mass interest about, pressure upon, and participation in, politics, government, and the decision-making process cannot be divorced from the equally compelling increased evidence of presidential policy during both the Ruiz Cortines and the López Mateos administrations of opening the political system to any and every Mexican who becomes sufficiently aware to demand entry to this process. In this sense, the ever-growing forces for democratic government, which well up from the general citizenry as social and economic conditions prepare them for an effective role in the political process, are being supplemented and encouraged by the chief executives who have won nomination to their high office precisely because they represent in their views and their past careers those same forces which make for representative, responsible, and limited government.

# *Epilogue*

About six years have passed since *Mexican Government in Transition* was written. Since then the presidential term of Adolfo López Mateos nearly has run its course and Mexico again is engaged in a national election campaign. Inevitably, during this period the political process has produced some changes, but there have been few surprises. The political system that by now governs nearly forty million Mexicans continues to follow the patterns formed during the decades since 1940.

In a few cases incipient trends have become more clearly defined. For example, the tendency toward increasing differentiation of attitude and exposition of viewpoints within the ongoing political system has continued apace. The right and left wings of the government party now tend to cluster in political "movements" that carry an identifiable title but carefully avoid any formal clash with the PRI. The challengers to BUO domination of the labor sector have won some recognition in the official party's councils. Both conservative Roman Catholic elements and radical leftists object openly and loudly, though unsuccessfully, to a government-

---

PUBLISHER'S NOTE: *This chapter was prepared in February, 1964, to bring the work completely up to date.*

307

sponsored free and compulsory primary textbook program that stresses nationalism, but in a centerist frame of reference.

On the other hand, deeply ingrained patterns continue to mold political activity, even in the face of changing circumstances. Despite the unfolding problem of Castro's Cuba and all of the pressures resulting from rapid change throughout the rest of Latin America, as well as from the United States' reaction through the Alliance for Progress, Mexico's politics remains almost entirely internally oriented, concerned mainly with domestic economic development and social integration and scarcely at all with foreign affairs.

The administration of Adolfo López Mateos (1958-1964) supplied a number of positive accomplishments, including distribution to *campesinos* of the greatest amount of land since Cárdenas' activities in the 1930's. The coverage of *seguro social*, the government health program, was extended to most of Mexico's cities and towns and even into several wide areas of the rural countryside. At the same time, the government acted to implement the constitutional provision requiring profit-sharing with workers in larger industrial firms. The period also was marked by greatly expanded educational activities, with the national budgetary allotment for education multiplying nearly four times until it totaled 25.4 per cent of the government's expenditures. This program included the distribution of some eighty-five million free texts and notebooks by 1964 and an eleven-year plan to provide primary schools for all children by the early 1970's. Politically, a constitutional amendment was adopted to encourage opposition parties to participate in congressional elections by allowing them up to twenty *Diputados de Partido* in the lower chamber, to be alloted not by electoral district but according to the national vote amassed. The plan grants each minority party five deputies if it captures 2.5 per cent of the votes, with an additional seat for each additional half per cent, to a total of twenty.

These accomplishments continue the reform aspects of the Mexican Revolution, but on balance and despite what some other commentators have suggested I believe that López Mateos' administration probably leaned slightly to the right though still clearly within the boundaries of a centerist position. The president's continuing support of industrial and commercial interests and his encouragement of foreign investment are indicators of the pattern.

Although the government took over the cinema-distribution and electric power industries, the former had been in economic difficulties and the latter was purchased in such a way that the foreign owners reinvested their money in other Mexican enterprises. Another indicator is the government's switch from neutrality to support of the United States' position during the Cuban missile crisis, as is the conviction of some twenty-five leftists arrested during the disruptive shakedown period early in the administration. After being held in jail for several years these men were tried and convicted in 1963 for the crime of "social dissolution." Among those involved were railroad strike leaders Demetrio Vallejo and Valentin Campa, the head of Mexico's Communist party, Dionisio Encina, and David Alfaro Siqueiros, the leftist muralist. Some persons also suggest that President López Mateos' selection of Gustavo Díaz Ordaz as his successor is further evidence of a drift to the right.

Events during the López Mateos administration point up an evolving pattern in Mexican politics that was not stressed in the original edition of *Mexican Government in Transition* because it had not taken so clear a form under President Ruiz Cortines. I refer to a weakness in governmental policy initiative. Raymond Vernon has called this problem "the dilemma of Mexico's development," suggesting that Mexico's political process is so concerned with balancing and representing all interests and viewpoints that they cancel each other and little if any innovating leadership emanates from government. Specifically, his thesis is that the country is passing through a period of economic stagnation that requires massive infusion of investments to stimulate continued economic growth, but that the president is hampered from encouraging the private sector to act for fear of the political left, or from encouraging the public sector to intervene for fear of the right. While I agree that a problem of sorts exists, I do not ascribe major responsibility to the balancing function in the political process.

As the Mexican political system operates, the president has ample authority and sufficient support from the center and the opposite extreme wing of the official party to support policies which are not pleasing to either the far right or the far left portions of the revolutionary movement, *if the chief executive is willing to take a firm stand*. The history of both the Cárdenas and the Alemán administrations clearly demonstrates this. The difficulty resides not so much in the power assigned to the president by the political process as in his psychological ability to use it, conditioned by the nature of his political experience. This in turn relates to the factors involved in the selection of presidential candidates by the PRI.

Over the years since the emergence of the revolutionary party a Mexican "governmental establishment" has grown up, consisting of a relatively small group of technical and administrative specialists and trouble-shooters. These members of the PRI have demonstrated their ability by completing successfully a variety of difficult government assignments and have proved their loyalty to the ongoing political system by willingness to accept transfer from one post to another as the needs of the country dictate. If an individual demonstrates competence in successive posts, he may be moved from appointive to elective office and back again, from state to national government positions, even from public to private duties, gradually climbing the ladder to ever more responsible and remunerative functions. The final step upward is, of course, to the presidency of the republic.

To some extent, all of the recent presidents of Mexico have been affected by this winnowing process. This assures that they have a certain degree of tested executive ability; but experience, first under Adolfo Ruiz Cortines and then under President López Mateos, suggests the existence of an unintended but increasingly evident by-product of the process. Almost by definition, success in the administrative sphere requires a very special, almost negative kind of political involvement. Effective manipulation of office and intersecretariat politics is essential for advancement, but not the talents needed for broader, give-and-take party politics and really competitive electioneering in which hard decisions must be made independently, with the individual ready to take the consequences of his actions. On the contrary, too much involvement in this sort of political activity can make a man less *presidenciable*, as chapter 7 points out. Once an individual attains the presidency, however, it is precisely experience in this aspect of politics that he needs.

Evidence that the selection-up process in the Mexican establishment tends to elevate administrative types rather than political men began to accumulate under Ruiz Cortines; the pattern became more defined during the administration of López Mateos. As president, the latter sought to accomplish his political goals through symbolic successes and conflict-minimizing compromises rather than by deciding on specific policies and pounding them into programs, as he had the political power to do. For example, although foreign affairs have little direct impact on Mexico's domestic politics, President López Mateos very effectively used his Asian and European state visits, his support for a denuclearized Latin America, and the settlement of the long outstanding El Chamizal border dispute between Mexico and the United States to bolster his personal status in domestic affairs. In like manner, he made frequent trips throughout the republic, strengthening his position by promising benefits to each region, apparently at times beyond the capacity of his administration to perform. On a functional basis he did much the same thing, attempting to give each competing interest some portion of what it sought.

Whether this method of governing is indeed a function of the process by which López Mateos rose in the government hierarchy, with corresponding influence upon his conception of the political process, or an outgrowth of the more general patterns imposed by the political system, can be tested fully only by comparing the political style of his administration with those of succeeding presidents. The fact is, however, that of the last four presidents only Alemán can be classed as a truly strong president in terms of the manner in which he exercised political power; Ruiz Cortines was intermittently strong and permissive, while Avila Camacho and López Mateos relied more on persuasion and compromise than upon the clout they could have utilized. And this during a period of growing complexity of Mexican life, as the society and economy developed more diversified functions, with a growing number of viewpoints and of organized groups to represent them.

Under López Mateos the trend toward public identification of specialized interests was clearly marked, particularly during the period just prior to the 1964 presidential election, which produced the usual crystallization of divergent views hoping to utilize the fluid political situation to maximize their positions. It already has been noted that conservative Roman Catholic lay groups are speaking out more openly in the textbook controversy; so did the forty-eight members of the hierarchy who in July, 1962, published a "Declaration of Catholic Principles" against communism. Similarly, the *alemanista* wing of the PRI set up a *Frente Cívico Mexicano de Afirmación Revolucionaria* to support private enterprise and attack communist tendencies, to which the *cardenistas* reacted by supporting a more radical left organization known as the *Movi-*

*miento de Liberación Nacional.* Again, a leftist agrarian group, the *Central Campesino Independiente* (CCI) rose to challenge the CNC, although its inroads among the rural population have not been so great as to threaten the agrarian sector of the official party; instead, the existence of the CCI has led to more energetic representation of small farmer interests by the CNC's *políticos.* Numerous other interests spoke out so openly and so loudly, particularly during the two years before the end of his term, that President López Mateos arranged a well-publicized act symbolic of national unity early in 1962, appointing all seven living ex-presidents (including both Cárdenas and Alemán) to government posts of varying degrees of responsibility.

Significantly, the appearance of a growing number of publicly identified interest organizations has not led automatically to a growing polarization of monolithic right and left movements. Not even the catalyst of impending presidential elections could overcome the inability of so-called left groups to unite, which was equaled only the tendency of religiously oriented and conservative factors to splinter. Illustrative of but by no means a complete record of the pattern are the following examples. During mid-1963 a group calling itself the *Frente Electoral del Pueblo* (FEP) attempted, unsuccessfully as it later resulted, to win legal registration as a national political party that could represent the radical left. It was attacked by the intellectual leadership of the *Movimiento de Liberación Nacional* as a tool of the unrecognized Mexican Communist party's plot to wreck the MLN, while at the same time Vicente Lombardo Toledano excoriated all three of the leftist movements as impeding the constructive development of the country. Almost identically, on the right, the *Partido Demócrata Cristiano,* which also failed to gain legal recognition, was unable to capture the support of a dissident group of former members of the PAN who formed the *Movimiento Social Demócrata Cristiano* or of another right group, the *Movimiento Cívico Social Mexicano,* much less of the recognized *Partido de Acción Nacional,* the present leadership of which rejects Christian Democracy as its political ideology.

If the preliminary skirmishing for the 1964 presidential election resembled that of six years earlier, the nominations and campaign were even more nearly carbon copies. Like his predecessor, President López Mateos managed to hold off the PRI's nominating convention until mid-November, 1963, although the political dam broke and the public knew that the party's candidate would be Secretary of *Gobernación* Gustavo Díaz Ordaz two weeks before the official action was taken, rather than one. As in the previous presidential election, all but one of the other legally recognized parties decided to go along with the official candidate. In fact, as early as the previous June Lombardo Toledano had hinted that his party, now renamed the *Partido Popular Socialista* (PPS), ought to support the revolutionary party's nominee. The PAN spoke for a time of avoiding the presidential contest but later decided to put up a candidate, a forty-four-year-old lawyer named José González Torres.

Gustavo Díaz Ordaz demonstrates all of the proven characteristics of a successful PRI pre-candidate. Born in 1911 in an important state, Puebla, he obtained part of his education in two other populous states, Oaxaca and Jalisco, after which he returned to his birthplace. His grandfather had been a collaborator of Juárez and his father a farmer and civil servant. Díaz Ordaz graduated in law and his public service included positions as both public prosecutor and judge. He also acted as head of his state's Arbitration Commission, as a law professor, and as vice-rector of the University of Puebla. After serving first as deputy and then as senator from his state, he entered the *Secretaría de Gobernación*, moving up the ladder to its top office during the administration of President López Mateos. As secretary he did an effective job, though he did not endear himself to the left with his vigorous actions against disrupting elements.

The early months of Díaz Ordaz' campaign followed the pattern established by previous revolutionary presidential candidates, with one exception. In moving from town to town, city to city, region to region, the nominee met with representative citizens, discussing their problems and seeking solutions. But this time the preliminary staff work was much more carefully organized. For most of the previous year, in anticipation of the campaign, the PRI had set about systematically to prepare a carefully documented study of the needs of the country. Both regional and functional representatives had been invited to submit discussions of national and local problems, together with recommendations for their solutions. These were worked over by a permanent staff at party headquarters and presented to a national meeting for final revision. This national program and its local components were the staff papers which provided a basis for discussion between the candidate and the persons with whom he spoke on his campaign tours.

In short, the political events which have occurred in Mexico during the administration of President López Mateos, since *Mexican Government in Transition* was written, continue rather than alter the established patterns of the country's political system. Some trends have followed their natural course, becoming more sharply defined; others have begun to peter out as they become outmoded. But few if any run counter to the increasingly deeply embedded political habits which the Mexicans have evolved since the Revolution of 1910 and particularly since the appearance of the revolutionary party.

What has changed since this book first appeared is the degree of sophistication found in theoretical approaches to the study of political development, a sub-field in political science that has advanced remarkably during the 1960's. Re-reading the book in light of today's conceptions convinces me, however, that if I were to write it now few if any basic changes would have to be made. Always excepting new material that becomes available with the passing of time and the steady appearance of new research reports on an intensely interesting country, the differences would center mainly in slight shifts in emphasis as regards interpretation of certain phenomena and the addition of materials on political culture that were not available earlier.

The availability of such works as Gabrial A. Almond and James S. Coleman, eds., *The Politics of the Developing Areas* (Princeton, 1960), with theoretical chapters by the two editors and an interesting section on Latin America by George I. Blanksten, or Lucian Pye, *Politics, Personality and Nation-building* (New Haven, 1962), or the several volumes in the Princeton Series on Political Development, which consider the influence on political change of such factors as communications, bureaucracy, education, political parties and the like, affects one's conception of change. The observer must now take into account as politically relevant many factors which once were glossed over as important and interesting but unmeasurable. The resulting new insights into the nature of the political development process do not replace previously held understandings, though they may shift accepted interpretations somewhat, but they do add important new dimensions.

One of the changes in emphasis which could result from the ex-: panding knowledge of political change might be the dropping of the dichotomy "Western" and "non-Western"—not because a better term has appeared, but because these words induce a false impression. Recent research demonstrates that political development phenomena are not geographically bound. Conditions and attitudes similar to those encountered in less developed countries of Asia, Africa, and Latin America have been described for certain European states; more significantly, even in so-called highly developed nations, less integrated regions and less educated or otherwise insulated portions of the population living in the most modernized sections of the country also may demonstrate traits more appropriate for traditional political systems. For these reasons, recent practice has been to replace the term "non-Western" with more ambiguous but also more neutral words such as "developing" or "modernizing."

Another shift in emphasis that might be considered would be to restate slightly the role of the revolutionary party in the political process. With our growing awareness of the high degree of interaction among all of the political structures—legal and extra-legal, formal and informal, organized and simply spontaneous reactions to a given political stimulus—one feels the need to stress explicitly what *Mexican Govenment in Transition* merely implies. The PRI is the most influential mechanism in Mexico's political system, the hard core around which other political structures operate, but it is only one of a large number of sub-systems that participate in the country's political process.

Closely related to this observation is another, relating to the nature of the role played in the political process by the functional interest associations, both those subsumed within the three sectors of the official party and those operating outside. Lucian Pye has pointed out that in most developing countries such groups have a different relationship to government than they do in a pluralistic democracy like the United States. Rather than operating more or less independently, attempting to influence both the formulation and implementation of public policy, they are what he terms "protective associations," dependent to large extent upon government and involved in the political process primarily in governmental output or implementation aspects of policy. That is, they seek to protect themselves from the consequences of governmental decisions instead of to influence the making of the policy. To my mind, this clearly is the case in Mexico, and the nearly captive relationship of the country's interest associations goes far to explain their relatively ineffectual role in the political process.

Beyond changing the emphasis given some of the materials found in *Mexican Government in Transition,* however, recent research also makes it possible to consider some factors scarcely touched upon. The most important of these is the way in which the concept of political culture can be used as a tool for studying the development process. In the case of Mexico, a happy combination of circumstances has resulted in an accumulation of data that makes an operational if not a definitive understanding of culturally inculcated political values and motivations feasible.

Recently, and probably directly as a result of the impetus toward national self-examination sparked by the Revolution, many Mexicans began to study themselves and their fellow citizens. These students, ranging from poets to psychologists and psychoanalysts, have produced an abundance of information, some emotional and impressionistic, some systematic and scientific. At the same time, North American political scientists—Gabrial Almond, Sidney Verba, Lucian Pye, among others—have attempted to adapt anthropological and social psychological findings to the study of political development. One key study by Almond and Verba, *The Civic Culture* (Princeton, 1963), used cross national surveys of five countries to compare national attitudes toward government, authority, and democracy with actual individual political practice, within the context of political culture. Fortunately—along with the United States, the United Kingdom, Germany, and Italy—Mexico was studied. As a consequence, theoretical formulations and substantive information were at hand for a somewhat more generalized discussion of the effects of the country's political culture on the political change resulting from the Revolution of 1910. This appears as "Mexico—the Established Revolution," a chapter which I prepared for Sidney Verba and Lucian Pye, eds., *Political Culture and Political Development* (Princeton, 1964).

It is impossible to present here what is described at length in that study. One can only suggest that it seems possible to relate certain attitudes toward government to given levels of political development, and to determine in rough proportions what part of the Mexicans share attitudes appropriate to each level of development. Thus, if we use the terms "parochial," "subject," and "participant" to describe the manner in which an individual relates to the political process, we can attempt to compare how many Mexicans fit each category at the outset of the Revolution in 1910 and how many do so now.

As used here, a parochial is a member of the traditional society, unaware of or, in a very few cases, rejecting the national political system. If a parochial has any reaction to the activities of national government, it may be suspicion or mistrust. The subject and participant, however, do relate to the national political process, but in different ways. The subject sees government in terms of output or implementation of policy. He is a consumer of services and a "victim" of responsibilities—taxes, military service, obedience to law—without influencing formulation of decisions. The participant also is a consumer of governmental output, but in addition shares in the political activities that influence or even control the making of policy. He participates actively in the operations of interest associations and political parties, voting, articulating attitudes toward issues of public policy. One can tenet that the more highly integrated a society and the more democratic a polity, the more likely one is to find participants.

In the case of Mexico, my estimate is that around 1910 some 90 per cent of the population were parochials, and of the remainder most were subjects, with no more than 1 or 2 per cent full participants in the political process. Fifty years later, the proportions were 25 per cent parochials, 65 per cent subjects, and 10 per cent participants. Several significant conclusions grow out of the analysis that produced these figures. In the first place, apparently it is comparatively easy to turn parochials into subjects by bringing the wide world to them, as the Mexicans did with their road-building and educational programs. Next, inducing subjects to take the next giant step and assume the role of participants in the political process is a great deal more difficult. This is particularly true when, as in the case of Mexico, many of the socializing influences in the non-political aspects of the culture tend to interact to encourage values appropriate to a subject political culture, and so do the operational political patterns. Finally and encouragingly, however, the evidence suggests that now, after some Mexicans have made the mental adjustments necessary if they are to operate effectively in a participant political system, an increasingly large number of subjects may follow. To understand the bases for these findings, see the study on Mexican political culture cited earlier.

One could continue this minor revisionism and exegesis upon a previously published work indefinitely, but the point of diminishing returns arrives all too speedily and obviously. For all of the efforts of its author, only the reader can decide for himself whether *Mexican Government in Transition* can stand the test of time and withstand the assaults of the wisdom of hindsight.

# Bibliography

## Books and Pamphlets

Alessio Robles, Miguel. *Historia Política de la Revolución.* Ed. Botas, Mexico, D.F., 1946.

Alexander, Robert J. *Communism in Latin America.* Rutgers University Press, New Brunswick, N. J., 1957.

Azuela, Mariano. *Las Moscas y Domitilo Quiere Ser Diputado.* Tip. de Carranza y hijos, Mexico, D.F., 1918.

———. *Los Caciques.* Cía. Periodística Nacional, Mexico, D.F., 1917.

———. *Los de Abajo.* Robredo, Mexico, D.F., 1938. (First published 1916.)

Barrales V., Josep. *Pensamiento Político de Adolfo López Mateos.* Ed. Porrúa, Mexico, D.F., 1959.

Bentley, Arthur F. *The Process of Government; A Study of Social Pressures.* University of Chicago Press, Chicago, 1908 [New edition, Principia Press of Illinois, Evanston, 1955].

Beteta, Ramón. *Pensamiento y Dinámica; Antología de Documentos Políticos-Sociales de la Revolución Mexicana.* Ed. México Nuevo, Mexico, D.F., 1950.

———. *The Mexican Revolution; A Defense.* DAPP, Mexico, D.F., 1937.

Booth, George C. *Mexico's School Made Society.* Stanford University Press, Stanford, 1941.

Braderman, Eugene Maur. *A Study of Political Parties and Politics in Mexico since 1890.* Unpublished Ph.D. thesis, University of Illinois, Urbana, 1938.

Brandenburg, Frank R. *Mexico: An Experiment in One Party Democracy.* Unpublished Ph.D. thesis, University of Pennsylvania, Philadelphia, 1956.

Cabrera, Luis (Pseud. for Lic. Blas Urrea). *Veinte Años Después*. Ed. Botas, Mexico, D.F., 1938.

Calero, Manuel. *Un Decenio de Política Mexicana*. No pub., New York, 1920.

Call, Tomme Clark. *The Mexican Venture*. Oxford University Press, New York, 1953.

*La Campaña Electoral de 1957-1958: Documentos-Programas-Plataformas*. Problemas de Mexico, Vol. I, no. 4 (15 July 1958), Mexico, D.F., 1958.

Chávez Chávez, Rafael. *La Intervención de la Corte en Materia Política*. Tip. Ortega, Mexico, D.F., 1946.

Clark, Marjorie R. *Organized Labor in Mexico*. University of North Carolina Press, Chapel Hill, 1934.

Cline, Howard F. *The United States and Mexico*. Harvard University Press, Cambridge, 1953.

Combined Mexican Working Party. *The Economic Development of Mexico*. Published for the International Bank for Reconstruction and Development by the Johns Hopkins University Press, Baltimore, 1953.

Correa, Eduardo. *El Balance de Avila Camachismo*. No. pub., Mexico, D.F., 1946.

————. *El Balance de Cardenismo*. Acción, Mexico, D.F., 1941.

Cumberland, Charles C. *Mexican Revolution, Genesis under Madero*. University of Texas Press, Austin, 1952.

Davis, Harold E. (ed.). *Government and Politics in Latin America*. Ronald Press Co., New York, 1958.

de Llano, Rodrigo. *México y las Elecciones de 1958*. Ed. Botas, Mexico, D.F., 1957.

de María y Campos, Armando. *Múgica, Crónica Biográfica*. Cía. de Ediciones Populares, S.A., Mexico, D.F., 1939.

Domínguez Rodríguez, Ricardo. *El Artículo 97 Constitucional y el Voto Público*. Ed. Claridad, Mexico, D.F., 1946.

Eisenberg, Ralph. *The Mexican Presidential Election of 1952*. Unpublished master's thesis, University of Illinois, Urbana, 1953.

Espinosa, Jr., Juan (Pseud. for Lic. Gustavo Arce Cano). *Presente y Futuro de México*. No. pub., Mexico, D.F., 1958.

Fitzgibbon, Russell H. *The Constitutions of the Americas*. University of Chicago Press, Chicago, 1948.

Fraga, Gabino. *Derecho Administrativo*. 6th ed.; Ed. Porrúa, Mexico, D.F., 1956.

Freeman, Joseph, Chávez Orozco, Luis, and Gutman, Enrique. *Lázaro Cárdenas Visto por Tres Hombres*. Ed. Masas, Mexico, D.F., 1937.

Fuentes Díaz, Vicente. *Los Partidos Políticos en México*. Two vols.; no pub., Mexico, D.F., 1956.

Gill, Mario (Pseud. for Carlos M. Velasco Gil). *Sinarquismo, Su Origen, Su Esencia, Su Misión*. 2nd ed.; Ed. del CDR., Mexico, D.F., 1944.

Gómez Morín, Manuel. *La Nación y el Régimen*. Bib. de Acción Nacional, Mexico, D.F., n.d.

González Luna, Efraín. *El Hombre y el Estado*. Bib. de Acción Nacional, Mexico, D.F., n.d.

Goodspeed, Stephen S. *The Role of the Chief Executive in Mexico: Politics, Powers and Administration*. Unpublished Ph.D. thesis, University of California, Berkeley, 1947.

Guzmán, Martín Luis. *La Sombra del Caudillo*. Cía. General de Ediciones, S.A., Mexico, D.F., 1951.

Haight, Charles H. *The Contemporary Mexican Revolution as Viewed by Mexican Intellectuals*. Unpublished Ph.D. thesis, Stanford University, Stanford, 1956.

Hidalgo, Ernesto. *El Caso de Guanajuato ante la Conciencia de la Nación*. Gráficas Guanajuato, Mexico, D.F., 1946.

*La Iglesia en America Latina; Trajectoria del Clero Político Mexicano hacia las Elecciones de 1958*. Problemas de Latino América, Vol. III, no. 3 (1 February 1956), Mexico, D.F., 1956.

Infield, Henrik F., and Freier, Koka. *People in Ejidos*. Praeger, New York, 1954.

Iturriaga, José E. *La Estructura Social y Cultural de México*. Fondo de Cultura Económica, Mexico, D.F., 1951.

James, Preston. *Latin America*. 3rd ed.; Odyssey Press, New York, 1959.

Jiménez Moreno, Wigberto. *Historia Antigua de México*. Publicaciones de la Sociedad de Alumnos de la Escuela Nacional de Antropología e Historia, Mexico, D.F., 1953 (mimeographed).

Johnson, John J. *Political Change in Latin America: The Emergence of the Middle Sectors*. Stanford University Press, Stanford, 1958.

Johnson, Marjorie C. *Education in Mexico*. U.S. Office of Education, Washington, D.C., 1956.

Ker, Annita M. *Mexican Government Publications, 1821-1936*. Government Printing Office, Washington, D.C., 1940.

Kluckholm, Frank L. *The Mexican Challenge*. Doubleday, Doran & Co., New York, 1939.

Lanz Duret, Miguel. *Derecho Constitucional Mexicano y Consideraciones sobre la Realidad Política de Nuestro Régimen*. 4th ed.; Imp. L.D., S.A., Mexico, D.F., 1947.

Lewis, Oscar. *Life in a Mexican Village: Tepoztlán Restudied*. University of Illinois Press, Urbana, 1951.

———. *Five Families: Mexican Case Studies in the Culture of Poverty*. Basic Books, Inc., New York, 1959.

López Aparicio, Alfonso. *El Movimiento Obrero en México*. Ed. Jus, Mexico, D.F., 1952.

Macridis, Roy C. *The Study of Comparative Government*. Random House, New York, 1955.

Mead, Margaret (ed.). *Cultural Patterns and Technical Change*. The New American Library (for UNESCO), New York, 1955.

Melgarejo Randolf, L., and Fernández Rojas, J. *El Congreso Constituyente de 1916 y 1917*. Secretaría de Fomento, Colonización e Industria, Mexico, D.F., 1917.

Mena Brito, Bernadino. *El PRUN, Almazán y el Desastre Final.* Ed. Botas, Mexico, D.F., 1941.

Mendieta y Núñez, Lucio. *Las Clases Sociales.* Instituto de Investigaciones Sociales, Universidad Nacional Autónoma, Mexico, D.F., 1947.

———. *Los Partidos Políticos.* Instituto de Investigaciones Sociales, Universidad Nacional Autónoma, Mexico, D.F., 1947.

Michels, Robert. *Political Parties: a Sociological Study of the Oligarchical Tendencies of Modern Democracy.* Hearst's International Library Co., New York, 1915.

Miñan García, Max H. *La Educación Rural en México.* Ed. de la Secretaría de Educación Pública, Mexico, D.F., 1945.

Morales Jiménez, Alberto. *Historia de la Revolución Mexicana.* PRI, Mexico, 1951.

Mosk, Sanford A. *Industrial Revolution in Mexico.* University of California Press, Berkeley, 1950.

Palavicini, Félix F. *Historia de la Constitución de 1917.* Two vols., no pub., Mexico, D.F., 1938.

Parra, Manuel Germán. *La Industrialización de México.* Imp. Universitaria, Mexico, D.F., 1954.

Ponce, Bernardo. *Adolfo Ruiz Cortines.* Biografias Grandesa, Mexico, D.F., 1952.

Portes Gil, Emilio. *El Gobierno Trabaja.* Bib. de Cultura Social y Política, Mexico, D.F., February, 1936.

———. *Quince Años de Política Mexicana.* 2nd ed.; Ed. Botas, Mexico, D.F., 1941.

Prewett, Virginia. *Reportage on Mexico.* E. P. Dutton and Co., New York, 1941.

Priestly, Herbert. *The Mexican Nation.* Macmillan, New York, 1938.

Quintanilla, Luis. *A Latin American Speaks.* Macmillan, New York, 1943.

Ramírez, José Ch. *Azúcar y Política.* La Impresora Azteca, Mexico, D.F., 1957.

Ramos, Samuel. *El Perfil del Hombre y la Cultura en México.* 2nd ed.; P. Robredo, Mexico, D.F., 1938.

Redfield, Robert. *The Folk Culture of Yucatán.* University of Chicago Press, Chicago, 1941.

Rivera Marín, Guadalupe. *El Mercado de Trabajo.* Fondo de Cultura Económica, Mexico, D.F., 1955.

Romanell, Patrick. *The Making of the Mexican Mind.* University of Nebraska Press, Lincoln, 1952.

Salazar, Rosendo. *Historia de las Luchas Proletarias de México.* Talleres Gráficos de la Nación, Mexico, D.F., 1956.

———. *La CTM: Su Historia, Su Significado.* Ed. T. C. Modelo, Mexico, D.F., 1956.

———. *Líderes y Sindicatos.* T. C. Modelo, Mexico, D.F., 1953.

Schaeffer, Wendell K. G. "National Administration in Mexico: Its Development and Present Status." Unpublished Ph.D. thesis, University of California, Berkeley, 1949.

Schurz, William L. *This New World*. E. P. Dutton and Co., New York, 1954.

Scott, Robert E. "Some Aspects of Mexican Federalism, 1917-1948." Unpublished Ph.D. thesis, University of Wisconsin, Madison, 1949.

Seller Rodríguez, Rodolfo. *La Crisis del Partido Revolucionario Institucional*. Talleres Galeza, Mexico, D.F., 1956.

Senior, Clarence. *Mexico in Transition*. League for Industrial Democracy, New York, 1939.

Servín, Armando. *Evolución Técnica del Sistema Impositivo Federal*. Fondo de Cultura Económica, Mexico, D.F., 1942.

————. *Las Finanzas Públicas Locales durante los Ultimos Cinquenta Años*. No pub., Mexico, D.F., 1956.

Sierra, Justo. *Evolución Política del Pueblo Mexicano*. Casa de España en Mexico, Mexico, D.F., 1940.

Silva Herzog, Jesús. *El Pensamiento Económico en México*. Fondo de Cultura Económica, Mexico, D.F., 1947.

————. *La Revolución Mexicana en Crisis*. Cuadernos Americanos, Mexico, D.F., 1944.

————. *Meditaciones sobre México*. Cuadernos Americanos, Mexico, D.F., 1948.

Simpson, Eyler J. *The Ejido, Mexico's Way Out*. University of North Carolina Press, Chapel Hill, 1937.

*Statistical Abstract of Latin America for 1957*. Committee on Latin American Studies, University of California at Los Angeles, Los Angeles, 1958.

Steward, Julian H. *Theory of Culture Change*. University of Illinois Press, Urbana, 1955.

Tannenbaum, Frank. *Mexico: The Struggle for Peace and Bread*. Alfred A. Knopf, New York, 1950.

Tax, Sol (ed.), and others. *Heritage of Conquest*. The Free Press, Glencoe, Ill., 1952.

Tena Ramírez, Felipe. *Derecho Constitucional Mexicano*. Ed. Porrúa, Mexico, D.F., 1955.

————. *Leyes Fundamentales de México, 1808-1957*. Ed. Porrúa, Mexico, D.F., 1957.

Townsend, William C. *Lázaro Cárdenas, Mexican Democrat*. George Wahr Pub. Co., Ann Arbor, 1952.

Truman, David B. *The Governmental Process*. Alfred A. Knopf, New York, 1951.

Tucker, William P. *The Mexican Government Today*. University of Minnesota Press, Minneapolis, 1957.

Vaillant, G. C. *The Aztecs of Mexico*. Penguin Books, Ltd., London, 1951.

Vance, John T., and Clagett, Helen. *A Guide to the Law and Legal Literature of Mexico*. Library of Congress, Washington, D.C., 1945.

Vasconcelos, José. *Breve Historia de Mexico*. Ed. Cultura Hispánica, Madrid, 1952.

————, and Gamio, Manuel. *Aspects of Mexican Civilization*. University of Chicago Press, Chicago, 1926.

Vivó, Jorge. *Geografía de México*. 3rd ed.; Fondo de Cultura Económica, Mexico, D.F., 1953.

Wagley, Charles, and Harris, Marvin. *Minorities in the New World*. Columbia University Press, New York, 1958.

Weyl, Nathanial, and Weyl, Sylvia. *The Reconquest of Mexico*. Oxford University Press, New York, 1939.

Whetten, Nathan L. *Rural Mexico*. University of Chicago Press, Chicago, 1948.

Williamson, René de Visme. *Culture and Policy*. University of Tennessee Press, Knoxville, 1949.

Zea, Leopoldo. *Del Liberalismo a la Revolución en la Educación Mexicana*. Bib. del Instituto Nacional de Estudios Históricos de la Revolución Mexicana, Mexico, D.F., 1956.

————. *El Occidente y la Conciencia de Mexico*. Porrúa y Obregón, Mexico, D.F., 1953.

## Articles

Almond, Gabriel A., Rapporteur. "A Comparative Study of Interest Groups and the Political Process," *American Political Science Review*, LII(March, 1958), 270-82.

Aubrey, Henry G. "Structure and Balance in Rapid Economic Growth," *Political Science Quarterly*, LXIX(December, 1954), 517-40.

Branch, H. N. "The Mexican Constitution of 1917 Compared with the Constitution of 1857," *The Annals of the American Academy of Political and Social Science* (supplement to issue of May, 1917).

Brandenburg, Frank R. "Organized Business in Mexico," *Inter-American Economic Affairs*, XII, no. 3 (Winter, 1958), 26-52.

Brito Foucher, Rodolfo. "El Sistema Electoral Mexicano," 64(May 14, 1938), 19 ff.

"Brito Foucher Ha Faltado a la Verdad, Dice Portes Gil," *Hoy*, V, no. 65(May 26, 1938), 14 ff.

Canchola, Antonio. "Relaciones Sociales y Económicas de la Ciudad y el Campo en México," *Revista Mexicana de Sociología*, XIX(January-April, 1957), 15-23.

Carreño, Alberto María. "Las Clases Sociales en México," *Revista Mexicana de Sociología*, XII(September-December, 1950), 333-50.

Comas, Juan. "Making Mexico One," *Américas*, 6(March, 1954), 19 ff.

Dotson, Floyd, and Dotson, Lillian Ora. "Urban Centralization in Mexico," *Rural Sociology*, XXI(March, 1956), 41-49.

Fitzgibbon, Russell H. "A Statistical Evaluation of Latin-American Democracy," *The Western Political Quarterly*, IX(September, 1956), 607-19.

————. "Measurement of Latin American Political Phenomena; A Statistical Experiment," *American Political Science Review*, XLV(June, 1951), 517-23.

Hewes, Gordon W. "Mexicans in Search of the Mexican; Notes on Mexican National Character Studies," *The American Journal of Economics and Sociology*, VII, no. 4(January, 1954), 209-23.

James, Earle K. "Church and State in Mexico," *The Annals of the American Academy of Political and Social Science*, 208(March, 1940), 112-20.

Kahin, George McT., Pauker, Guy J., and Pye, Lucian W. "Comparative Politics in Non-Western Countries," *American Political Science Review*, XLIX(December, 1955), 1022-41.

Lewis, Oscar. "México desde 1940," *Investigación Económica*, XVIII, no. 70(segundo trimestre de 1958), 185-256.

———. "The Culture of the Vecindad in Mexico City; Two Case Studies." A paper read at the 33rd International Congress of Americanists in San José, Costa Rica, July, 1958.

———. "Urbanization Without Breakdown," *Scientific Monthly*, LXXV (July, 1952), 31-41.

Lombardo Toledano, Vicente. "The Labor Movement," *The Annals of the American Academy of Political and Social Science*, 208 (March, 1940), 48-54.

Mangham, Herbert J. "Decentralizing Mexico," *Mexican American Review*, XXIV(September, 1958), 30-34.

"El Mausoleo de la Democracia," *Hoy*, no. 855(11 July 1953), 8-11.

Mendieta y Núñez, Lucio. "La Clase Media en México," *Revista Mexicana de Sociología*, XVII, nos. 2 and 3(May-December, 1955), 517-31.

Monypenny, Phillip. "Political Science and the Study of Groups; Notes to Guide a Research Project," *The Western Political Quarterly*, VII (June, 1954), 183-201.

Palerm, Angel. "Notas Sobre la Clase Media en México," *Ciencias Sociales*, III, nos. 14 and 15(April-June, 1952), 18-27, and no. 18(December, 1952), 129-35.

Scott, Robert E. "Budget Making in Mexico," *Inter-American Economic Affairs*, IX, no. 2 (Autumn, 1955), 3-20.

Seligman, Daniel. "The Maddening, Promising Mexican Market," *Fortune*, LIII(January, 1956), 103 ff.

Tax, Sol. "The Problem of Democracy in Middle America," *American Sociological Review*, 10(April, 1945), 192-99.

Wagley, Charles, and Harris, Marvin. "A Typology of Latin American Subcultures," *American Anthropologist*, 57, no. 3(June, 1955), 428-51.

Whetten, Nathan L. "Internal Migrations in Mexico," *Rural Sociology*, XXI(June, 1956), 140-51.

———. "The Rise of the Middle Class in Mexico," in Volume 2 (1950) of Theo R. Crevenna, *Materiales para el Estudio de la Clase Media en América Latina*. 6 vols.; Pan American Union, Washington, D.C., 1950-52. (mimeographed)

## Government Reports and Documents

*Anuario Estadístico de los Estados Unidos Mexicanos, 1946-1950.* Dirección General de Estadística, Secretaría de Economía, Mexico, D.F., 1953.

*Diario Oficial de la Federación.* 1920 to present. Official publication of the national government, in which all laws, decrees, and administrative regulations must be published before they take legal effect.

*Diario de los Debates del Congreso Constituyente; Publicado Baja la Dirección del C. Fernando Romero Garcia.* Imprenta de la Cámara de Diputados, Mexico, 1917. Two vols.

*Diario de los Debates de la Cámara de Diputados del Congreso de los Estados Unidos Mexicanos.* 1915 to present.

*Diario de los Debates de la Cámara de Senadores del Congreso de los Estados Unidos Mexicanos.* 1915 to present.

*Directorio del Gobierno Federal; Poderes Legislativo, Ejecutivo y Judicial, 1956.* Sría. de Bienes Nacionales, Mexico, D.F., 1956.

*Informe que Rinde al H. Congreso de la Unión el C. Presidente de la República.* 1920 to present. Annual "State of the Union" message opening the congressional session, September 1, and reproduced in every major newspaper and news magazine.

*Informe Rendido a la Suprema Corte de Justicia de la Nación por su Presidente . . . al Terminar el Año. . . .* 1921 to present. Annual report of the Supreme Court, both Full Bench and *Salas,* discussing principal cases and other business considered during the year.

*Jurisprudencia Definida de la Suprema Corte, Apéndice al Tomo LXXVI del Seminario Judicial de la Federación.* Antigua Imprenta de Murguía, Mexico, D.F., 1944.

*Memoria de la Secretaría de Gobernación . . . Presentada al H. Congreso de la Unión por el Secretario del Ramo. . . .* 1920 to present. Annual report of the Secretariat of *Gobernación.*

*México en Cifras.* Dirección General de Estadística, Secretaría de Economía, Mexico, D.F., 1938, 1952, 1953.

*Reglamento para el Gobierno Interior del Congreso General de los Estados Unidos Mexicanos.* Imprenta de la Cámara de Diputados, Mexico, D.F., 1954.

*Seis Años de Actividad Nacional.* Secretaría de Gobernación, Mexico, D.F., 1946.

*Seis Años de Gobierno al Servicio de México, 1934-1940.* Secretaría de Gobernación, Mexico, D.F., 1940.

*Seminario Judicial de la Federación.* 1917 to present.

*Séptimo Censo General de Población, 1950; Resumen General.* Dirección General de Estadística, Secretaría de Economía, Mexico, D.F., 1953.

## Laws and Decrees

*Constitución Política de los Estados Unidos Mexicanos, 1° de Mayo de 1917.* Ed. Información Aduanera de México, Mexico, D.F., 1958. This annotated edition by Lic. Manuel Andrade includes latest amendments. A somewhat out-of-date English-language version may be found in Fitzgibbon, *The Constitutions of the Americas,* cited above.

*Decreto que Aprueba la Suspensión de las Garantías Individuales Consignadas en Varios Artículos Constitucionales, Diario Oficial,* June 2, 1942.

*Decreto que Levanta la Suspensión de Garantías Decretada el 1° de Junio de 1942, y Reestablece el Orden Constitucional, Ratificando y Declarando Vigentes las Disposiciones que el Mismo Especifica, Diario Oficial,* January 21, 1946.

*Ley Electoral de Poderes Federales, 1° de Julio de 1918,* DAPP, Mexico, D.F., 1947.

*Ley Electoral de Poderes Federales, Diario Oficial,* December 31, 1945.

*Ley Electoral Federal, 3° de Diciembre de 1951, con Reformas Publicadas en el Diario Oficial el 7° de enero de 1954,* Secretaría de Gobernación, Mexico, D.F., 1955.

*Ley de Secretarías y Departamentos de Estado.* In effect 1 January 1947. In *Directorio del Gobierno Federal . . .,* pp. LVII ff.

*Ley de Secretarías y Departamentos de Estado, Diario Oficial,* December 23, 1958. In effect 1 January 1959.

## Political Party Publications

The Revolutionary Party. *La Democracia Social en México: Historia de la Convención Nacional Revolucionaria.* PNR, Mexico, D.F., 1929.

———. *Memoria de la Segunda Convención Nacional Ordinaria del Partido Nacional Revolucionario.* Edición Oficial del PNR, Mexico, D.F., 1934.

———. *Plan Sexenal del Partido Nacional Revolucionario.* PNR, Mexico, D.F., 1934.

———. *Segundo Plan Sexenal, 1941-1946,* PRM, Mexico, D.F., 1940.

———. *33 Meses al Servicio de la Revolución. Memorial del Partido de la Revolución Mexicana, 1940-1943.* No pub., Mexico, D.F., 1943.

———. *Memoria del Partido de la Revolución Mexicana, 1943-1944.* PRM, Mexico, D.F., 1944.

———. *Declaración de Principios, Programa de Acción y Estatutos del Partido Revolucionario Institucional.* PRI, Mexico, D.F., Febrero de 1946.

———. *Ibid.,* 1953.

———. *Ibid.,* 1957.

Partido de Acción Nacional. *Acción Nacional; Principios de Doctrina, Aprobada por la Asamblea Constituyente en sus Sesiones del 15 y del 16 de Septiembre de 1939.* PAN, Mexico, D.F., n.d.

———. *Programa Mínimo de Acción Política.* PAN, Mexico, D.F., 1952.

———. *Plataforma que Sostendrá el PAN en la campaña electoral . . . en 1952.* . . . PAN, Mexico, D.F., 1951.

———. *Principios, Programa y Estatutos del PAN.* Mexico, D.F., 1958.

Partido Popular. *Razón Histórica, Principios, Programa y Estatutos del Partido Popular.* No. pub., Mexico, D.F., 1948.

———. *Ibid.,* 1957.

Partido Nacionalista de México. *Ante una Nueva Actitud Política.* No. pub., Mexico, D.F., 1952.

## Newspapers

*Excelsior*, Mexico, D.F., 1915-1959.
*El Nacional*, Mexico, D.F., 1935-1958.
*Novedades*, Mexico, D.F., 1940-1958.
*El Popular*, Mexico, D.F., 1944-1958.
*La Prensa*, Mexico, D.F., 1930-1958.
*El Universal*, Mexico, D.F., 1915-1959.
*The New York Times*, New York, 1931-1959.

## Periodicals

*Hoy*, Mexico, D.F., February, 1937-1959.
*La Nación*, Mexico, D.F., 1944-1959.
*Mañana*, Mexico, D.F., 1950-1959.
*Tiempo*, Mexico, D.F., 1950-1959 (known in the United States as *Hispano-Americano*).
*Time*, New York, 1950-1959.

# Index

ward change as differentiating factor, 10

Polyfunctionalism, 25, 76

Pope John XXIII, 174, 186

Popular Front, 130

Popular participation: pressure on official party for, 139-45

Popular primaries: abandonment of concept of nominations on basis of, 131

Popular sector (PRI): role in political process, 31; individual farm members, 69; competition for support of rural Mexicans, 73; possible assimilation of urban proletariat, 77; favored position of government bureaucrats in, 81; political mechanism for middle class, 82; percentage of elective officers named by, 89; membership of, 133; diversion of local revenues to national capital, 135; individual memberships in, 142; general discussion of, 168-70; position of government workers in, 169-70; dependence upon president, 261

Population of Mexico, 43-44

Portes Gil, Emilio: election as Provisional President, 121; *cacique* in Tamaulipas, 122; order requiring financial support of PNR by government employees, 124; suggests abolition of sector system of PRM, 139; President of Central Executive Committee, 157; mentioned, 123, 247

Positivism: and General Díaz, 57

Powers, disappearance of, 137-38

Prerevolutionary aristocracy: role in political process, 23-24

Prerevolutionary Mexico: social and political system, 56-58; power of *caciques* in, 102-3

*Presidentes municipales*: 1957 elections for, 89

Presidential Office, 288

President of Mexico: as spokesman for Revolution and revolutionary party, 136-37; double function, 146-47; increase in political authority, 209; qualifications for, 211-20; change in nature of function, 246; change from military to administrative leaders, 247-48; sources of authority, 256-57; exercise of control function, 258-61; domination of national legislature, 262-63; rarity of vetoes, 263; power to initiate legislation, 263; policy-making, 279-93; executive departments assisting, 281 and n, 282; consultation with CONCAMIN and CONCANACO, 285

Prieto Laurens, Jorge, 119

Primaries: change to under PRI, 140-41; barred by election law, 152

Production Council, 290

Professional class: role in political process, 24

Proletarian Defense Committee, 129

Puebla: population of, 43

Querétaro, 49, 99, 101, 122

Quezada, Abel, 204, 287

Quintanar, Father Antonio, 232

Quintana Roo, 41, 42

Rabadán, Macrina, 191

Railroad strike, 25, 167-68, 192, 254, 304

Ramírez y Ramírez, Enrique: seeks union of Communists and non-Communists, 189; attack on Lombardo Toledano, 191; ousted by PP, 191

Ramos, General Matías, 125

Ramos, Segundo, 242

Real income: changes in, 90-91

Regionalism: as cause of national